Driving Ambition

Life in the slow lane

Craig Briggs

Copyright © 2018 Craig Briggs
Updated 2020
The moral right of the author has been asserted. This is a work of non-fiction that recounts real events and experiences. Some names, places, conversations, and identifying characteristics have been changed to preserve anonymity of those concerned.

Copy editing/proofreading by Louise Lubke Cuss at wordblink.com
Cover design and Photography by Craig Briggs
Portrait photo by Melanie Briggs
All rights reserved.
ISBN: 1726398730
ISBN-13: 978-1726398732

By the same author

The Journey series

Journey To A Dream

Beyond Imagination

Endless Possibilities

Opportunities Ahead

Driving Ambition

The Discerning Traveller

A Season To Remember

An Excellent Vintage

Life In A Foreign Land

The Accidental Explorer

Seasons To Be Cheerful

Here To There And Back Again

Fiction

Pandora's Box

Short story

Roast Pig and Romance

Hardcover

**Journey To A Dream
Special Tenth Anniversary Edition**

In Memory

Arnold Edward Price
(6 May 1912 – 5 Dec 2011)

Gifts are for occasions,
memories are for life.

CONTENTS

	Introduction	1
1	Pharaohs and Mummies	7
2	A Knight's Quest	18
3	Birthday Celebrations	29
4	Ollie the Octopus	42
5	Uncle Craig	52
6	Fiesta, Fiesta	67
7	He's Gone	78
8	Preparations Begin	86
9	Land's End	98
10	Midnight Moonshine	107
11	Dognapped	118
12	The Office Party	130
13	Are You Pedro?	144
14	Bounce	156
15	Visa Visit	168
16	Fireplace Overload	178
17	Bequests Addressed	188
18	Dinner Time	198
19	Shanghai Surprise	211
20	Bunny Hop Carnival	225
21	What's in a Name?	235
22	Traditional Aussie	248
23	Ships in the Night	261
24	A Period Feature	275
25	Signs of Age	286
26	Close Call	300
27	Manolo the Magnificent	316
	Continue the Journey	332
	About the Author	338

Introduction

If life deals you a bad hand, don't fold, take a chance; a good player will always come out on top.

I entered this world on the 12th of July 1962, in St. Luke's Hospital, Huddersfield. The second child, and only son, of Donald and Glenys Briggs. Donald, a humble lathe operator, worked for one of the town's largest employers, David Brown Tractors of Meltham.

The birth of their first child, Julie, had been a joy. The arrival of a son would make the family complete. Donald couldn't wait to groom his boy for sporting success. Notification of my arrival came via a phone call to his work, a call that dashed his parental hopes. Young Craig was not a 'normal' lad: he'd been born with congenital feet deformities. I cannot imagine a crueller message.

Unaware of my disability, I got on with life as any infant would. My first birthday brought a gift that would change my life forever. Not a cuddly toy from Mum and Dad, nor a silver-plated trinket from friends or relatives. My life-changing gift was a marvel of modern engineering, manufactured by J. E. Hanger and Co. of London for and on behalf of the National Health Service. Bespoke footwear gave me what the Vespa had given the youth of the fifties: freedom and independence. They weren't quite as stylish as an Italian built scooter but I didn't care. From now on, Master Briggs was on the move and no one would hold me back.

Over the next five years a series of surgical procedures changed the way I moved. Recollections are few but these infant experiences would influence the rest of my life. In the 1960s bedside visits were restricted to one person for one hour per day. The anguish of a young mother listening to the tortured screams of her infant son begging her to stay must have been horrific; it wasn't much fun for me either.

When the time came, Mum walked me to school like other proud mothers. For his part, Dad gave me his first and only piece of worldly advice. 'If anyone hits you, hit 'em back.'

With one exception, my mind proved sharper than my boxing prowess. Kids can be cruel, particularly to those who stand out, but only once did I break down in tears and ask, 'Why? Why me?' It's a question I sometimes ask myself today, but for very different reasons. Academia was not my thing. I found it difficult to concentrate on anything that didn't interest me.

I left secondary education with a mediocre haul of four 'O' levels and drifted aimlessly into an 'A' level course. It seemed preferable to starting work. If my 'O' level tally was disappointing, my 'A' level results were pitiful. I blamed a perforated appendix, two months before my finals, but if truth be known I'd had my fill of education.

In May 1980 I left college and entered the employment market. Margaret Thatcher was busy dismantling British industry and unemployment was running at a post-war high. I signed on to receive unemployment benefit and spent the summer lounging around the house watching the

Wimbledon Tennis Championship on telly. As the tournament drew to a close, parental pressure to find work intensified. In September, during one of my many visits to the Job Centre, a job card caught my eye: 'Wanted: trainee retail managers'. The idea of becoming a manager appealed, so I applied.

Five hundred and sixty applicants chased six positions. I pleaded my case at an interview and ended up being selected. After a two-week training course in the seaside town of Southport, I passed with honours, achieving the rank of assistant manager. When asked where I'd like to ply my newfound retail skills, I chose London, a city paved with gold.

In October 1980, I left Huddersfield a naïve child and returned three and a half years later a wiser and more mature young man. A brief period of letting my hair down followed, catching up on lost time and lost youth. During these wild and hedonistic months, I met the love of my life and future wife, Melanie.

My career in retail spanned six and a half years with five different companies. Each one expanded my experience and knowledge but to realise my dream I would have to go it alone. Not long after my twenty-sixth birthday, I handed in my notice. My future lay in leather jackets. Unfortunately, no one shared this vision and my aspirations fell at the first hurdle.

The prospect of returning to the retail trade pushed me into pursuing a different path. I reached a compromise and worked as a self-employed agent for one of the nation's largest insurance companies. The job title, Financial Consultant, exaggerated the role. In reality I was nothing more than a desperate insurance salesman. Life was hard and the insurance industry ruthless. Trying to sell a product that nobody wants, and which by its nature will never benefit the payee, is not easy. Unlike most recruits, I managed to survive and learnt some difficult but valuable lessons.

My 'Big Break' came when two of my clients asked me to invest in their fledgling printing business. The first year's accounts showed greater losses than actual sales. Against all professional advice I jumped at the chance, re-mortgaged the house and bought an equal stake.

By accident rather than design, I'd finally found my true vocation. The company was losing money hand over fist. The bank had taken a second charge on the partners' homes and my investment was swallowed up in a black hole of debt. Just when things couldn't get any worse, the bank called in the overdraft. While others worried, I applied myself to the problem. Through hard work and determination, we weathered the storm, but casualties were high.

After thirteen years of blood, sweat, and holding back the tears, I ended up owning a modestly successful little business. The time was right to begin my journey to a dream.

In May 2002 my wife Melanie and I decided to sell up and chase our dream. We packed all our worldly belongings, including our dog Jazz, into my ageing executive saloon, and headed off to Spain.

Not for us the tourist-packed Costas of the Mediterranean or the whitewashed villages of Andalucia. Our destination was Galicia: a little-known region in the northwest corner of Spain.

The contrast in lifestyles from England's industrial north to Spain's rural interior proved far more traumatic than either of us had imagined. Three and a half years at night school studying the Spanish language was little help. Galicia has its own language, gallego. A proudly spoken tongue that has more in common with Portuguese than Spanish.

Dubious estate agents and questionable property descriptions turned our search for a new home into a lottery. Clear objectives became blurred and after several failed attempts to buy a property, we were forced to reassess our goals.

Eventually, we found our dream house, a tiny bungalow on the outskirts of the sleepy village of Canabal. Coping with Spain's laid-back approach while managing a building project tested our resolve. What could go wrong did and by Christmas we were ready to throw in the towel and head back to Blighty. But Yorkshiremen are made of sterner stuff.

A timely visit from my dad re-energised our ambitions. Twelve months and ten days after arriving in Galicia, we moved into our new home and completed the first part of our *Journey To A Dream*.

Choosing a name for our renovated property proved difficult; eventually we settled on *El Sueño* (The Dream). After the challenges of the first twelve months, we settled into a more relaxed lifestyle. Drinks at sunset, or Teatime Tasters, became an integral part of our daily lives and the warmth and generosity of our village neighbours made us feel at home.

With Melanie's help, I set about transforming our barren plot into a garden paradise. It wasn't all plain sailing and dealing with Spanish bureaucracy proved difficult. As time drifted by we started to enjoy a life *Beyond Imagination*.

For the first time in a long time, I had the freedom to take up some hobbies. Little did I know that writing and viniculture would become my pastimes of choice. With help from our neighbour, Meli, I took my first tentative steps on the road to winemaking. The success of my fledgling hobby was left in the hands of Mother Nature. Initial results were encouraging. My love of winemaking had begun.

As with viniculture, my efforts at writing took time to develop. Under the tutorage of Peter Hinchliffe, former editor in chief of Huddersfield's daily newspaper and founder of an online magazine, my writing slowly improved.

Hobbies are one thing but the financial requirements of day to day living were never far from our thoughts. After successfully buying, renovating, and selling a second property, we decided to look for another. Eventually, we found the ideal project, a romantic ruined farmhouse with *Endless Possibilities*.

Events have a way of keeping our lives in perspective, and this was particularly so when Melanie's dad was diagnosed with terminal cancer. A surprise fortieth birthday party turned into an emotional, but happy, final family reunion.

Later that year we offered to help our friends, Bob and Janet, convert their unloved house into a luxury holiday rental. Weeks before the first guests were due to arrive, the builder had a serious on-site accident. We had no alternative but to roll up our sleeves and finish the job. A season that could have turned into a disaster ended in success and satisfied customers. The question was, could we duplicate that success and build our own holiday rental property?

Finding the perfect place was challenging; buying it proved far more difficult. The lack of official paperwork led to lengthy delays. Thirteen months after agreeing the purchase, we finally took possession. That's when the problems really began. The wisdom of buying a house without water or electricity was put to the test. By the time we resolved those issues another twelve months had passed. The time had come to put the frustrations of the past behind us and concentrate on the *Opportunities Ahead*.

Throughout the wait we'd kept ourselves busy. There can't be many people who can add moonshine distillation to their curriculum vitae. Our second year in property management presented an unexpected opportunity, a house swap to the far side of the world. All we had to do was make the arrangements. After all, how difficult could it be to organise the trip of a lifetime?

1

Pharaohs and Mummies

The two most important requirements when deciding to restore a Spanish ruin are a vivid imagination and a great sense of humour. A healthy bank balance helps, as do limitless patience, unyielding determination, and nerves of steel. Above all, be prepared to sacrifice your sanity: if you're not crazy when you start, you will be by the time you've finished.

In that respect, Melanie and I are gluttons for punishment. Two previous projects had driven us to the brink of insanity, and our current undertaking threatened to push us over the edge. Problems securing an electricity supply had led to major delays. Twelve months on and the restoration had only just begun.

Our ruin of choice was a once charming farmhouse, long since abandoned to the ravages of time. The main contractor was a local builder called Manolo. He was charged with breathing new life into our decaying wreck. Alfonso, a local stonemason of high regard, would rebuild the boundary walls and landscape the garden. We'd decided to manage the project ourselves and take up the slack, as and when required.

Today's mission, should we choose to accept it, was to explore a strange new world, to avoid new lifeforms and old accumulations, and boldly go where no one had gone before.

'We'd better make a start on cleaning out the *bodegas* (cellars),' I announced over morning coffee.

Melanie looked decidedly unenthusiastic.

'Do we have to?'

'Someone has to do it.'

In common with most rural properties in the area, the ground floor *bodegas* had been used for stabling livestock, while the living accommodation was on the first floor. At the moment, Manolo was busy replacing the old roof. Ripping up the rotten floors was next on his agenda. Before then, the two *bodegas* needed mucking out and Melanie and I were the designated shit shovellers.

Most dictionaries would have you believe a *bodega* is a wine cellar. To many this conjures up images of wealthy aristocrats deliberating over which vintage to serve with dinner. Here in the Galician countryside, nothing could be further from the truth. These windowless cellars maintain a relatively even temperature throughout the year making them ideal for housing livestock. During the long summer months, they remain comfortably cool and in winter, bovine body heat helps warm the living accommodation. The only drawback to this cheap, renewable energy is the stomach-churning odours steaming through the floorboards.

Melanie's lack of enthusiasm was directly linked to these former inhabitants. The property hadn't been lived in for decades, unlike the *bodegas* which had been in regular use. Damp cellars and animal effluent make unpleasant bedfellows but ours contained something far worse.

During our initial viewing of the house we'd stumbled across a 1970s mint green bathroom suite tucked away in a small room next to the kitchen. It caught our attention for a number of reasons, not least of which was why anyone would choose mint green. The glass-panelled door was quite an unusual feature but most curious of all was the question of waste. In a house devoid of plumbing and running water, where did it go?

Shortly after buying the place we found out. The soil pipe from the toilet went through the floorboards and into the *bodega*. Evidence of this unique sewage system was clearly visible, splattered down the cellar wall.

'What's left to do?' asked Melanie.

Earlier in the year we'd cleared out everything flammable and burnt it. That's when we uncovered a highly sought-after artefact. Hidden under a pile of woodworm infested boards was a handcrafted stone drinking trough, two metres long, sixty centimetres wide, and half a metre deep. We couldn't believe our luck. The house only cost 12,000 euros and the trough was probably worth 2,000.

'We can start by dragging that stone trough outside and putting it somewhere safe,' I replied.

'You've got to be joking. It must weigh a ton.'

'Don't worry, I've got a plan.'

'What plan?'

'The ancient Egyptian stone moving plan.'

'Really.'

I could tell from her tone that she wasn't impressed but if I waited long enough she was bound to ask.

'Go on then, what exactly is the ancient Egyptian method for moving Galician stone troughs?'

'Not troughs, blocks.'

Her glare widened.

'When the pharaohs built the pyramids, they used rollers to move the heavy stones.'

'And your point is?'

'If it worked for them, I'm sure it'll work for us.'

'And what about the slaves?'

'What slaves?'

'The slaves to pull the blocks?'

'That's where you and I come in.'

'Ha, ha. Very funny.'

'I'm not joking.'

Melanie's reluctance to work at the weekend was understandable but if the plan failed, only we would be any the wiser.

'Now, you be good,' said Melanie to the dog, as we prepared to leave.

Jazz wagged her tail and stared back as if to say, aren't I always?

On a bright summer's morning, the twenty-minute drive from home to the sleepy village of Vilatán is a joy. When we arrived, there wasn't a soul in sight.

The two *bodegas* occupy the length of the house and are divided equally by a metre-thick stone wall. An internal doorway connects the two sides. From outside, two large wooden doors secure the left-hand *bodega* and a smaller door the right. The stone trough was in the one on the left.

Opening the *bodega* doors is a nerve-racking experience.

'Are you ready?' I asked, after freeing the padlock.

'Just get on with it.'

That was easy for her to say; she was standing metres away. I stood on the half-turn, ready to make a speedy retreat should anything untoward rush out. As usual, my imaginary demons surrendered to a shaft of daylight. The morning sun hadn't yet risen above the roofline but the open doorway illuminated all but the darkest corners.

'That's buggered that up,' remarked Melanie.

Fortunately, the trough was very close to the entrance. Unfortunately, it was right behind the door.

'We'll have to take the door off.'

'*We* will, will *we*?'

Despite their age and patched-up appearance, the two wooden doors were significant pieces of joinery. Each one was held in place with two iron hinges slotted over rusty pegs that were attached to the door frame. Removing them would be relatively easy; all I had to do was lever the hinges off the pegs.

'Hold it here and keep it upright and whatever you do, don't drop it,' I said to Melanie, showing her where to position her hands.

'If it's that important perhaps you should hold the door and I'll lever it off.'

'OK darling, whatever you say.'

Alfonso was using the *bodega* to store his tools. Of interest to us was a long steel bar and two metal pipes. We would use the bar to jimmy off the door and the pipes to roll the trough outside.

'The lever is over there,' I said, pointing at the metal rod leant up against the *bodega* wall.

Melanie grabbed it and pulled.

'It's heavier than it looks,' she said, straining to lift it.

'Perhaps I should do that, darling, and you hold the door.'

Begrudgingly she agreed.

I positioned the bar at a shallow angle under the door.

'Are you ready?' I asked.

'As ready as I'll ever be.'

'After three. One, two, three.'

The heavy steel lever made light work of lifting the door.

'Are you alright?' I asked.

'Just hurry up.'

I let the rod fall to the ground and grabbed the other end.

'Let's slide it outside and lean it up against the wall.'

Carefully we dragged it across the ground and leant it against the house.

'I told you it would be easy,' I said, catching my breath.

Melanie wasn't impressed.

'Has that made it any easier?' she asked.

That was a good question. The trough was resting on two stones. We needed to drag it off the stones and onto the two pipes; only then could we push it outside. I explained my plan.

'And how exactly are you going to move it away from the wall?'

The trough was wedged tightly against the dividing wall between the two *bodegas*.

'I'll use the lever.'

'Rather you than me,' she replied. 'There could be anything hiding behind there.'

'Thanks for that.'

Opening the *bodega* doors was scary enough; now I had to get up close and personal with whatever was hiding behind the trough.

'I'm only joking,' she replied, before wandering outside.

'I see you're not taking any chances.'

'Just get on with it.'

I laid the pipes on the floor and wedged the lever behind the trough. It took less effort than I expected to prise it away.

'Watch your toes,' cautioned Melanie.

She needn't have worried. If it came to saving my toes or the trough, I knew which I would choose. Everything was going to plan until out of the corner of my eye something large dropped from a hole in the wall and onto the floor. My reaction was quicker than a speeding bullet. Without hesitation I dropped the lever and raced outside. Startled by my sudden movement, Melanie let out a shriek.

'What is it?' she asked.

'Didn't you see it?'

'What?'

'That thing.'

'What thing?'

'I don't know and I wasn't hanging around to find out.'
'Well what did it look like?'
'It was massive.'

I could tell from Melanie's expression that she was starting to doubt my apparition.

'So, what now?' she asked.
'You'll have to find out what it was.'
'Why me?'
'Because you don't mind spiders.'
'I thought you said it was massive.'
'It was.'

Melanie looked unconvinced.

'Go on, you'll be fine,' I said.

Melanie found a stick in the garden and crept slowly towards the doorway.

'What's that for?'
'Protection.'

Cautiously, she stepped inside the *bodega* and peered behind the tough.

'I can't see anything,' she said.
'Go around the other side and have a look.'

My suggestion meant venturing deeper into the *bodega*. If anything leapt out, her escape route was cut off.

Step by step she moved further inside, banging the stick on the floor as she went.

'Well?' I asked, as she neared the far end of the trough.
'I can't see anything.'
'Give it a minute. Let your eyes adjust to the dark.'

No sooner had the words left my lips than Melanie jumped backwards.

'What is it?'

Slowly she inched forward, squinting into the darkness.

'Oh, that's gross.'
'What is?'
'Put it this way, I think you're safe.'
'Why? What is it?'

'A mummified rat.'

The poor creature had found its way between the wall and the trough and perished.

'Are you sure there's nothing else?'

'I can't see anything.'

Crisis over, I finished levering the trough off the stones and onto the pipes.

'What now?' asked Melanie.

'We push.'

We took up station at the back of the trough and braced ourselves to move it forward. On the count of three we gave an almighty shove. Lo and behold, it moved. I couldn't quite believe it; perhaps those ancient Egyptians knew a thing or two after all.

'That's it. Go on,' I said, encouraging Melanie to keep up the pressure.

As the back of the trough rolled off the first pipe it dropped to the floor.

With hindsight, three pipes would have been preferable but beggars can't be choosers.

'Put that pipe at the front and I'll lever it forward.'

Slowly but surely the ancient stone trough emerged into the daylight. Every forward inch required an almighty effort but we were getting there.

'Where are we going to put it?' asked Melanie.

'Anywhere,' I said, 'providing it's on its current trajectory.'

Shifting this weighty monolith left or right of its present course was out of the question. Moving it forward was difficult enough.

'Let's put it halfway between the house and the boundary wall,' I said.

It wasn't ideal but at least Manolo and Alfonso would have equal space to work around it.

Less than two metres from the house, our steady progress came to an abrupt halt.

'Put your back into it,' I said.

'It's stuck,' she replied.

It wasn't immediately obvious but the ground outside the *bodega* inclined ever so slightly downwards before climbing again. When the first pipe reached the upslope, the earth was too soft to support its weight.

'There's a dip in the ground,' I said.

'And the earth is too soft to take the weight.'

'We need to put something under the pipe,' I replied.

'Like what?'

I looked around the garden, then inside the *bodega*.

'This should do,' I said, picking up a plank of wood.

Melanie looked confused.

'I'll use the lever to lift the trough and you slip the plank under the pipe.'

Her expression didn't alter. 'What are you doing now?' she asked.

I'd found a rock in the garden to act as a pivot.

'You'll see.'

With the rock in place, I slipped the iron rod under the trough and lifted it with ease.

'OK, slip the plank under.'

'Are you sure it's safe?'

'Of course it is. Look.'

To emphasise the point, I took one hand off the bar and kept the trough aloft with the other.

'Show off.'

Melanie pulled out the pipe, slipped the plank under the trough and then replaced it. Slowly, I lowered it back down. The plank creaked under the weight before snapping in two.

'Bugger!'

We needed to rethink our strategy. That's when I remembered a sheet of aluminium I'd found during the house clearance.

'Wait here,' I said, before disappearing into the house.

'This will do,' I said, waving my find in the air.

'Are you sure?'

'What do you mean?'

'It looks a bit on the flimsy side.'

She had a point.

'It's only to stop the pipe sinking into the ground,' I replied.

Once again, I lifted the trough. Melanie cleared the splintered plank and replaced it with the sheet of aluminium. Slowly I lowered the stone trough. The thin metal sheet crumpled under the weight but the pipe held fast.

'OK, let's give it go.'

On the count of three Melanie pushed and I used the lever to inch it forward. We were on the move again.

'That'll do,' I said.

It had taken us the best part of the morning to move this huge lump of granite less than six metres. We were shattered but there was more still to do. After a short break, we got back to work cleaning out the *bodega*.

Metaphorically speaking, I've done my fair share of shovelling shit but this was the first time I'd done it for real. I filled the wheelbarrow and Melanie pushed it outside and tipped it out in the corner of the meadow. At times like this, working in the dark is preferable to knowing where you are and what you're doing. Every time I plunged the shovel into the damp dung, I half-expected to unearth human remains but this excavation revealed something far more unusual.

I'd expected to discover a floor of some description but all I found was an uneven surface pitted with holes and covered with rocks. To do a thorough job, all these stones would have to come out.

By the time we called it a day, the first of the two *bodegas* was cleaner than it had ever been. The second would wait until tomorrow.

The following morning, I could hardly walk. The extraordinary efforts of the previous day had taken their toll. Every muscle ached and my feet felt like the slightest pressure would cause them to shatter. People with pinned ankles are not designed to walk over uneven ground, never mind spend all day working on it. Enough self-pity; there was work to be done.

'Are you ready?'

'Do I have a choice?' replied Melanie.

As we drove through the village, the faithful were making their way to church. The tuneless bell had been tolling for a good ten minutes. The menfolk were conspicuous by their absence. Perhaps women are more in need of redemption.

The second *bodega* was equal in size to the first but access was nowhere near as good.

'What are you waiting for?' asked Melanie, as I built up the courage to enter.

Muscles tensed and shovel at the ready, I stepped into the darkness. Melanie followed. Once again, I shovelled and she wheeled the barrow.

At lunchtime we stopped for a quick bite to eat before continuing. Five hours after arriving we were almost there.

'That's it,' I said, loading the last of the stones into the wheelbarrow.

'Thank heavens for that. Can we go home now?'

I shared her sentiment.

'What are we going to do with all these stones?' she asked, as we walked past a metre-high pile of rocks.

'We can use them as hardcore when we build the terrace,' I suggested.

That evening we sat in the garden watching the sun sink behind the woody knoll. After such a hard day's graft, I felt we'd earned a special Teatime Taster. Cooling in the fridge was a rather fine locally produced white wine. I pulled the cork and we relaxed.

'*Salud* (Cheers).'

2

A Knight's Quest

Striking the right work-life balance is essential during a long-term building project. If you're not careful, you can end up working all hours God sends, and a few more besides. Melanie and I promised ourselves that wouldn't happen. We'd spent all weekend working so decided to take Monday morning off.

Melanie had been asking me for weeks what I wanted to do on my birthday. With less than a fortnight to go, I needed to decide. One thing had been on my mind for some time but I hadn't had the chance to check it out. This morning provided the perfect opportunity to do some research. I began my quest by booting up the computer.

'Guess what I've found?' I said, as I walked into the kitchen.

Melanie was busy preparing lunch, a rather tasty-looking salad.

'What?'

'Guess.'

'I don't know, you've found that sock you were looking for?'

'Ha, ha, very funny.'

'What then?'

'I've just discovered the whereabouts of the Ark of the Covenant and the Holy Grail.'

'Really.'

'Is that all you can say? Medieval knights dedicated their lives to unearthing these sacred artefacts.'

'Lovely, and where exactly did you find them?'

'On the internet.'

'The internet?'

'You might well scoff, but I know exactly where they're going to be next weekend.'

'And where's that?'

'Ponferrada.'

'Ponferrada?'

'That's right, Ponferrada.'

Ponferrada is a city 100 kilometres east of us in the province of Castilla and León. It's located on the Camino de Santiago (Way of St. James), the pilgrimage route from France to the cathedral city of Santiago de Compostela. During the Middle Ages, the Order of the Knights Templar were charged with protecting pilgrims travelling the route. They established a garrison in Ponferrada and in the 12th century built a rather impressive castle.

Legend has it that every year, Fray Guido de Garda, Master of the Order of the Templars, returns to the city to fulfil an eternal pact. For reasons that aren't exactly clear, he brings with him the Ark of the Covenant and the Holy Grail. To mark this historic event, the city holds an annual fiesta called La Noche Templaria (Night of the Templars) on the first weekend following the summer solstice. This year's fiesta fell on the weekend of the 7th, five days before my birthday.

Despite her scepticism, Melanie listened while I explained my findings.

'So, what do you think?' I asked.
'It sounds interesting.'
'In that case, let's do that for my birthday.'
'OK, why not?'

Returning to work at 3:30 pm might seem strange to some but here in Spain it's considered quite early. Take Manolo for example. Every day at exactly one o'clock he downs tools and heads home. After a family lunch and the occasional siesta, he returns to work at precisely half past three.

By the time we arrived at Vilatán, Manolo was on the roof. Over the last few weeks he'd straightened the sagging roofline, realigned the joists and was busy refitting the chestnut boards that would support the new terracotta tiles.

'*Buenos tardes* (Good afternoon),' I called, as we strolled towards the house.

'*Hola.*'

'Is this OK here?' I asked, pointing at the stone trough.

'No problem but what are you going to do with all those stones?'

Nothing gets past Manolo.

The next job on our list was to build a sun terrace on the south facing side of the house. We knew from day one that work at this end of the property would be problematic. Access was poor and building materials would have to be brought in by hand. Employing someone to do that would be expensive so we volunteered ourselves for the donkey work.

At the moment, the living accommodation had two entrances, a back door and another at the northern end which was accessed by climbing a flight of stone steps. We were keeping the back door but replacing the other entrance with an internal staircase rising from the *bodega*. The idea was to move the redundant stone steps from one end of the house to the other and use them to reach the new terrace. To level the site, we planned to build a retaining wall and backfill it with hardcore. That's when the rocks would come in handy. I explained our thinking to Manolo.

'You can do that if you want,' he said.

I sensed there was a but coming.

'But I think they were put in the *bodegas* for a reason,' he replied.

'To level the floor?' I asked.

'More than that.'

Melanie and I looked at each other. Had our actions compromised the building's structural integrity? Was a catastrophic collapse imminent?

'More?' I asked.

'They were put there to help with drainage.'

'Drainage?'

Manolo climbed down the scaffolding to explain.

'Do you see all these natural channels?' he asked, pointing at the floor of the *bodega*.

We nodded.

'During the winter months, they let water escape.'

Manolo was referring to water that leaked into the *bodegas* from the natural fissures in the bedrock.

'We were hoping to concrete the floor,' I said.

Manolo assured us that providing we replaced the stones, water would quickly find its way outside even with a concrete floor.

'It's only moisture,' he said. 'All *bodegas* get damp in the winter, it's natural. You'll only get problems if you don't put them back.'

It had taken all weekend to clean the *bodegas* and clear out the stones, and it took the rest of the morning to reinstate them.

Before heading home, we took a long hard look at the stone steps.

'I think you're going to need some help,' said Melanie. 'They're far too heavy for me to move.'

She was right; a stone trough on rollers was one thing but manhandling these would take brute force. Fortunately, I knew just the man for the job.

'I'll give Steve a call and see if he can help. It shouldn't take us long.'

Steve jumped at the chance and picked me up at 9:00 am the following morning.

'Top or bottom?' I asked, as we stood at the foot of the steps, surveying the job in hand.

Starting at the top would mean carrying each granite block down the height of the staircase. Starting at the bottom risked the whole lot collapsing on us. With each step weighing between 100 and 150 kilos, we decided to work from the top down.

With the aid of a pickaxe, I levered the first step loose.

'Perhaps if we turn it around, we can slide it to the bottom,' I suggested.

Carefully, we turned the heavy stone through ninety degrees and balanced it on the edge of the step below.

'Watch your fingers,' I said, as we nudged it closer to its tipping point.

Steve stood on one side and I the other.

'Ready?'

'I'm ready.'

The lightest touch tipped the block over the edge. Steve and I hung on to it for dear life as it bounced down the steps one after another until it thumped into the grassy earth at the bottom, sending me flying.

'Are you alright?' asked Steve, as I picked myself up.

Only my pride was injured on this occasion.

I'd thought that between us we could carry them to the other end of the house or at least lift them into the wheelbarrow but they were too heavy and awkward.

'We could try rolling them,' suggested Steve.

End over end we manhandled each step the length of the house. By lunchtime, we'd moved them all and built a new flight of steps at the opposite end of the house. Manolo looked suitably impressed.

'*Bastante bien* (Not bad),' he remarked.

Removing the staircase revealed a mound of rubble. It's uncanny how completing one job often creates another. For now, lunch beckoned and an afternoon of rest and relaxation.

When we turned up for work on Wednesday morning, Manolo's wife Julia and their eldest son Manuel were standing in the meadow.

'I wonder what they're doing here,' said Melanie.

My mind flashed back to Manolo's accident, a double leg fracture sustained three years ago while working for us. I needn't have worried. He was standing at the top of the scaffolding. As I pulled up behind his van I noticed two pallets of roof tiles had been delivered.

'*Buenos días*,' I called, as we walked toward the house.

'*Hola*,' replied Julia.

'*Muy buenos*,' called Manolo from the top of his tower.

Roof tiles had never been so interesting. After due consideration, we'd opted for a simulated weathered look. They were slightly more expensive but appearance was important.

'What do you think?' I asked Manolo.

'It's a good brand but they don't make them like they used to,' he commented.

Not quite the reply I was expecting but it didn't matter.

'You can start loading now,' he called to Julia.

Manolo had secured an electric winch to the top of the tower and attached a steel bucket to that. Julia and Manuel were here to work. Without them, he would be up and down the scaffolding for days.

The metal bucket was crafted from half an oil drum and held about twenty tiles. While Julia and Manuel reloaded, Manolo distributed them in small piles across the roof. By lunchtime, the first pallet load was aloft.

'*Hasta luego*,' they said, as they left for lunch.

Melanie and I had spent the morning removing the mound of rubble from the side of the house. I provided the brawn and Melanie the transport.

'One more barrow and we'll call it a day,' I said.

The next morning it was the turn of Manolo's youngest son, twelve-year-old Javier, to be pressganged into helping.

By the end of the week, the front half of the roof was tiled and Melanie and I had shifted all the rubble, exposing the beautiful granite stonework. The old entrance was now above head height.

'Come on,' I said to Melanie.

'Where?'

'Let's walk down the lane to get a better view of the roof.'

The transformation left us speechless. There was plenty of work still to do but finally our dream was becoming a reality.

After such a physically demanding week, I figured we'd earned our awayday to Ponferrada and our quest for the Holy Grail. It's said that an army marches on its stomach. With that in mind I'd made some enquiries and found a Chinese restaurant. What at one time was taken for granted has become an infrequent culinary treat. Leaving nothing to chance, Melanie rang and reserved a table.

The drive to Ponferrada takes about an hour along one of our favourite roads, the *carretera nacional* 120, more commonly referred to as the N120. From home, it climbs into the mountains before descending into the valley of the river Sil. As the seasons change so does the scenery. No two journeys are ever the same. After meandering through the countryside, following the course of the river, it rises once again into the Massif mountain range before descending into Ponferrada.

We left home after lunch and quickly found a parking space close to the city centre. Between the hours of one and four most Spanish cities fall silent and Ponferrada was no different. We made our way along the quiet streets and up into the old town. The focal point of the daytime activities was the Plaza Ayuntamiento. The square was deserted when we arrived.

'Are you sure this is the right place?' asked Melanie.

The abandoned market stalls were a bit of a giveaway. Lunchtime security relied on a dust cover and honesty.

'They must have left for lunch. Let's get a coffee until they reopen,' I suggested.

Wandering through the narrow lanes of the old town felt like we'd stepped back in time. We found a table outside an establishment called Bar Chelsea and ordered a *café con leche* (coffee with milk).

'What are we going to do now?' asked Melanie as we finished our drink.

'Let's see what's down there,' I said, pointing down a narrow lane.

The further we strolled from the square, the quieter the alleyways became. Before long we found ourselves at the site of the evening's main event, the Castillo de los Templarios (Castle of the Templars).

'At least we know where it is now,' I said.

'It looks brand-new,' remarked Melanie.

We wandered across to an information board to find out more. Construction began in the 12th century and finished in the 15th. The current restoration work would take somewhat less time to complete.

'Restoration? It looks like they're rebuilding it,' commented Melanie.

I had to agree. Mind you, they were doing a great job.

'Let's go to the square and see what's going on,' I suggested.

We mooched back at a steady pace, admiring the architecture. For a split second my faculties were caught off-guard when two Knights Templar wandered past. They were dressed in white tunics with a red cross emblazoned on the front. I had to look twice to make sure I hadn't inadvertently slipped through a hole in space and time. A pair of prescription spectacles and a modern timepiece gave the game away.

As we neared the square the number of partygoers increased. Lunchtime was over. We were greeted by a surreal mix of modern and medieval. Squads of Knights Templar were grouped together chatting over refreshments and aristocratic noblemen walked hand in hand with velvet-clad ladies. Even the children were dressed in costumes. It seemed as if the entire population had made the effort to participate in this period drama.

In the square, the fiesta was in full swing. Falconers entertained the crowds with their regal birds of prey, blacksmiths hammered at glowing rods of steel and stonemasons amazed onlookers with their skill. The market stalls were bustling with potential customers as artisan traders sold their handcrafted wares. Before long, the sound of medieval folk music drifted through the crowd, rising in volume as a troupe of players entered the square accompanied by street performers. When a ten-foot-tall witch arrived, young children hid behind their parents as she wielded her magic broomstick. The rest of the afternoon slipped away in a mêlée of medieval frivolity. By the time I looked at my watch, the hour had ticked around to eight.

'Are you feeling peckish?' I asked.

'Why, what time is it?'

'It's just gone eight.'

Melanie could hardly believe it. 'I'm ready when you are,' she replied.

Like many Chinese restaurants, the Restaurante Chino Gran Muralla is located in a less salubrious part of town on Calle Gral. The place was quiet; evening service had only just begun. A smartly dressed waiter showed us to a table.

Every dish on the menu looked familiar as did the interior décor. We made our choices and waited. The food was excellent. With time on our hands we dined at a leisurely pace, savouring each mouthful as if it was our last. After settling the bill, we headed back to the Plaza Ayuntamiento.

'So, where's this Ark of the Holy Grail?' asked Melanie, as we made our way along the narrow streets.

'It's the Ark of the Covenant and the Holy Grail.'

Melanie was teasing which was hardly surprising given the dubious provenance of these mythical artefacts.

'Fray Guido de Garda doesn't show his face until eleven,' I added.

'Who?'

'Fray Guido de Garda, Master of the Order of the Templars. He's the bloke who brings them.'

'And what time is it now?'

'Quarter past ten.'

'What are we going to do until then?'

The stallholders in the square were doing a brisk trade but we'd browsed them twice already. The craftsmen were still busy hammering metal or chiselling lumps of stone, and while their workmanship was undeniable, once you've seen one butter dish hewed from a granite block it's not quite as amazing the second time around. As for the birds of prey, they'd gone home for a well-earned rest.

'Let's get a drink,' I said.

We wandered back to Bar Chelsea which was much livelier than earlier in the day. As time drifted by, the flow of people walking towards the castle increased.

'I think we ought to make a move. We don't want to miss anything.'

Melanie agreed and we joined the exodus.

On the approach to the castle, crowds had gathered behind hastily erected barriers. We picked a spot and waited patiently.

'What time is it supposed to start?' asked Melanie.

I glanced at my watch.

'Ten minutes ago.'

In typically Spanish fashion, a further twenty minutes passed before a battalion of Templars appeared on the horizon, with each knight carrying a flaming torch. Leading these men at arms was none other than Fray Guido de Garda.

'He looks pretty good for his age,' I remarked.

'He's got some lovely shoes as well,' replied Melanie.

As the army approached the Ark of the Covenant came into view, carried on the shoulders of eight proud knights. The solid, gold coloured casket had more than a passing resemblance to an ornate blanket box. As for the Holy Grail, that arrived on the shoulders of six more soldiers. A rather underwhelming goblet of tarnished steel. As the procession turned to enter the castle, fountains of fire led the way.

The evening ended with a spectacular fireworks display as the relics disappeared from view, lost to humanity for another twelve months.

Considering the number of onlookers, I was surprised how quickly we got back to the car. We arrived home in the early hours. Jazz was excited to see us and we were delighted to be back. We'd had a fabulous day but we couldn't wait to hit the sack.

3

Birthday Celebrations

Clear blue sky and bright sunshine made returning to work all the more difficult. We'd had a great weekend but the sun terrace wouldn't build itself.

'Are you ready?' I asked.

Melanie was pulling on her working boots.

'One minute.'

We left Jazz in the garden and called at the builder's merchant on the way to Vilatán. Manolo had advised me that a mix of three aggregate to one cement would be ideal for the foundations of the retaining wall.

'I need a pallet of breezeblocks, a cubic metre of aggregate, and fifteen bags of cement,' I said to the sales assistant. 'Can you deliver them at nine o'clock tomorrow morning?'

'No problem.'

When we arrived at the house, Manolo was on the roof. We said hello and got straight to it.

The site of the proposed terrace was nothing more than a steep grassy banking, with the newly built stone steps climbing up one side. Digging the foundations was easier than I'd expected.

'We can build the wall on the bedrock,' I said.

'Are you sure?'

At times like this, Manolo's knowledge is invaluable so I asked him.

'You'll need to drill some holes in the rock and hammer steel reinforcing rods into it. That will prevent the wall from slipping,' he said.

Why hadn't I thought of that?

'I've got some rods you can use,' he added.

By lunchtime, I'd drilled the holes, hammered in the rods and shuttered the channel with boards to create a mould. First thing tomorrow we could mix the concrete and pour the foundations.

'Are we coming back this afternoon?' asked Melanie, on the drive home.

'No, we can't do anything until the materials are delivered.'

Harder days lay ahead so we enjoyed the time off while we could.

Stumbling across a Chinese restaurant in Ponferrada had got me thinking. If a city that size could accommodate one, perhaps I might find another in Chaves. Since discovering this Portuguese border town earlier in the year, it had become our favourite awayday destination. It had some great shops and prices across the border were excellent. Furnishing a house is expensive and every penny saved would be a penny earned. That afternoon I decided to take a look.

'Guess what I've found?' I said, as I stepped outside.

Melanie was lying on a sunlounger with her head in a book.

'That sock you were looking for?'

'Very funny.'

'I give in. What have you found?'

'A Chinese restaurant in Chaves.'

That pricked her curiosity.

'Whereabouts?'

'Rua Tabolado.'

'Never heard of it.'

'I've looked on Google Maps and it's at the bottom end of town close to the river.'

'We'll have to give it a go next time we visit,' suggested Melanie.

'It's funny you should say that.'

'Why?'

'I've been thinking. Would you like to go for my birthday?'

Manolo told us that once we'd poured the concrete foundations, it would need time to cure. Other than keeping it wet, I wasn't exactly sure what curing entailed or why it was necessary but according to him it was *muy importante* (very important).

'I thought the Ark of the Holy Grail was your birthday treat.'

'That doesn't mean to say that we can't do something on the 12th. And it's the Ark of the Covenant and the Holy Grail.'

'OK, let's go. We can have a look for a barbecue while we're there.'

Pricing up barbecues seemed a little premature but it couldn't harm to take a look.

The promise of a midweek trip to Portugal made an early start that little bit easier.

'Will you need me this morning?' asked Melanie, as I readied to leave.

Her tone dictated my reply.

'I'm sure I can manage without you.'

'It's just I've got all the bedding to iron for the other house.'

Melanie was referring to *Casa Bon Vista*, the holiday home we manage for our friends Bob and Janet. We had a party of four arriving that weekend and everything was still to iron.

'No problem.'

When I arrived at Vilatán, Manolo was putting the finishing touches to the roof and the results looked stunning. He'd turned his attention to the back porch, the new addition that would add a little character to an otherwise regular shaped building. I parked behind his van and went to say hello. The materials I'd ordered had already arrived.

'*Hola*,' I said, as I rounded the corner of the house.

'*Muy buenos*. Here's the delivery note from Otero's,' he said, handing it to me.

'*Gracias*.'

'When you mix the concrete it's better to have it too wet than too dry,' he advised.

The wet concrete found its own level inside the shuttering and by lunchtime I'd finished.

Before heading home, Manolo came to inspect my handiwork.

'Is that enough?' I asked.

Manolo gave it his seal of approval.

Stress-free summers are one of the reasons we moved to Spain, along with stress-free autumns, winters, and springs. Today was one of those lazy, pseudo-holiday days. While my concrete baked in the sun, I bathed in the heat. Manolo had offered to keep it moist to prevent it from cracking. Frequent dips in the pool ensured my crust received the same treatment. Hot summer days and warm still evenings had raised the water temperature to a very agreeable twenty-nine degrees Celsius; one more would be a record.

'What's for lunch?' I asked.

'I thought we could barbecue some chicken.'

The gas barbie had been worth its weight in gold. The heat was instant, controllable, and clean. A peaceful siesta followed lunch, dozing on a sunlounger in the shade of a parasol. The afternoon drifted seamlessly into early evening and a Teatime Taster.

'Red or white?' I asked.

Melanie chose white; I joined her. As the sun dipped over the horizon Jazz began to stir. A wander around the village before dinner seemed in order. More food, a few games of Scrabble and before we knew it, it was time for bed. I'm not sure we could live every day like this but it would be fun finding out.

'Happy birthday,' said Melanie, as she emerged from the kitchen carrying two mugs of coffee.

Birthdays aren't really my thing. I prefer celebrating other people's rather than my own.

'Thank you.'

Jazz followed her in and leapt onto the bed.

'Here you go,' said Melanie, handing me a few greetings cards and some presents from the UK.

I read through the cards and ripped open the presents. My sister Julie is always very generous on these occasions.

'What time are we setting off?' asked Melanie.

One of the great things about a trip to Portugal is the time difference. Spain is one hour in front which means after a sixty-minute drive we arrive in Chaves at the same time as we left home. The hour we lose on the return journey doesn't seem to matter.

'What about eleven?' I suggested. 'That will give us plenty of time to have a look around the shops before lunch?'

The scenery en route to Chaves is beautiful and even in the height of summer the roads are quiet and free flowing. As we approached the outskirts of the town we stopped at a garden centre to take a look at their extensive range of barbecues.

'They're more expensive than I expected,' I said.

'You're not kidding, look at the price of that one.'

Melanie was pointing at what I can only describe as the Rolls Royce of pre-cast concrete barbecues complete with prep area and a sink.

'It's hideous and besides which, where would we put it?'

Within minutes of arriving we'd hopped back into the car and driven off.

'There looks to be a place coming up on the left,' said Melanie.

Standing on the roadside verge were all manner of concrete ornaments from a life-sized mother goose and half a dozen goslings, to a five-tier fountain standing two metres tall. I pulled up alongside and we walked into a courtyard littered with garden ornaments.

'Hello, my name is Amelia, can I help you?' said a woman in Portuguese.

Her sudden appearance caught us by surprise.

'Do you have any barbecues?' I asked.

She gestured us to follow her and led us to a yard at the back of the shop. The amount of stock was overwhelming. As well as a comprehensive selection of barbecues there were all manner of replica religious artefacts and an extensive range of ornamental fountains. Nothing caught our eye.

The price of each item had been handwritten on a white self-adhesive label. The weathered appearance hinted at their age. Most had been bleached by the sun to such an extent that the prices were almost illegible and winter moisture had made them curl at the edges.

'This one's nice,' said Amelia, trying to drum up trade.

'It's not really what we're looking for,' I replied.

Melanie had started edging back towards the car.

'What about this one?' she asked.

As barbecues go, they were all very nice but none of them fitted our vision for the house.

'It's too big,' I said politely, 'but thanks for showing us around.'

Melanie took the hint and made a beeline for the exit; that's when I spotted it.

'Hang on a minute,' I called.

'What?'

'Look at this.'

'It's a fireplace.'

Amelia saw her chance.

'I can do a good price on that one,' she said.

'How much?' I asked.

'Craig, it's a fireplace.'

'I know it's a fireplace but don't you think it's stunning?'

Melanie took a closer look.

This was exactly what I'd envisaged for the new lounge. A statement piece crafted from solid granite. It was magnificent.

'Have you seen the price?' she whispered.

Someone had scribbled 1250 in pencil on one corner of the plinth.

Amelia had taken a calculator from a desk and was tapping on the keys. She showed us the result. Melanie and I peered at the LCD display and then at each other.

'What do you think?' I asked.

'It's a good price.'

'But do you like it?'

'It's gorgeous but can we afford it?'

'Can we afford not to buy it?'

Amelia had reduced the price to 650 euros.

'Let's go for it,' said Melanie.

'Can we reserve it and collect it later?' I asked.

Amelia's eyes lit up.

'Sure, no problem.'

In our best Portuguese-Spanglish we explained it would be some time before we could collect it.

'We don't have any floors at the moment,' I explained.

From the look on her face, that fact was lost in translation. The terms of the sale were a minor consideration; Amelia was just relieved to have closed a deal. We agreed a deposit of 100 euros with the balance payable on collection.

'We'll phone you before we come,' I said, as we left.

The clock had ticked around to 12:50 pm.

'We'd better see if we can find the restaurant,' I said.

'I thought you knew where it was?'

At times like this, I wish I'd printed out a map. Too late now.

'I do,' I replied.

We drove through town, passed the castle and headed towards the river.

'According to Google, it's somewhere along here, so keep your eyes peeled.'

The town centre was quite busy, forcing me to drive quicker than I wanted.

'Perhaps it's a little further than I thought,' I admitted.

We reached the end of the road and neither of us had seen anything remotely like a Chinese restaurant.

'Where now?' asked Melanie.

I had little choice but to carry straight on.

'We can ask there.'

'Where?'

I'd driven past a sign marked tourist information. If anyone knew its whereabouts, they would.

'Tourist information.'

'Where's the tourist information?'

'One hundred metres down here.'

The office was situated in a small leafy square. I parked nearby.

'It's closed,' said Melanie, 'what time is it?'

I glanced at my watch.

'Six minutes past one.'

'They close at one,' she said, pointing at a notice taped to the window.

'Bugger!'

I looked around the square for signs of life. All the shops had closed for lunch. We were just about to leave when I spotted movement inside a kiosk on the far corner of the square.

'There,' I said, pointing at the kiosk, 'let's ask if they know where it is.'

The chap in the kiosk was a cheery-looking bloke in his late fifties. He listened patiently to my ramblings before replying.

'That's right,' he said, 'there is a Chinese restaurant.'

At last.

'Do you know where it is?' I asked.

The man looked thoughtful. Melanie and I waited.

'I think it's in Rua Tabolado,' he replied.

I could have told him that.

'Has it moved?' I asked.

'No, I don't think so. I'm sure it's on Rua Tabolado but I couldn't tell you exactly where.'

We thanked him for his insight and made our way back to the car.

'That was helpful,' remarked Melanie.

'We must have missed it,' I said. 'Let's take another look.'

The roads were much quieter by now; everyone had gone home for lunch.

'Just check that this is Rua Tabolado,' I said, as we neared our starting point.

'Yes, this is it,' she replied.

Slowly, I trundled along the road, one eye in front and the other searching for the eatery.

'It's there!' called Melanie.

'Where?'

'You've just passed it.'

Reversing was out of the question. I turned next right and parked. We could only hope the food justified our efforts. Walking towards the restaurant, it was easy to see how we'd missed it. The signage was hidden under the portico of a modern apartment block.

The interior decoration was exactly as we'd expected, so too the menu. The food, however, was very different. From the spring rolls to the chicken with cashew nuts, the dishes were absolutely delicious and very different to anything we'd eaten before. The Jing Huà Chinese restaurant was instantly elevated to our favourite eatery, justifying the 280-kilometre round trip.

Now that's my idea of a birthday celebration.

Having recharged our batteries, we were raring to go. Even Melanie had a spring in her step. When we arrived at Vilatán, Manolo had finished the roof and was busy power-washing the outside walls. Clothed in an oversized waterproof jacket, matching green trousers and black wellies, he looked more like a deep-sea fisherman than a builder.

'Wow,' said Melanie, as we stepped from the car.

Wow indeed. Even in its ruined state the house was photogenic. With its brand-new roof, it had become a budding supermodel.

'*Hola*,' we called, over the noise of the compressor.

Manolo tried to wave but as soon as he took one hand off the high-pressure pistol it recoiled into the air.

'At least the roof's watertight,' I joked.

The foundations had set solid and there wasn't a crack in sight. While I mixed some cement, Melanie loaded three blocks into the barrow and wheeled them from the meadow to the far end of the house.

'Where do you want these?' she asked.

'There will be fine.'

An hour into the morning, the compressor fell silent. Manolo took his break at the same time every day. His choice of snack was almost as predictable. A large chunk of bread with either cheese, ham, or chorizo, washed down with a can of cheap beer. As usual, he wandered across to see what we were doing.

'Is it OK?' I asked.

'It's very good. When you've finished the first row I'll show you a quicker way.'

Manolo had watched me using a spirit level which was slow and laborious. His adjustable line level resulted in the second row being laid in less than half the time.

We spent Saturday morning fulfilling our duties as property managers by cleaning *Casa Bon Vista* in readiness for the new arrivals. On Sunday we did the 'Meet and Greet', a phrase we'd coined for welcoming new guests to the house.

All too soon we were back at Vilatán. I quickly found my rhythm, mixing cement and laying blocks. By Wednesday, Manolo had finished cleaning the stone and made a start on repointing. Each dollop of cement seemed to breathe new life into the old farmhouse. Watching his progress was like seeing blood flowing through the veins of a living entity. Whatever happened, Melanie and I had to ensure the new terrace continued this sympathetic evolution and avoided a visual revolution.

By the end of the week, my blockwork had reached the required height. Manolo was making good progress but that was about to end. When he agreed to undertake the restoration, it had been on the proviso that he could take a couple of months off during the summer. August and September are his busiest time of year. Property owners who don't reside in the area arrive for their annual escape and Manolo is overwhelmed with requests to patch up the previous year's wear and tear. These regular clients are an important part of his annual income. Two months away wouldn't affect our timetable so we were happy to agree.

Before leaving he advised us not to use the old roof tiles to backfill the terrace.

'They'll turn to dust in no time,' he said.

'Will gravel do the job?' I asked.

'Perfect.'

'How much are we going to need?' asked Melanie.

Manolo stared into the void.

'About four cubic metres should do it,' he replied.

'Is that four Big Bags?' whispered Melanie, realising she'd be barrowing it.

A Big Bag contains a cubic metre of aggregate. They're a bit more expensive than buying it loose but far more convenient and the weight is accurate.

'That's right,' I replied, 'but don't worry, I'll have them delivered at the top of the track. It'll be downhill from there.'

That wasn't strictly accurate but there is a slight downward slope.

'Anyway, we need to sort out the drainage before then.'

The concept of drainage is often overlooked in Galician rural properties. Many homes don't even have gutters, something we'd insisted on. I was determined to divert as much water away from the house as possible. The guttering at the back would flow through a series of underground pipes into the adjacent track.

Before heading home for lunch, we thanked Manolo for his efforts and looked forward to his return.

'If you're stuck for something to do you can always come back for a few days,' I said.

Manolo smiled.

No sooner had we returned home than the phone rang. Melanie rushed to answer it.

'That was Di,' she said.

Di and her husband Bill moved to the area a couple of years after us. They live in a small village on the outskirts of Ferreira.

'What did she want?'

'She asked if we'd like to join them for their village fiesta.'

'That sounds fun. When is it?'

'Next Friday.'

Small village fiestas are usually great fun, especially the

first night. The atmosphere is always very friendly. As for the entertainment, that could be anything.

On Monday morning, I hitched up the trailer and we drove to the builder's merchant in Monforte. The trade counter was busy when we arrived. I began by ordering the gravel.

'Loose or Big Bags?' asked Marcus, our favourite sales assistant.

'Big Bags please. And delivery?'

He looked at the schedule.

'First drop tomorrow afternoon.'

'Is that the best you can do?'

'I'm afraid so.'

'OK.'

'Anything else?'

'We need these,' I said, handing him a list of plastic pipes, elbows, and a drain.

I secured the five metre lengths of plastic pipes to the trailer and we left for Vilatán.

Before the day was out, all the pipework was in place. Backfilling could now begin.

4

Ollie the Octopus

Without Manolo's van parked in the meadow, the house looked abandoned. We'd left home at 4:00 pm. With a bit of luck, the delivery driver would be waiting for us when we arrived. I should have known better.

'It seems strange without Manolo here,' I remarked.

The place was eerily quiet. We wandered across to the far end of the house and stared up the track.

'What time did Marcus say they'd deliver?' asked Melanie.

'First drop after lunch.'

'And exactly what time is that?'

Melanie was alluding to the fact that I hadn't asked. Even if I had, it wouldn't have made any difference.

'I thought they might be here,' I replied.

'What time is it now?'

'Five o'clock.'

The delivery finally turned up at 6:00 pm.

'Where do you want them?' asked the driver.

'Over here,' I said, pointing to a patch of spare ground at the top of the track.

The lorry's hydraulic arm made light work of unloading the heavy bags.

'Where now?' he asked.

He'd managed to squeeze three bags into the space, but unloading the fourth would block the track. It probably wouldn't be there very long but I couldn't take that risk. When it comes to obstructing a public right of way, the locals get a little prickly. We had no choice but to drop it in the meadow.

'Can you take it around the front?' I asked.

'No problem,' he replied.

Ten minutes later he'd finished unloading and was on his way. By now the clock had ticked around to 6:30 pm.

'Right then, we'd better get cracking. It's not going to move itself.'

The distance from the top of the track to the site of the new terrace was about twenty-five metres. I shovelled the gravel into the wheelbarrow, Melanie pushed it to the house and I tipped it. Time and time again we tramped back and forth.

'That's enough,' she said, as I emptied one more shovelful into the barrow.

Shifting half a tonne of gravel didn't seem much for half a day's work but by 7:30 pm we'd had enough.

It took two more days to empty the three bags at the top of the track.

'What are we going to do about the other?' asked Melanie.

'You'll have to wheel it through the village.'

'You've got to be joking, it must be half a mile.'

A slight exaggeration but of course I was joking.

'I'll fill the trailer and drive it round.'

Using the trailer turned out to be a great idea. It held a lot more than the wheelbarrow and was narrow enough to fit down the track. By the time we headed home on

Thursday, we'd shifted the lot. All we had to do now was top it with a concrete base.

When your body talks it's important to listen. The previous day's efforts had left us feeling battered and bruised.

'Let's take the day off and start again on Monday,' I suggested over breakfast.

A relaxing day at home was the perfect tonic for a fiesta night out with Bill and Di.

The focal point of the night's activities was the village green in front of the church. Like many villages in the area, Següín is little more than a hamlet of a dozen or so properties scattered over an ill-defined area. It surprises me how well attended local fiestas are but the offer of free food and drink helps boost the numbers. Tonight's offering was crispy rashers of pancetta atop a wedge of crusty bread washed down with local red wine. The fatty aromas from the table-sized griddle were tempting enough to challenge the most stoic vegetarian.

A Spanish fiesta wouldn't be complete without music. The night's entertainer was a female vocalist of generous proportions. Her repertoire of popular tunes was delivered from the top of a farm trailer dragged onto the green by a 1940s Massey Ferguson tractor. A makeshift electricity supply had been wired into a nearby streetlight providing the power to a row of low voltage lightbulbs and an overworked amplifier. After a couple of hours, the congregation began to thin as people drifted home for their fiesta feast, so we took our cue and did the same.

A late night and copious amounts of wine are not conducive to an early start but needs must. The guests were leaving *Casa Bon Vista* that morning and new arrivals were due later in the day. In between time we had to make sure everywhere was spick and span. Two and a half hours after arriving, the place looked spotless.

On days like this an afternoon siesta is impossible to resist. I positioned a sunlounger in the shade and quickly nodded off.

Ring, ring ... Ring, ring!

I opened my eyes in time to see Melanie running into the house. Five minutes later she reappeared.

'That was Yvonne.'

Yvonne and Richard are the parents of Melanie's goddaughter Erren and her brother Mason. Since our move to Spain they've become regular summer visitors. Aged four and seven, they've taught me the joy of chaos and the need, if only briefly, to challenge the boundaries of normal living.

'When do they arrive?'

'Next Thursday.'

'What!'

'I know, it doesn't seem two minutes since she told me they'd booked.'

'What did she want?' I asked.

'To see if there's anything we'd like them to bring.'

'A pork pie wouldn't go amiss,' I replied.

'That was top of my list. Mason said hello and asked if we still have Gary Gator.'

It surprises me what kids remember.

Gary Gator is an eight-foot-long inflatable alligator we bought in 2004. Despite Melanie's reservations, he instantly became a family favourite and has given the kids hours of fun.

'I know exactly where he is,' I replied.

'That's good. We also ought to start thinking about somewhere to go; you know what Yvonne's like.'

If it were up to the kids they'd spend every waking hour in the swimming pool but Yvonne thinks it important for them to get a little more from their Spanish holiday.

'What about Ourense?' I suggested.

'Ourense?'

'The old town is really nice and we could catch the tourist train to the hot springs.'

Ourense has two claims to fame, an inordinate number of bridges joining the two halves of the city across the river Miño and natural hot springs that possess magical healing properties, or so they claim. The tourist train is actually a road-going truck disguised as a steam engine. It tows half a dozen carriages through the pedestrianised streets and along the riverbank to the out of town hot springs.

'That's not a bad idea,' said Melanie.

She made it sound like I never have them.

'Where does the train set off from?' she asked.

'I don't know but I can find out.'

A quick internet search revealed it left the Plaza Mayor four times a day, twice in the morning and twice in the afternoon. If Yvonne wanted the kids to explore new horizons, we had a plan.

Mason's enquiry got me thinking. Gary Gator was getting a bit long in the tooth, so to speak. Perhaps it was time to add to our inflatable collection. On our next trip to the supermarket, I took my chance. While Melanie queued at the deli counter, I sloped off to browse the non-food section. The choice of inflatables was mind-boggling, from flotation aids to luxurious armchair recliners. One toy caught my eye. The illustration on the box showed a giant octopus with eight multicoloured tentacles. Priced at under ten euros, how could we go wrong?

'Look what I've found,' I said, when I finally caught up with Melanie.

'What is it?'

'A child-eating octopus.'

'Really.'

Melanie seemed unimpressed, which was hardly surprising given the size of the box.

'Well don't count on me blowing it up,' she added.

A clear indication that she was happy for me to add it to this week's housekeeping budget.

Back home I couldn't wait to see what it looked like. I tugged it out of the box and unfolded the tightly packed toy. There's something quite appealing about the smell of rubber. The eight tentacles were much longer than I'd expected. As for the body, that would remain a secret until I'd blown it up.

'Teatime Taster?' asked Melanie.

'Why not.'

'Red or white?'

'White for me.'

Melanie disappeared into the kitchen and I got to work.

There's a knack to blowing up inflatables. Inlet valves work best if they're nipped between finger and thumb but if it's a small valve and you have large fingers, it can be tricky.

'Here you go,' said Melanie, placing a glass of white wine on the table.

I nodded my head and continued blowing. After five minutes I paused to catch my breath.

Given the effort I'd expended, the result was pitiful.

'You haven't got very far,' commented Melanie, as she stared at the limp toy.

'It's massive,' I replied. 'You can have a go if you like.'

'No chance. It's your idea; you can blow it up.'

I took a sip of wine to lubricate my lips. As time passed my efficiency waned. Failure to synchronise the nipping and releasing of the valve with inhaling and blowing led to bubbles of saliva leaking from the corners of my mouth.

'That's disgusting,' said Melanie. 'Why don't you take a break?'

Her offer was tempting; my cheeks were aching and I was sure I'd split my lip. I held the inflatable at arm's length to check my progress. The difference since my last pause was hardly noticeable. The enormity of the challenge was becoming apparent.

Given its size, I would have expected each tentacle to have a valve and another for the body; no such luck. If I didn't hurry up the Kershaws would have been and gone by the time I'd breathed life into this monster.

Another five minutes of lung-busting effort revealed the outline of a shape. It looked like an enormous, bright yellow, flat bottomed beach ball decorated with blue circles. Five minutes later two huge eyes stared back at me.

'Look at that,' I said, pointing at the base of the domed head.

'What is it?'

'It's a hosepipe connection.'

Melanie looked puzzled.

The picture on the box showed a fountain of water spouting from the top of its head. Not for one minute did I think it was possible. It seemed I was wrong.

'Look at the picture,' I said, handing her the box.

'You're kidding,' she replied, staring at the image.

'Apparently not.'

This unexpected discovery spurred me on. One by one the giant tentacles filled with air. As they did the creature began to snare me in its grasp. Ever so slowly the head, body and two-tone tentacles became as firm as a wine gum.

'What do you think?' I said proudly.

'I think you look shattered.'

'You're not kidding.'

I felt like I'd spent the last hour diving for pearls. The result, however, was magnificent. The creature was at least three metres in diameter and a metre tall.

'Give it a go then,' urged Melanie.

'Let me catch my breath.'

Melanie stared at me.

'OK,' I added.

'What are you going to call it?' she asked, as I dragged it towards the pool.

I thought for a moment.

'Ollie.'

'Ollie?'

'Ollie the Octopus of course.'

I placed it on the edge of the pool, pushed the hosepipe onto the connector and launched him into the water.

'Are you ready?' I asked.

'Go on then,' she urged.

When I opened the tap, jets of water erupted from Ollie's head exactly as illustrated.

'Wow! That's great,' said Melanie.

I had to agree.

'That's one way to top up the pool,' she added.

Melanie had a point. With two kids jumping in and out, topping the water level up would be a regular chore. That evening Ollie slept under the porch, held in place with a few garden chairs. The last thing we wanted was a gust of wind taking him on a walkabout. Everything was ready for the arrival of our guests.

The next day began bright and sunny. Throughout July the temperature had risen steadily and continued into August. Soon our quiet and orderly lives would be tipped upside down.

'Are you ready for the little people?' I asked Jazz, as she waited for me to open the back door.

In a week's time, she would be as exhausted as us.

'Here you go,' I said, pushing open the door.

'Would you like another coffee?' asked Melanie.

'Yes please.'

'I'll bring it out.'

When I stepped outside, Jazz was lying on the terrace basking in the morning sunshine. Ollie was where I'd left him but something wasn't quite right. His egg-shaped dome had lost its form and at least one of the tentacles looked almost flat.

'I think we've got a problem,' I shouted from the terrace.

'One minute,' called Melanie.

I moved the chairs out of the way and dragged the limp sea creature into the sunshine.

'What's happened?' asked Melanie, as she emerged from the kitchen with two mugs of coffee.

'I think he's sprung a leak.'

'You're kidding.'

I wish I was; blowing him up had almost put my lights out.

'Oh well, at least it wasn't very expensive,' said Melanie.

'That's not the point.'

I paused for a moment thinking what to do next. We were expecting our guests to arrive at lunchtime. Whatever we decided, we needed to be quick about it.

'I want another,' I said.

'There isn't time.'

'Of course there is. Come on, let's get him into the back of the car.'

'As it is?'

'Well I'm not letting any more air out. It took me long enough to blow it up. Come on, grab a leg.'

'What about the coffee?'

'Coffee can wait.'

Reluctantly, Melanie put the mugs down on the garden table and sauntered across to give me a hand.

'Careful,' I said, as we squeezed him through the side gate.

'Yes sir. We wouldn't want to puncture him, would we?'

I lifted the car's tailgate and unceremoniously stuffed him in the back.

'It's not going to fit,' said Melanie.

Ollie was a mere shadow of his former self but in the world of inflatables, he could still hold his own.

'Oh yes he will,' I replied, pushing my body weight into the deflating inflatable.

As I pushed, a tentacle leapt from the car.

'Don't just stand there,' I said.

Melanie grabbed the flailing limb and thrust it back into the car. As she did another popped out the other side.

'You're going to have to undo the valve,' she said, doing her best not to laugh.

Explaining the problem to the supermarket cashier would have been easier with the valve closed but Melanie was right. Ollie's refusal to cooperate left me no choice. I opened the valve and wrestled with his head, while Melanie grappled with his tentacles. After several minutes of stiff resistance, he finally succumbed.

'When I let go, you close the tailgate. After three, one, two, three.'

Like an Olympic sprinter launching himself off the starting blocks I recoiled from the car as Melanie slammed the tailgate.

It had taken the best part of half an hour to restrain Ollie. I jumped in the car, reversed out of the driveway and sped through the village. When I opened the tailgate at the supermarket Ollie was no more, gone forever on a whiff of stale air. I dragged him out and did my best to tuck him under my arm. The shop assistant was very understanding.

'Would you like to choose another?' she asked.

I wandered into the shop to find his twin brother. As I walked back to the checkout I heard giggling on the next aisle. Three shop assistants were fighting to get Ollie back in the box. Even in deflation Ollie had brought joy to the world.

Back home doubts began to surface as my lungs clamoured for air. Within two hours of my fateful discovery Ollie was reincarnated to his former glory. It would take me somewhat longer to recover.

'I'll have that coffee now.'

5

Uncle Craig

The calm before the storm. Our peaceful world would soon be shaken to its core and to be honest, I couldn't wait. A clang on the doorbell announced their arrival.

'They're here,' called Melanie from the kitchen.

Ollie was floating serenely on the still water of the swimming pool. I rushed over to the outside tap and slowly opened the valve. Jets of water erupted from the top of his head, creating a symmetrical shower of droplets. By the time I'd walked around to the front, Mason had unbuckled the restraint on his booster seat and jumped out of the car. Without saying a word, he ran to the back, opened the tailgate and tugged his carry-on out of the boot.

'Mason, just wait,' said mum Yvonne, as she fought to undo Erren's baby seat.

Her words fell on deaf ears. Mason was far too excited to pay attention.

'Don't I get a kiss?' asked Melanie.

'Mason, slow down,' demanded his dad, Richard.

Mason knew exactly what was expected of him. He dropped his case and flung his arms around Aunty Melanie. She scooped him off the ground and gave him a big kiss. One down, one to go. He ran to me; instinctively I offered him my hand. His initial surprise quickly changed to pride. He pouted his chest out and reciprocated my adult greeting. Duty performed, he ran back to his case, grabbed the handle and dragged it towards the house. By now Erren was free. She copied her big brother's actions. Firstly, running to Melanie and then to me before bolting back to the car to retrieve her carry-on case.

'Here you go,' said Richard, lifting it out for her.

Erren grabbed it and chased after Mason.

'What do you say?' called Yvonne, as Erren bumped it up the doorstep.

'Thank you,' she shouted, before disappearing into the house.

No sooner had Erren vanished than Mason reappeared.

'Mummy, Mummy, come look at this,' he said excitedly.

Yvonne glanced at me as if to say, What have you been up to?

'What is it?'

'Come and look,' he replied before running back inside the house.

Yvonne turned to Melanie. 'What is it?'

'Wait and see.'

The four of us walked through the house and into the back garden. Ollie was floating in one corner with water spouting from his head.

'Oh, my word! Couldn't you find anything bigger?' joked Yvonne.

'Uncle Craig, what's his name?' asked Erren.

'That's Ollie,' I replied, 'Ollie the Octopus.'

'Uncle Craig, have you still got Gary Gator?' asked Mason.

'We have,' I replied. 'He's sleeping in the laundry room.'

By the time I'd extricated Gary from his hiding place, Mason and Erren had unzipped their suitcases, pulled out their swimming costumes and were hurriedly stripping.

'Here you go,' I said, hurling Gary into the pool. 'Be careful he doesn't bite, he hasn't had his lunch yet.'

Mason was first to brave the water in his brand-new Union Jack patterned swimming trunks.

'Mason, have you put some suntan lotion on?' asked Yvonne.

A rhetorical question to prepare him for a smothering.

'Beer, Richard?' I asked.

'It would be rude to say no.'

Yvonne took control of the situation. Erren wriggled uncontrollably while Mum daubed her in cream and Dad breathed life into her buoyancy aids. Overenthusiasm meant he had to let some air out so she could squeeze her arms through.

'Mason, come and have some cream put on,' called Yvonne.

'Just a minute.'

'No, now.'

Yvonne's tone struck the right note. Reluctantly, Mason dragged himself away from the pool. Another competition ensued as Mason wriggled and Yvonne wrestled until every inch of his alabaster flesh had been covered.

'And put your hat on.'

'Aww Mum.'

'Mason, do as you're told,' said Richard.

With the immediate challenges resolved we took a seat and enjoyed a refreshing drink.

'Are you coming in Dad?' asked Mason.

'Not just yet.'

'But when?'

'Soon.'

After a long drive, all Richard wanted to do was relax.

'How soon?'

'When I've finished my drink.'

'Come on Dad.'

'Yeah, come on Dad,' said Erren.

'When I've finished my drink.'

Mason and Erren had no trouble entertaining themselves but Mum and Dad weren't about to get away scot-free.

'Mum, watch this,' said Mason, before jumping into the pool.

'Look at me Dad,' called Erren, mirroring her brother's water bomb.

Before long, Richard had downed his beer, an act that didn't go unnoticed.

'Are you coming in now, Dad?' asked Mason.

'Yeah, come on Dad,' called Erren.

Richard's excuse had slipped away as easily as the cold beer.

'OK,' he said before nipping inside to change.

His reappearance was greeted with excited cheers. He walked to the deep end, took up a starting position and dived straight in. Seconds later he emerged, shock etched into his face.

'It's freezing.'

'No it's not,' replied Mason.

'It's not Dad, really it's not,' confirmed Erren. 'It's only when you first get in.'

Such wisdom from a young mind.

Dad played with the kids until they'd worn him out.

'Teatime,' called Melanie.

Chicken nuggets and baked beans, the perfect fuel to keep two human dynamos energised.

Their first fun-filled day came to an end at about 8:00 pm when the adults finally got a moment's peace.

'Can Uncle Craig read us a story?' asked Erren.

I'd spoken too soon.

The pair rested quietly in their beds while Uncle Craig read a short story.

'Can we have another?' asked Mason, as I closed the book.

'If you go to sleep now, I'll read you another tomorrow.'

Not quite the answer they wanted but a deal was struck.

For the first time since they'd arrived, *El Sueño* fell silent.

'Who'd like a drink?' I asked, as I stepped outside.

With all the orders filled we finally got a chance to relax and catch up on news.

The peace and quiet lasted until seven the following morning. Batteries recharged, they were off again. By the time I rose, they'd been playing in the pool for the best part of two hours.

'Uncle Craig, can we have paella for lunch?' asked Mason, as I stepped outside.

'Yeah Uncle Craig, can we?' echoed Erren.

I glanced at Melanie. It seemed the question had been well rehearsed.

'Of course we can,' I replied.

'Yeah!'

I hadn't yet had breakfast and lunch was planned.

Since our move to Spain, paella has become one of my speciality dishes. It's a great alternative to lighting the barbecue.

At noon, I made a start. A few years ago, I treated myself to a double ringed burner and a forty-six-centimetre paella pan. I began by bathing the pan with extra virgin olive oil before adding chopped onions and garlic and sweating them until the onions were soft. Then I added the chicken. Chopped boneless breast is not exactly traditional but as I'm not a lover of fiddling with my food, boneless meat makes perfect sense. After sealing the diced chicken I added a packet of saffron. The colour change was instant. I followed this with chopped tomatoes and a bowl of frozen peas.

As soon as I'd added the rice, speed was of the essence. I mixed in two teaspoons of pimiento powder and stirred everything together before pouring in enough chicken stock to fill the pan to the brim. After bringing it to the boil, I left it to simmer until the rice started to catch on the bottom of the pan. As a finishing touch I created a sunburst effect using alternate strips of red and yellow peppers.

'Come and get it,' I called.

Strangely enough, I didn't need to ask twice.

In between mouthfuls, conversation turned to our upcoming trip to Australia.

'Tell me again, Craig, how exactly did you manage to blag a free holiday to Oz?' asked Yvonne.

'I believe it's called synchronicity.'

Richard rested his fork on the edge of his plate and stared at me.

'I thought that was underwater ballet,' he quipped.

'You're thinking of synchronised swimming. Synchronicity is when a series of seemingly unrelated events coincide resulting in something unexpected happening.'

'And how does that explain a free holiday to Australia?'

'Well, in this instance the seemingly unrelated events were Bob and Janet's holiday let, a roof terrace extension, a rental enquiry from a family in Australia and a planned working holiday to the Costa Blanca.'

'You've lost me,' said Yvonne.

'All those events culminated in an Australian family staying in our house for a fortnight in exchange for us staying in theirs for a month.'

'And they agreed to that?'

'Not only did they agree but they said we could go for as long as we liked and use their car for the duration.'

'You jammy so and so's,' replied Richard, mindful of little ears.

'I know. We couldn't have asked to meet a nicer family.'

'So how long are you going for?' asked Yvonne.

'We set off from the UK on the 7th of February and get back on the 15th of March.'

'You're flying from the UK?'

'Yes, the flights were much cheaper and Melanie's mum is looking after Jazz.'

The conversation moved seamlessly on to Richard and Yvonne's gap year. Both had spent it in Australia, but not with each other.

'You went with someone else?' asked a surprised Mason.

'I didn't know your dad then,' replied Yvonne.

'You had a boyfriend?' he asked, clearly struggling to imagine Mummy with a boyfriend who wasn't Daddy.

'That's right, we toured the country in a campervan.'

Mummy's revelation left Mason and Erren open-mouthed.

'We had a great time,' she added.

A nervous giggle followed their astonished silence. The innocence of youth.

'We thought you might like to visit Ourense after lunch,' interrupted Melanie.

Her suggestion was less well received than my paella but Yvonne seemed keen. The kids said nothing. They knew from experience that at some point during their stay Mummy would drag them away from the pool.

'What's the matter?' I asked. 'Don't you want to take a train ride?'

Mason's eyes lit up.

'What train?' he asked.

'A little train that goes from the town centre to the hot springs.'

Mason paused for thought.

'Uncle Craig, what are hot springs?'

'They're big paddling pools that fill with water from wells that are so deep the water comes out hot.'

Mason looked at his dad for confirmation.

'Uncle Craig, is it a real train?'

'It's a special train with carriages that can drive through the narrow city streets and along the riverbank.'

All of a sudden, a trip to the hot springs didn't seem such a bad idea after all.

'And guess what's coming to town this weekend,' I said.

'What?' asked Erren.

'It's the Monforte fiesta.'

'Uncle Craig, what's a fiesta?' asked Mason.

'It's a Spanish party with music, dancing, market stalls, and an enormous funfair.'

This was more like the cultural activity Mason and Erren were interested in.

'There's only one drawback,' I added.

'What?' they asked.

'It doesn't start until really late so you'll have to do what all the Spanish kids do and have a siesta in the afternoon.'

'Uncle Craig, what's a siesta?'

'It's a short nap.'

Mason thought I was pulling his leg.

'Do we?' he asked his mum.

'If you want to stay out late you do,' she replied.

'All the kids in the village have a siesta and then they're allowed to stay out until really late,' I explained.

It seemed the idea of an afternoon siesta had some merit.

The drive to Ourense is stunning. The main road climbs out of the Val de Lemos, then drops over 1,300 feet in less than seven kilometres to the banks of the river Miño. When we arrived, the streets were quiet.

We made our way to the Plaza Mayor in the centre of the old town. It was quite a relief to see the tourist train parked there. We wandered around the vehicle looking for ticket information or a timetable. As usual, there wasn't either.

'Do you think we'll be able to buy tickets from the driver?' I asked.

'Let's hope so,' replied Melanie.

'Let's get a drink while we wait,' I suggested.

On one side of the square is the town hall. Opposite and adjacent are a number of bars. We walked to the nearest and took a table in the shade. Shortly after, a young waiter came to take our order.

Within ten minutes of our arrival a young couple walked into the square. They too circled the train looking for information before waiting nearby. At least we weren't the only ones without tickets. By the time the driver turned up, a small crowd had gathered. We settled the bill and joined them.

'Six please,' said Melanie.

Mason had already jumped aboard and Erren was keen to follow. The carriages quickly filled and the train departed.

Most of the streets leading away from the Plaza Mayor are pedestrianised. Alluring window displays flashed past as the train weaved through the paved alleyways tooting its horn at unsuspecting passers-by. Before long we reached the river Miño. The crossing point was Ponte Vella, a bridge that dates back to the Roman occupation in the first century. Once across, the driver stopped to let passengers alight and others board. I got the impression that those departing used the train as a convenient commute from one side of the city to the other.

Half an hour after leaving the Plaza Mayor we arrived at the natural hot springs at Burga de Canedo, a free council facility comprising four outdoor pools of increasing water temperature.

'This is lovely,' remarked Yvonne as she dipped her feet in one of the pools.

Even the kids seemed to enjoy the warm water.

The train departed shortly after arriving and returned an hour later. Just long enough to keep two young children occupied.

We arrived back at *El Sueño* in time for a dip before dinner. Breaded fish shapes and more baked beans. As promised, the day ended with another bedtime story.

Saturday morning followed a similar pattern to Friday. The kids had been in and out of the pool for over an hour by the time I showed my face.

'When can we see the house?' asked Yvonne, referring to our latest project.

'We can pop up this morning if you'd like but there isn't much to see,' I replied.

She seemed to think I was joking, but nothing could have been further from the truth. An hour later we were trundling through the lanes of Vilatán. I pulled into the driveway and Richard followed.

It wasn't yet lunchtime and the temperature had rocketed past thirty degrees Celsius. Stepping out of the air-conditioned car was like walking into a warm oven.

'Well?' I asked.

The silence was deafening.

'I told you there wasn't much to see,' I added.

Even Mason was lost for words.

'We've widened the driveway,' I said.

Richard turned to look but still seemed in a state of shock.

'The roof's finished,' I added, trying to find something positive to say.

'Remind me again, why did you buy it?' asked Yvonne.

'It's not that bad,' I replied.

In front of the house were piles of old roof tiles. Manolo's cement mixer stood in a dried-up puddle of grey cement which had leaked across the meadow, leaving it looking like an aerial view of the Amazon delta.

'That's the borehole over there,' I said, pointing at the wellhead cover.

'How deep is it?' asked Richard, who seemed to have recovered from his initial shock.

'Two hundred metres.'

I explained the problems we'd had and the extra costs we hadn't budgeted for.

'And this will be the new terrace.'

If they weren't traumatised when they arrived, they were now. The sight of a three-metre-high breezeblock retaining wall situated less than a metre from the southern end of our beautiful granite farmhouse was a step too far. I could almost feel their disdain at what we'd done.

'It looks pretty ugly at the moment but when it's clad with natural stone it should look like it has been there for years.'

They weren't convinced.

We walked back to the front of the house and I unlocked the *bodega* doors.

'I'm afraid there's not much to see in here.'

'You're not kidding,' remarked Yvonne as she stepped inside.

Trying to explain how much effort it had taken to get the *bodegas* looking like this proved fruitless.

'Is anyone ready for lunch?' I asked, changing the subject.

'Yeah!' sang Mason and Erren.

'We need a loaf from town on the way back,' said Melanie.

'Aunty Melanie, what are we having for lunch?' asked Erren.

'We're going to have different types of cured meat and cheeses with crusty bread.'

Erren looked apprehensive.

'Aunty Melanie, can I have some sliced carrots with mine?' she asked.

'Of course you can.'

'And sweetcorn. Can I have some sweetcorn?'

'You can have whatever you want.'

Alfresco family lunches are a real treat. Conscious of their pending siesta, the kids made full use of the pool before Mummy brought a halt to proceedings. Once they were settled, the adults took a nap of their own.

The evening began with dinner at our favourite restaurant, La Maja. The town was busy and parking was at a premium. Pizza and pasta are a great way to keep kids quiet for a while.

'Do you two want another drink?' asked Yvonne.

'Yes please,' said Mason. Erren nodded her head.

'Uncle Craig, can I ask for mine?' asked Mason.

'Of course you can.'

'How do I say it?'

'*Una* Coca Cola Lite*, por favor.*'

Mason practised his line and I called the waiter.

'*Una* Coca Cola Lite, *por favor*,' said Mason, before the waiter had opened his mouth.

'*Si señor*,' he replied with a smile.

Ten minutes later Mason was itching to repeat his newly acquired linguistic skills.

'Dad, can I have another drink?'

'That didn't last long,' replied Richard, before calling the waiter.

'*Una* Coca Cola Lite, *por favor*,' blurted Mason.

'*Si señor.*'

No sooner had he brought it than Mason was guzzling it down.

'Mason, slow down,' said Yvonne.

Mason did as he was told, for a while at least.

'Mummy, can I have another drink?' he asked sheepishly.

'No, you can wait,' she replied.

He'd pushed his luck too far and resigned himself to a lengthy wait.

By the time we asked for the bill, he'd forgotten all about it.

'*Hasta luego chicos*,' said the waiter as we left.

Mason clung to his mum's arm.

'Say *adios*,' she whispered.

'*Adios!*' he said boldly, which brought another smile from the waiter.

Outside the evening air was warm and still. The streets were busy with partygoers. We followed the crowds heading towards the Escolapios College using the bright lights of a Ferris wheel to guide us. Latino rhythms lured us towards the funfair. The college carpark had been commandeered by a mesmerising array of mechanical wonders lurching from side to side and twirling round and round. Appetising aromas, both sweet and savoury, drifted through the crowds from street vendors.

'Can we go on the big wheel Dad, can we?' asked Mason.

'Come on then.'

'Uncle Craig, are you coming?'

How could I refuse?

Some years earlier, I had surprised Melanie with a trip on the London Eye. At a height of 135 metres it's one of the world's tallest Ferris wheels. Each of its thirty-two passenger capsules affords twenty-five guests stunning views of the city of London. It's a marvel of modern engineering. This in contrast was a relic of a bygone age. Measuring less than twenty metres in diameter, its birdcage-sized baskets held passengers in extreme discomfort. That said, Mason marvelled at the Monforte de Lemos night sky in exactly the same way Melanie and I had enjoyed London's cityscape.

High on a hill in the centre of town is the former palace of the Counts of Lemos. Illuminated with bright spotlights, it looked like a magical floating castle. To our right was the imposing 16th century Escolapios College and below were the flashing neon lights and ear-splitting sounds of the travelling fair.

Unbeknown to us, while we were gently rotating, Mason had chosen his next ride. Back on terra firma he wasted no time asking.

'Can we go on the dodgems, Dad?'

'Yeah can we?' echoed Erren.

All day the kids had been as good as gold; they taken a siesta without complaining and sat quietly through an hour-long dinner. Who could deny them a little fun?

'OK, but take it in turns to drive.'

They waited patiently for the cars to grind to a halt then ran across the track and jumped into a bright red car with the words 'Coca Cola' emblazoned across the front and the number one down both sides.

'Oh look,' said Yvonne, '*una* Coca Cola Lite *por favor.*'

The four of us laughed and watched as Mason and Erren set about bumping into anything that moved. When they finally rolled to a stop, they jumped out and ran across to us.

'Can we do it again?' asked Mason, hardly able to control his excitement.

'Yeah, can we Mum, can we?'

'Go on then.'

'Yeah!'

Richard gave them a few more coins and they raced back to their favourite car. Six turns later, Mum and Dad persuaded them to walk a little further.

'They smell nice,' said Richard, as we strolled past a mobile catering van. 'What are they?'

'Churros. They're similar in taste to doughnuts,' I replied.

'I think I'll try some of them.'

'Hold up,' I called.

Yvonne, Melanie and the kids stopped and turned. The sight of food tempted them back to the van.

'What are you getting?' asked Yvonne.

'Some of them,' said Richard, pointing at the churros.

'They look nice.' A pan of caramelised almonds had caught her eye. 'I'll have some of those Richard. Do you want anything?' she asked Mason and Erren.

The kids moved forward and stared at an array of treats.

'Popcorn,' said Erren.

'What do you say?'

'Please.'

'And what about you, Mason?'

Mason was struggling to decide.

'Can I have some candy floss, please?'

Before heading home, we wandered around the street-side stalls browsing trinkets made in China and knitwear from Peru. By the time we pulled into the driveway the clock had ticked around to 2:00 am. Time for everyone to hit the sack.

A late night did little to curb the enthusiasm of youth. By 9:00 am they were splashing about in the pool. Their final two days passed in a heartbeat and before we knew it, we were sitting quietly on the front porch watching the sun set on another August day.

Peace and tranquillity had returned to *El Sueño*.

6

Fiesta, Fiesta

The departure of the Kershaw family coincided with renters leaving *Casa Bon Vista*. After such a hectic week, it would have been nice to have the day off but no such luck. In less than twenty-four hours new guests would be arriving. Melanie and I spent the morning cleaning and the afternoon at home dozing in the shade.

That evening, I pulled the cork on a fruity white and we decamped to the far end of the garden to watch the setting sun. Listening to the sounds of nature made a refreshing change from endless questions and bedtime stories. Croaking frogs, chirping crickets and the twitter of songbirds filled our world, until...

Ring, ring ... Ring, ring.

Melanie raced into the house.

'It's your dad,' she mouthed, handing me the phone.

'Hello,' I said chirpily.

'Hiya. I thought you ought to know, I've had a letter from the hospital with a date for my op.'

Dad was waiting to undergo heart bypass surgery. Several years ago, he'd been successfully treated for an irregular heartbeat. More recently he'd complained of breathlessness. Following extensive tests, he was diagnosed with damaged arteries. The cardiologist suggested surgery was his best option. After weighing up the pros and cons, he decided to take his advice.

'When is it?' I asked.

'The 28th of August.'

Dad sounded disappointed.

'That's good news, isn't it?'

'I suppose so but it means I'll have to cancel my trip to you.'

'That doesn't matter. There'll be plenty of time to visit once you're better. Did you take out holiday insurance?' I asked.

'Yes.'

'If you explain the circumstance, I'm sure they'll refund your money.'

'I suppose so. Anyway, I just rang to let you know. I'll speak to you again at the weekend. Bye for now.'

I said goodbye and put the phone down.

'Dad's got the date for his op, 28th of August,' I said to Melanie.

'I thought it might be that,' she replied.

Incoming phone calls are quite rare in our household but later that evening we received another.

'Hello.'

'Hello, it's Ian.'

Ian lives in the UK but owns a holiday home in the area. We'd met him and his family a few years ago and hit it off.

'It's our village fiesta at the weekend and we're having a get-together. Would you and Melanie like to join us for lunch?' he asked.

'That would be lovely. What time?'
'Come at one o'clock; we'll eat about half past.'

One consequence of a routine-free lifestyle is losing track of time. A midweek clean at *Casa Bon Vista* had thrown our week out of kilter.

'What day is it today?' I asked, as Melanie nudged open the bedroom door carrying two coffees.

She thought for a moment.

'Friday, I think.'

'Already.'

'I know. I don't know where this week has gone.'

'I'm going to order the materials for the terrace this morning. With a bit of luck, they'll deliver them first thing on Monday,' I said.

Once we started pouring the concrete for the base of the terrace I wanted to continue to a finish. The materials would have to be dropped at the top of the track; the less time they were there the better. If everything went to plan, we should have the whole thing finished in three or four days.

'And then I'll nip up to Vilatán to do some pointing,' I added.

I'd decided to renovate the boundary wall at the back of the house myself. Legally it didn't belong to us so we couldn't rebuild it even if we'd wanted to. We'd spoken with the owner and they were happy for us to clean our side and repoint.

'Do you need me?' asked Melanie.

'Not if you've got something better to do.'

'It's just there's the laundry from *Casa Bon Vista* to sort out,' she replied.

'That's fine.'

On my way to Vilatán, I called at Otero's and ordered two Big Bags of aggregate and twenty bags of cement.

'Can you deliver them first thing Monday morning?'

'No problem,' replied Marcus.

The outcome might not mirror his intention but at least I'd asked.

I spent the rest of the morning pointing the boundary wall, a mind-numbing job which made the prospect of tomorrow's fiesta lunch at Ian's even more attractive.

Ian and his wife Kathy own a house in Doade, a small village high above the canyon of the river Sil in the heart of the Ribeira Sacra region. By the time we arrived, preparations were well underway. Their daughters, Rebekah and Rachel, were flitting between kitchen and dining room carrying plates of food. Rebekah's boyfriend James was chatting to Penelope, and Roy and his wife Maria were joining in the conversation.

The feast began in typical Galician style with *empanada*: an eighteen-inch diameter pie made with bread dough and stuffed with an onion-based filling containing meat or fish. The main course was less traditional: chicken curry and boiled rice. Homemade desserts finished off a great meal.

'Right then, who's for a stroll to the viewing point?' asked Ian.

'Viewing point?' I asked.

'Have you not been? It's fantastic.'

The beauty of the Ribeira Sacra is recognised throughout Spain. A landscape of deep river valleys, lush rolling hills and high mountains afford visitors unparalleled scenery. Some of the best sights can be seen from *miradors*: designated viewing points chosen for their outstanding outlook. We'd been to quite a number in the area but had no idea that Ian and Kathy's house was within walking distance of one. Always on the lookout for new discoveries, Melanie and I jumped at the chance.

Less than 200 metres from their front door, an unmade track left the village lane and headed into the forest. A sunny afternoon in August is hardly the best time to go exploring on foot but tall pine trees provided some welcome shade. After a twenty-minute stroll the track came to a disappointing end.

Was this it?

'Up there,' said Ian, pointing at an elevated outcrop.

The track melted into a narrow, overgrown footpath, wide enough for single file. The gentle incline steepened and all of a sudden the panorama opened out. The scenery was breathtaking.

'Carry on,' said Ian, encouraging me upwards.

We climbed a series of stone steps which took us past the tiny chapel of San Mauro and up to the viewing platform. It felt as if we were standing on top of the world.

Almost a thousand metres below was the river Sil, snaking through the valley like a giant anaconda. From the banks of the river, row upon row of narrow terraces planted with grapevines climbed the steep valley like a stairway to heaven. On the opposite side of the canyon, the silhouette of the medieval castle at Castro Caldelas was clearly visible.

'Wow!'

Words seemed inadequate. Not for the first time the Ribeira Sacra had surprised us with its outstanding natural beauty. From now on, the Mirador Pena do Castelo would become top of our family and friends' tourist attractions.

All too soon the weekend was behind us and we were readying ourselves for another week of building work.

'Are you ready?' I asked.

'As I'll ever be,' replied Melanie. 'Remind me again, why are we leaving at such an ungodly hour?'

'If Otero's deliver the materials in the meadow instead of at the top of the track, we'll have a hell of a job moving them to the other side of the house.'

Marcus had promised me an early drop. If we were late, you could guarantee they wouldn't be. My fears proved unfounded. A little after 9:30 am the delivery lorry arrived.

'Can you drop them at the other side of the house?' I asked.

'No problem.'

Ten minutes later we were ready to start. Manolo had offered us the use of his cement mixer, a large petrol-powered machine that weighed a ton. We had opted instead to borrow Roy's electric mixer. As cement mixers go, it was relatively small and reasonably portable. That said, it still took some shifting. Between us, Melanie and I manhandled it out of the *bodega*, up the stone steps, and dragged it to the top of the track.

'Will the extension cable reach this far?' asked Melanie. We would need an electricity supply.

Melanie's question sent a shiver of uncertainty down my spine. Up until then, it hadn't crossed my mind. An equipment oversight now would mean a forty-five-minute round trip home to collect whatever we needed.

'I'm not sure,' I confessed.

'And what about the hosepipe?' she asked.

The materials had been delivered and the cement mixer was ready for action, but without water and electricity they were both redundant.

'Water shouldn't be a problem. I can couple two hosepipes together,' I replied.

'Are you sure two will be long enough?'

The only water source was from the borehole in the middle of the meadow.

'I think so,' I said, wandering back to the house.

Using a coupler, I joined the hosepipes, attached one end to the valve on the top of the borehole and dragged the hose across the meadow, up the steps, over the gravelled terrace, and up the track.

'That's going to work,' I said, with a sigh of relief.

'And electricity?'

When the contractor installed the mains supply, we'd asked them to rig up two temporary sockets. They were screwed to a piece of old timber and mounted on the wall inside the *bodega*. A Heath Robinson affair but at this stage, appearance came a distant second to functionality. I plugged in the extension cable and headed up the track. Ten metres from the mixer, the cable ran out.

'Bugger! We're going to need another extension. I'll have to drive home and get one.'

Two hours after arriving on site, we finally started mixing.

The day's efforts went well. Using wooden shuttering I divided the terrace into four strips, each a metre wide. I was only glad Manolo wasn't around; I knew he wouldn't approve. I mixed the concrete and poured it into the wheelbarrow, Melanie wheeled it down the track to the terrace and I tipped it. By the end of the day we'd completed one strip and used up a third of the materials.

'Another three days should do it,' I said, on the drive home.

What I hadn't counted on was our work-life mix interfering with our aggregate-cement mix.

Ring, ring … Ring, ring.

'Hello, this is Penelope, I'm organising lunch at my place for our village fiesta, would you like to come?'

'When?' asked Melanie.

'This Wednesday. I'm sorry the invitation is late but I've only just decided.'

How could we refuse?

'That would be lovely Pen, count us in.'

Aches and pains reminded us of yesterday's exertions. One more day and Penelope's fiesta lunch would provide a short respite. By mid-afternoon, we'd poured the second metre-wide strip of concrete and used another third of the materials.

'I don't think we're going to have enough,' I said.

The first bag of aggregate was empty and I'd made quite a dent in the second.

'You'll have to get some more.'

On reflection, I decided to see how things went before placing an order.

That evening Mother Nature treated us to one of the most spectacular thunderstorms we'd ever seen. Atmospheric pressure had been building for days. Temperatures were high and increasing humidity made the lightest work a chore. Something had to give.

'Did you see that?' asked Melanie.

A burst of light flickered across the southern night sky.

'How could I miss it?'

Within seconds a rumble of thunder rolled across the heavens.

'How far away do you think it is?' she asked.

I'd grown up believing the distance between a flash of lightning and a clap of thunder equated to one mile per second. One of Dad's pearls of wisdom. How true it is, is anyone's guess.

'I'll tell you next time there's a flash,' I replied.

'There,' said Melanie, as the sky lit up.

My silent count began: 1,001, 1,002, 1,003… At 1,009, the distant thunder let out a menacing groan.

'It's about nine miles away.'

'What's that in real money?'

'About fifteen kilometres.'

'That's miles away,' she replied.

'Don't you mean kilometres?'

Every flash initiated a new count. Slowly but surely the storm crept closer. As it did, the frequency and intensity of both light and sound increased.

'Wow!'

Like a disco strobe light, flash after flash ignited the night sky and the cracks of thunder threatened to split the earth in two. Jazz had long since taken herself off to bed. Raindrops the size of golf balls exploded on the terrace and collided into the swimming pool like meteors. Gusts of cool air strengthened as the storm passed overhead.

Each crack of thunder bounced off the ground like a bass speaker at a rock concert.

Within half an hour, the night fell silent and the cool wind was replaced by warm still air.

'That was fantastic,' said Melanie.

I had to agree.

Ring, ring … Ring, ring.

'I'll go,' I said.

Dad had arranged to call. This would be our last chance to speak before his operation. The conversation was fairly mundane. I told him about the storm; he said he was looking forward to his grandson's eighteenth birthday party, scheduled for tomorrow. Neither of us said anything profound. I felt he'd told me everything he intended to on his last visit. We said goodbye and I ended by telling him I'd see him soon.

Penelope's fiesta lunch afforded us a leisurely start to the day. I couldn't remember the last time we'd had a lie-in.

'I'm going to nip into town to pick up some groceries. Do you want to come?' asked Melanie.

'No thanks.'

I was happy to stay at home and avoid the drudgery of supermarket shopping.

'Is there anything you want?'

'I can't think of anything.'

'OK, see you soon.'

And off she went.

After checking my emails, I sat outside on the back terrace and relaxed in the morning sunshine. Before I realised, I'd dozed off.

Ring, ring … Ring, ring.

The phone woke me. I rushed into the house and glanced at the clock: 12:30 pm. In half an hour we were meant to be joining Penelope for lunch. Why hadn't Melanie woken me?

Ring, ring ... Ring, ring.
I picked up the receiver.
'Hello.'
'It's me,' said Melanie.
'Do you know what time it is?' I asked.
'The car's broken down.'
That wasn't the answer I was expecting.
'What do you mean?'
'I mean, the car's broken down.'
'Where are you?'
'I'm in town and the car has broken down.'
Melanie's tone stiffened.
'What do you mean, broken down?'
'I don't know. It won't start.'

By inference, it seemed that I was to blame for this inconvenience or at the very least I should know how to remedy it.

'When you say it's broken down, what exactly is it doing?'
'It's not doing anything, it's broken down.'
'What are you going to do?' I asked.
'What do you mean, what am *I* going to do? It's your car.'

It's my car when it's broken down and hers when she wants to go shopping. Arguing the point wouldn't solve the problem. I went into diagnostic mode.

'Can you unlock the door with the remote?'
'Yes.'
That alone led me to believe it wasn't the battery.
'And what happens when you insert the key and push the start button?'
'Nothing.'
'Nothing?'
'Nothing.'
'That's strange.'
I thought for a moment.

'You'll have to call a breakdown vehicle. The emergency phone number is in the glovebox.'

Melanie's anger turned to angst and her voice began to break.

'How am I going to get home?'

'Give them a call and see what they suggest,' I replied calmly. 'And don't worry, everything will be fine.'

Ten minutes later the phone rang again.

'Hello?'

'It's me, the driver of the tow truck has asked if I want the car brought home or taken to the Renault garage.'

'You'd better take it straight to the garage and see what they say.'

'But what about getting home?'

'If they can't fix it, you'll have to get a taxi.'

The time was approaching one o'clock; the garage would soon be closing for lunch. I crossed my fingers and hoped they got there in time. Minutes later the phone rang again.

'It's me. They think it's the battery but they're closing for lunch so we'll have to pick it up later. They've called a taxi for me.'

'OK. When you get home stay in it. It'll have to take us to Penelope's.'

Drama over, we arrived at Penelope's fashionably late and thirty euros out of pocket.

7

He's Gone

Isolated properties in far-flung places have a certain romantic charm but romance is rarely practical. If your car is towed to the repair shop, isolation becomes a pain in the backside. Fortunately, we don't have that problem. Through accident rather than design, the quaint, if somewhat neglected railway station in Canabal provides a much-appreciated lifeline. Despite offering a limited service of only two trains a day, one inbound and one out, the early train to Monforte de Lemos has become a godsend.

'What time does the train arrive?' I asked, as I wandered into the kitchen.

Melanie glanced at the clock.

'Nine thirty-seven.'

I looked at my watch.

'We'd better be making a move then.'

'It's only twenty past.'

'I know but we don't want to miss it.'

Jazz was on the back terrace, basking in the morning sun.

'Come on lass,' I called.

She hauled herself off the floor, ambled through the house and found an equally sunny spot in the front garden. Melanie and I said goodbye to her and we headed off to the station.

'I told you we'd be too early,' said Melanie, as we waited on the platform.

Nine thirty-seven came and went. A further fifteen minutes passed before the locomotive appeared on the horizon.

The journey takes less than ten minutes, just long enough for the conductor to collect our fare. The walk to the dealership took about the same.

'We had to replace the battery,' explained Javier, the garage manager, 'but everything is fine now.'

I was a little surprised but pleased it wasn't more serious. Having paid the bill, we left for Vilatán. A late start resulted in a late finish. By the time we headed home, we'd poured another metre-wide strip of concrete. The end was in sight, so too the materials. We would definitely need more.

The events of the last twenty-four hours helped take our minds off Dad's surgery. Over lunch we had time to reflect.

'Are you going to give the hospital a ring?' asked Melanie.

'What time was he going in to theatre?'

'Nine o'clock this morning.'

'If I leave it a bit longer, I might be able to speak to him.'

Dad's cardiologist was unable to say exactly how long the procedure would take. The full extent of his condition wouldn't become apparent until they'd opened him up. I waited until 6:00 pm before calling. A softly spoken ward sister informed me that Dad hadn't yet regained consciousness and was under observation in intensive care. He'd been in theatre for seven and a half hours. As well as performing a triple bypass the surgeon had replaced two heart valves. His condition was serious but he was being well looked after and closely monitored.

'Is it alright if I ring back later?' I asked.

'Of course. Feel free to ring at any time.'

I explained the situation to Melanie.

'Perhaps we should stay in tonight,' she suggested.

We'd been invited to dinner at Gerry and Carol's, a couple we met a few months after moving to Galicia. We'd hit it off straight away and have been good friends ever since. They own a holiday home and make a point of getting in touch whenever they're here. The thought of waiting by the phone didn't appeal; better to be with friends at a time like this.

'No, let's go,' I replied. 'If nothing else, it'll take our minds off things.'

Gerry's signature dish is Coq au Vin and he didn't disappoint. Succulent pieces of chicken marinated in Spanish red wine, delicious. Carol's brother Malcolm was his usually mischievous self. Malcolm was born with Down's syndrome and Carol and Gerry have dedicated their lives to enriching his. Every time Gerry left the dining table, Malcolm hid his napkin or put his fork on his chair.

'Malcolm, stop it,' instructed Carol.

He stared back as if to say, What, me?

Earlier in the day, he'd filled Gerry's trainers with Coca Cola, a prank he'd found particularly amusing. The three of them were great hosts and helped ease our concerns, albeit for a short time.

As soon as we returned home I rang the hospital. Dad was stable but very ill and still hadn't regained consciousness.

'I'm going to look for a flight,' I said to Melanie.

The shorter the time to departure the more expensive the fare. Ticket prices for flights leaving tomorrow were astronomical. I checked all the carriers and a mesmerising combination of airports, both departure and arrival.

'There's nothing you can do now,' said Melanie. 'Wait until the morning and see how he is.'

She was right. The clock had ticked around to 1:00 am. Availability was unlikely to change between now and then. We'd spent so much time focusing on the challenges of managing his convalescence, it hadn't crossed our minds his surgery might not go to plan. All we could do now was hope he got to that stage.

First thing in the morning I rang the hospital. His condition hadn't changed.

'I've just spoken with your sister,' said the ward sister. 'She's travelling up from London this morning.'

Knowing she would soon be with him was reassuring.

'What do you want to do?' asked Melanie.

'I'll wait until Julie gets there and see what she thinks.'

It would be hours before she arrived at the hospital. The thought of sitting around twiddling my thumbs was intolerable.

'Let's go up to Vilatán and do some work,' I suggested.

'Are you sure?'

'Certain.'

No sooner had we driven to the house than the heavens opened. It never rains but it pours. Summer showers are rare and usually pass as quickly as they arrive, and that morning was no different. But before long we had to stop again. This time we'd run out of materials.

We hadn't been home long when Julie rang. She'd caught the early train from London to Leeds. His condition had worsened overnight.

'They've put him on dialysis,' she said.

'I've been looking at flights. What do you think I should do?'

'It's too early to say. I have to return to London this afternoon but I'm coming back this evening. As soon as I know anything I'll call.'

At six the following morning the phone rang.

'It's me, I've spoken with the surgeon.'

'What did he say?'

'He's going to give Dad some different drugs but if he doesn't respond soon he's going to die.'

The line fell silent. I didn't know what to say. Leading up to his operation Dad had been uncharacteristically optimistic. Not for one minute had we envisaged this scenario.

'I'm going to book a flight. I'll see you soon.'

Flights from Galicia to the north of England are few and far between. My best option was to fly from A Coruña to Heathrow, hire a car and drive the 200 miles to Leeds. The earliest flight departed that afternoon at 16:25. Taking into account the one-hour time difference between Spain and the UK, the flight was scheduled to land in Heathrow at 17:00 hours. With a bit of luck, I'd get to Leeds at around 10:00 pm.

Melanie would join me later, depending on how things went. En route to the airport she phoned Julie with our plans. Dad's condition remained unchanged.

Boarding was chaotic. I'd paid a small fortune for the ticket and had to fight my way on board.

Within fifteen minutes of landing, I'd collected the hire car and informed Melanie of my arrival. Traffic on London's M25 outer ring road was nose to tail. By the time I reached the M1 heading north, any hope of getting to Leeds by 10:00 pm had gone. On current progress, I'd be lucky to get there before midnight.

Hour after hour passed without a word from either Julie or Melanie. I could only assume Dad was hanging on. By 8:00 pm the sky darkened. Progress was slow. When I reached Nottingham, things began to improve.

The city of Leeds boasts two outstanding hospitals, St. James's University Hospital, immortalised in the eighties TV series *Jimmy's* and Leeds Teaching Hospital NHS Trust. Dad was in the latter.

As I approached the city suburbs my search for signage began. I'd travelled all this way but hadn't a clue where to find the hospital. When the motorway ended, I followed signs for the city centre and breathed a sigh of relief when I picked up one for the hospital.

Unbeknown to me, Leeds Teaching Hospital is one of the biggest NHS trusts in the UK. I drove up and down streets searching for the cardiology department. By accident I stumbled across the right building. The surrounding roads were lined with parked cars and there was neither sight nor sound of a carpark. I'd come all this way to be thwarted by a lack of parking. Suddenly, out of the corner of my eye, I saw a vehicle pulling away. I glanced at the time. A quarter past eleven. The notice read Staff Parking. I had no choice but to risk it. I pulled into the space, switched off the engine and headed towards the entrance. I'd been on the go since before six that morning but the crisp night air gave my weary frame a new lease of life. I pushed open a door and entered. The hospital corridors were dimly lit and deserted. A noticeboard directed me to the intensive care unit. I approached reception where a young nurse was filling out paperwork. She looked up.

'Hello, my name's Craig Briggs. I'm here to see my dad.'

'Ah yes, your sister's waiting for you,' she replied.

The nurse rounded the counter and led me to the waiting room.

'I understand you've travelled from Spain,' she said.

'That's right,' I replied, somewhat surprised.

She pushed open the door and ushered me inside. Julie was sitting on a chair. She rose, stepped forward and before I could say a word, flung her arms around me.

I was frozen to the spot, flabbergasted by her actions. The Briggs family don't do lovey-dovey. Before I could compose myself, she spoke.

'He's gone.'

The meaning of her statement was clear. I couldn't speak. She tried to explain what had happened but I wasn't taking it in. She finished by asking if I wanted to see him. Her question cut through my dumbed-down senses.

'No,' I said, without hesitation.

'Are you sure?'

I was certain. Vivid memories of being pressured to see Mum flooded back. As far as I am concerned, the dead have no place amongst the living. Remembering someone's life-force is far more important than viewing a lifeless corpse.

'I'm certain,' I replied.

'We might as well go then.'

Outside in the carpark I rang Melanie. She knew. Julie had rung her at eight thirty. For safety reasons they had decided not to tell me.

The next seven days were filled with practical issues which left little time for reflection or grief. In many ways that was a good thing. Preparing Dad's eulogy changed that. A week of maintaining a stiff upper lip collapsed in an emotional heap.

Melanie's arrival gave both of us the support we needed. She'd informed family and friends so I hadn't had to. We kept ourselves busy sorting through Dad's belongings. He'd joked that we shouldn't throw anything away without checking it first; he wasn't kidding. Every drawer and cupboard yielded small sums of cash. A brown envelope here and a rusty tin there. In the end we unearthed over one thousand pounds scattered throughout the house.

His clothes went to a charity shop along with ornaments and other personal items. Julie and I divided family photos and the rest were thrown away: a lifetime of memories personal to him. Much of the process felt shallow and superficial. Dad was gone; souvenirs and keepsakes seemed woefully inadequate.

Clearing out the attic posed a new problem. When Melanie and I left for Spain, what couldn't be squeezed into the car found its way into Dad's attic. All those indispensable items that five years later were still here.

'What are we going to do with all this junk?' I asked Melanie.

'It's not junk.'

Perhaps not but we hadn't needed any of it for the past five years and were unlikely to need it in the next.

'We'll have to send them to Spain,' she added.

'Are you sure? It's not like we've needed any of it.'

Melanie opened one of the boxes.

'We can't throw this away,' she said, staring at a mass-produced piece of porcelain her mother had given her one Christmas.

I was in no mood to argue or spend hours sorting through each box. We moved them from the attic into the spare bedroom and pushed them to the back of our minds.

Dad's funeral took place eleven days after he passed away. He'd made his views quite clear.

'Don't waste money burying me,' he'd said.

At 2:00 pm a line of cars followed the hearse through Huddersfield to the crematorium. Dad was a popular figure, a typical working-class Yorkshireman, outspoken and opinionated but never rude. His popularity was measured by the number of mourners. For a seventy-five-year-old widower, a good number turned out to pay their final respects and say goodbye.

After a short service, family and close friends returned to Dad's for a late lunch. Pork pies and sandwiches, washed down with a mug of tea: typical Yorkshire fare for a typical Yorkshireman.

8

Preparations Begin

Three days after the funeral, Melanie and I flew home. The previous two weeks had slipped away in a semi-conscious daze. Practical matters had kept us busy and family and friends occupied the time in between. The flight back gave me time to reflect. It seemed ironic that months earlier Dad and I had reached a level of mutual understanding previously missing from our relationship. I was looking forward to the future and he was too. For him to be taken now seemed grossly unfair.

Thankfully, there were plenty of things to keep us occupied on our return but Dad was never far from our thoughts. Heartfelt condolences were frequent and sincere. In some ways it helped to keep talking about him. Bob and Janet, the owners of *Casa Bon Vista*, were on the final week of a two-week break and Rajan and Mitty, the American couple who bought our first property project, were on an extended visit from their home in California. Dinner invitations and day trips were frequent. In between engagements we kept ourselves busy at Vilatán. Within a week of our return we'd finished pouring the concrete base for the terrace. Our next task was to enclose the area with a breezeblock wall.

'What are we going to do about all that stuff?' Melanie was referring to the boxes of household non-essentials we'd unearthed in Dad's loft.

'We'll have to get them shipped over here.'

'How?'

'I don't know, there must be companies that do that sort of thing.'

'It sounds expensive.'

Was Melanie having second thoughts?

'Perhaps we can find a man with a van,' I suggested.

'A man with a van who just happens to be driving from Huddersfield to Canabal?'

She had a point. It would probably be easier to send a parcel to the moon.

'It was your idea to keep it all,' I said.

'We can't just throw everything away.'

'We could have donated it to charity.'

Melanie's facial expression said it all. We'd just given away Dad's lifetime of collecting. This wasn't the time to be donating ours.

'I'll have a look on the internet and find out how much it'll cost, then we can decide what to do.'

That afternoon I trawled the web searching for a carrier. I found a number of companies that made regular trips from the UK to Spain but none of them mentioned Galicia. One operator caught my eye. Elite-European offered part-load options. Within an hour of making an enquiry I'd received a reply and raced outside to tell Melanie. She was relaxing in the sunshine with her head in a book.

'I've found one,' I announced.

'One what?'

'A carrier.'

Melanie came straight to the point. 'How much?'

'They do part loads as well,' I replied.

'That's good, but how much?'

'Three hundred pounds for up to one cubic metre.'

Melanie looked surprised.

'That sounds cheap. What's the catch?'

'I couldn't find one.'

'Did you tell them where we live?'

'No, I gave them someone else's address.'

'Tsk.'

'Of course I told them.'

'And they'll deliver it here, for 300 pounds?'

'That's what she said.'

'Do they know where Galicia is?'

'When I asked, she said she'd looked on a map and we were just above Madrid.'

'Madrid! I know I'm rubbish at geography but Galicia is nowhere near Madrid.'

'She said they were happy to deliver. What do you want me to do, talk her out of it?'

'Are you sure it's going to be safe?'

I hadn't a clue and didn't really think it mattered.

'It'll be fine. We just need to organise somewhere for them to pick it up.'

'Can't they collect it from your Dad's?'

'It has to be somewhere with access for an articulated lorry.'

It was difficult to park a car in Dad's narrow cul-de-sac, never mind a forty-footer.

'When will they collect it?'

'That's the other thing.'

'What other thing?'

'They only come to Spain once a month. Their next collection date is the 5th of November.'

Between now and then we had to pack everything securely, label it, and find somewhere for them to pick it up.

'Perhaps Richard and Yvonne can help,' suggested Melanie. 'They have lorries delivering all the time.'

Richard and Yvonne's dairy farm would be the perfect collection point.

'I'll ring Yvonne tonight and ask if we can use their address,' she added.

'You realise we'll have to go back to England to get everything ready,' I said.

'You'd better look for some flights then.'

Ryanair, the low-cost carrier, had recently started a service from Valladolid to Liverpool. I checked availability towards the end of the month. Prices were ridiculously high. At this rate we'd spend more money flying to and from the UK than we would transporting the stuff. Perhaps this wasn't such a good idea after all. That's when the notion of flying from Madrid came to me.

Throughout the summer we'd whiled away many a warm evening watching the distant headlights of traffic speeding along the main road. Mysterious night drivers heading to unknown destinations. Such was the appeal of these midnight travellers that I'd often toyed with the idea of driving to the Mediterranean coast to watch the sunrise: dinner in Canabal and breakfast by the sea. A romantically nonsensical 2,000-kilometre round trip induced by too much wine. Perhaps this was the perfect opportunity to fulfil my driving ambition, or at least half of it.

I checked the timetable from Madrid to East Midlands Airport. Bingo! I found a flight departing Madrid Barajas International Airport at 07:20 and landing at East Midlands at 08:37. We couldn't have wished for better flight times. The drive to Madrid takes four and a half to five hours. We could leave home at midnight, drive through the night and arrive at the airport in perfect time to check in; best of all the air fares were next to nothing.

'I've had an idea,' I said, as I pushed open the lounge door.

'Really.'

Melanie knew me too well. What off-the-wall scheme had I come up with now?

'The flights from Valladolid are really expensive so I thought we might fly from Madrid.'

'Madrid!'

'We can do what we've always talked about and drive through the night.'

'Excuse me?'

'OK, we can do what *I've* always talked about. What do you think?'

'As long as you're not expecting me to drive, that's fine.'

'No worries, you can sit back and enjoy the journey. Have you spoken with Yvonne yet?'

'She said we can use their address, no problem.'

Having got all our ducks in a row, I booked the flights, 31st of October returning on the 7th of November.

Keeping busy helped take our minds of things. Building the wall around the terrace was a welcome distraction, other activities less so. It's surprising how good memories can be the most painful. That was certainly true of a trip to Chaves. We'd gone to give ourselves a break from building and to have a Chinese meal at our favourite restaurant. After lunch we decided to take a tour of the town on the road-going tourist train. We'd seen it before, trundling through the streets, and thought it might be fun. Everything was going great until it stopped in the main square close to the castle and gardens. The driver announced a ten-minute break to let passengers have a wander. Less than five months earlier, we'd been here with Dad. The three of us had strolled around the gardens and Dad really enjoyed it. How quickly life can change.

'Come on love, don't be sad,' I said, trying to comfort Melanie.

'I can't help it,' she replied.

I felt her sadness but tried to stay calm.

Our next emotional hurdle came a few days later when we harvested the grapes. Dad had been keen to help us for years but his visits hadn't coincided with picking. Last year his wish came true. Knowing we wouldn't share that experience again put a dampener on the whole event but life is for living and as long as I'm able, that's exactly what I intend to do.

'Let's take a trip to the coast,' I suggested one evening after dinner.

We'd talked about touring the Costa del Muerte since moving to Galicia. For one reason or another we hadn't got around to it.

When it comes to names, the Galician coastline has been hard done by. The Mediterranean has such alluring titles as the Coast of Light, Coast of Gold, Coast of Sun, and White Coast. Here in Galicia we ended up with the Coast of Death. I challenge any marketing executive to make that sound attractive. Personally, I think it should be renamed Costa Preciosa (the Beautiful Coast).

'When?'

'Soon.'

'The whole coast?'

'Why not? We should be able to drive it in a couple of days.'

'Where are we going to stay?'

'There'll be plenty of places, particularly at this time of year.'

'OK.'

The following day I searched the internet for suitable accommodation and stumbled across Casa de Trillo, a charming rural hotel in the village of Santa Mariña, eight kilometres from the coast and ninety kilometres west of A Coruña.

'What do you think?' I asked, showing Melanie the photos.

'It looks lovely.'

'OK, how does Monday the 15th sound?'
'Sounds great.'
'Right then, I'll book.'

On the second day of October I placed the last breezeblock on the wall surrounding the terrace.

'That's it,' I said proudly. 'What do you think?'
'It's hideous.'

She wasn't kidding. Row upon row of dreary grey breezeblocks did nothing to enhance the appearance of our rustic farmhouse.

'Wait until it's clad, it'll look great.'

We'd chosen a natural stone cladding. At ten euros a square metre it wasn't cheap but if the result matched my mind's eye it would look perfect. We'd seen other buildings finished with the same material and in most cases, it was difficult to distinguish between cladding and a stone-built wall.

Eager to see how it would look, we mixed up some mortar and I made a start.

'It's going to look lovely,' said Melanie.

I stepped back to admire my handiwork and couldn't have agreed more.

'I might ask Roy to give me a hand,' I said on the drive home.

Roy's background was in the building trade and cladding is a slow job. It had taken me most of the morning to complete less than two square metres. With over seventy to do, if I didn't get help I'd be at it for months.

'That's a good idea,' replied Melanie.

That evening I rang him. He was happy to work five half-days per week which suited me down to the ground.

'I can't start until the 11th,' he said.
'No problem, that's fine.'

With Roy on board, my attention turned to Manolo the builder, and Alfonso the stonemason. Manolo's two-month break was coming to an end; as for Alfonso, we hadn't seen sight nor sound of him for ages. The following day we called to see Manolo.

'I've got a roof to finish but should be back by the 11th,' he said.

That was great news. Once started, he would see the project through to completion. Later that day I rang Alfonso.

'I should be able to start on the 15th,' he said.

We'd waited all this time for him to return only for him to choose the day we were heading off to the coast. At least when we returned we'd have a full complement of workers; then things should really start moving along.

Melanie and I were enjoying breakfast on the back terrace when the bell rang.

Clang, clang, clang, clang!

Jazz leapt to her feet and raced around the side of the house.

Woof, woof, woof, woof!

'I'll go,' I said, springing to my feet.

By the time I'd walked around to the front, Jazz had stopped barking and the post-lady was stroking her head.

'I've got a parcel for you,' she said.

I took it and walked back to the house.

'Who was it?' called Melanie.

'The post-lady.'

Parcels from the UK are eagerly anticipated.

'That's from Claire,' said Melanie.

'How do you know?'

'I recognise the handwriting.'

I ripped open the packaging and pulled out a book.

'What is it?'

'A guidebook for Australia.'

'That's so thoughtful.'

'That reminds me, we must sort out some travel insurance.'

Our trip to Australia was less than four months away. What had seemed like a distant dream was fast becoming a reality.

'And don't forget the hotel.'

How could I? We'd changed the outbound flight to give ourselves an extra night in Shanghai. As well as finding a hotel I was keen to organise an itinerary to make sure we made the most of our stopover.

'I'll have a look on the internet this afternoon,' I replied.

There were hundreds of places to choose from but only a few met my strict criteria. The hotel in question had to be within walking distance of the Huangpu River and have a view of the Pudong skyline.

'Come and take a look at this,' I called to Melanie who was lounging in the sun.

She wandered through into the office and sat at the computer. On screen were photos of The Bund Riverside Hotel, a five-star establishment in the heart of the city.

'That looks really nice,' she said.

'And look how close it is to the centre.'

Melanie stared at the street map. I could see from her expression she hadn't a clue what she was looking at.

'This is The Bund,' I said, pointing at the map, 'where all the old colonial buildings are. Opposite that is the river quay where the cruise charters depart from and across the river is the Pudong District.'

'Pudong?'

'That's where all the futuristic skyscrapers are. Look how near the tube station is. We should be able to walk to the hotel from there.'

'And how much is it?'

'Less than 100 dollars per night.'

'Dollars?'

'Everything seems to be quoted in dollars.'

'What are you waiting for, get it booked.'

Five minutes later our reservation was confirmed.

Sourcing affordable travel insurance proved much more problematic. It seems that Spanish residents are unable to take advantage of cheap UK travel insurance. I spent hours trying to find a workaround without success and finished up coughing up a fortune.

My next challenge was airport transfers. I had to find a way to get from Shanghai Pudong International Airport to the hotel. That's when I stumbled across the Maglev or magnetic levitation train. It sounded like something out of *Star Trek*, a train propelled by magnets on a cushion of air to create near frictionless locomotion. This futuristic technology makes the Maglev the fastest commercially operated train on the planet. The line travels from the airport to Longyang Road Station in the heart of the city. At a speed of 430 kilometres per hour it takes seven minutes and twenty seconds to cover the thirty kilometres. Less than half the time it takes for the morning train from Canabal to Monforte to be late.

At Longyang Road Station we could transfer to the underground and take Line Two to East Nanjing Road Station which was less than 300 metres from the hotel – perfect. The only cloud on an otherwise clear horizon was the departure time of the last Maglev. Any flight delay and we'd miss it. I figured we'd cross that bridge if and when we came to it.

My search turned to organising an itinerary. If everything went to plan we would have the first evening free, the whole of the following day, and a good half of the day after that. The hotel's location gave me an idea for our first evening, a romantic river cruise along the Huangpu River. Online booking was simple and remarkably cheap.

Next, I typed the phrase "Shanghai sightseeing tour" into Google. The top search result was a company called Viator. I scrolled through the various tour packages looking for the most appropriate. The Full Day Shanghai Tour was exactly what we were looking for. An eight-hour trip including lunch, taking in all the major tourist sites.

The package was available in two options, private or group tour. The price difference was staggering: almost five times more expensive for the private tour. Organised trips aren't our thing, even less so as part of a group, but I couldn't justify the extra expense. Reluctantly I booked the group tour.

The only major attraction missing from the package was the Oriental Pearl Tower. Constructed in 1994, this radio and TV tower is China's tallest building and the third tallest in the world. This symbolic building forms the centrepiece of the Shanghai skyline and was within easy walking distance of the hotel. On our day of departure, I figured we could leave the luggage at the hotel and visit this iconic landmark before collecting it and travelling back to the airport on the Maglev.

I couldn't help but marvel at the ease at which independent travellers can arrange and book all these services and activities. From my spare bedroom in deepest Galicia, it had taken me less than a day to book a city break in Shanghai, organise an itinerary and ensure we were insured against all eventualities. Fifteen years ago, that would have been impossible. The World Wide Web has to be one of the greatest advancements in human development since some clever bugger invented the wheel. I've no idea how this technology will develop in the future but for the time being I can't praise Tim Berners-Lee enough – thanks Tim.

'All booked,' I announced, as I stepped out onto the back terrace.

'That's good.'

'I think it's about time for a Teatime Taster. What do you think?'

'That sounds like a great idea.'

As we watched the sun dipping behind the woody knoll one thought kept recurring.

'You do realise that if something happens to us we'll be worth a fortune.'

Melanie looked confused.

'The life insurance alone is worth over one and a half million euros each.'

'What life insurance?'

'The cover on the travel insurance, it's worth 1.5 million.'

'Wow! That's good.'

'Apart from the fact we have to be dead to claim it.'

The thought tickled us both.

'But seriously, we'll have to decide who to leave it to,' I said.

'You can leave yours to me and I'll leave mine to you,' she replied.

'That's fine, as long as the plane doesn't crash.'

'Don't even go there.'

Nominating beneficiaries could wait for another day.

9

Land's End

The first part of our trip to the far side of the world was organised. Preparations for our time in Australia required broad brushstrokes rather than fine details. We had four months to write a wish list. Final arrangements could be made during our stay. Between now and then, our priority was to progress the work at Vilatán.

Just-in-time ordering is a system that hasn't yet reached rural Galicia. With Roy agreeing to work with us, it was vital to have the materials we wanted, when they were needed.

'Can I order one pallet of stone and five bags of cement for delivery tomorrow morning?' I asked over the phone.

I was speaking to Moncho, owner operator of a builder's merchant in Escairón, a large village four kilometres from Vilatán. His prices were similar to Otero's but he had one major advantage; he owned a URO. A unique, multi-purpose all-terrain delivery vehicle that was narrow enough to drive down the track at the side of the house and deliver the materials over the new wall and onto the terrace.

'No problem,' he said.

The following morning, he failed to turn up.

'I can bring them this afternoon,' he said over the phone.

Hanging around on the off chance he'd keep his word wasn't an option.

'Can you deliver them tomorrow morning?' I asked.

'No problem.'

'Are you sure?'

'Certain.'

The day after, he showed up as agreed.

Roy picked me up from home on the 11th as arranged. Manolo had already made a start when we arrived at Vilatán. He never lets us down. During his morning break he came to inspect the new terrace. The last time he'd seen it, there was a cavernous void behind the retaining wall. Things had moved on since then.

'Good job,' he said, nodding his appreciation.

High praise indeed from a man who always gives an honest opinion.

'*Gracias*,' I replied.

Roy and I divided our labour. He worked on cladding the outside of the wall and I inside.

At the end of the week I reminded him that we'd be away on Monday and Tuesday.

'OK. See you Wednesday at 9:30 am,' he said.

Weather forecasters were predicting a poor week ahead. On Monday morning nothing could have been further from the truth. After a leisurely start, I put the overnight case into the back of the car and Jazz jumped in alongside. Our route took us north towards A Coruña and then west along the coast. By lunchtime we'd reached the coastal town of Malpica.

When it comes to the sea, Jazz possesses a sixth sense. She sat up in the back of the car, staring out of the window and whining with excitement.

'We'll have to let her out,' said Melanie.

'Why don't we stop here for lunch?' I suggested.

'That's a good idea.'

Coastal resorts in the off season are like ghost towns, and Malpica was no different. I drove up to the harbour and parked. A fleet of small fishing boats were anchored in the safe haven. Out to sea a layer of mist floated above the gently undulating waves. If ever a scene deserved the description ethereal, this was it.

Jazz jumped from the car, tail up and nose down.

'Leave them alone,' said Melanie, pulling on her lead.

Perched on the harbour wall were a number of seagulls basking in the midday sun.

'There doesn't seem to be a beach,' I said.

Jazz was keen to stretch her legs.

'Over there,' said Melanie.

A sign marked *Playa* pointed to a road leading into the town.

'Come on then,' I said, heading back to the car.

The road rose steeply out of the harbour. Narrow streets led us over a headland before descending to a wide expanse of golden sand.

'This is more like it,' said Melanie.

I parked by the side of the beach and lifted the tailgate. Jazz jumped out and bolted towards the sea. The beach was deserted.

'Jazz, come here,' I called.

The last thing I wanted was a damp dog festering in the back of the car. She stopped and stared back at me.

'She'll be alright,' said Melanie.

Jazz loves water but rarely swims. She's far more comfortable with her paws on the ground. We'd carried her into the swimming pool a few times to make sure she knew how to get out but she wasn't happy about it.

The view across the beach and out to sea was beautiful. A golden sandy bay was hemmed in with low lying hills to the west and tall cliffs to the east. Overhead the morning sun had burnt away the clouds to reveal a deep blue sky, a colour also reflected in the calm water. The shallow angle of the beach created white-topped breakers that lapped the shore in three distinct crests. Fringing the shoreline was a lace-like carpet of bright green seaweed. Jazz ran around on the deserted sand like an excited puppy.

The beauty offshore contrasted sharply with the scene onshore. The town had developed haphazardly with a contrasting mix of architectural styles, none of which were particularly pleasing to the eye. The harbour was pleasant enough but the beach was bordered by an ill-conceived promenade open to traffic. Behind that was a mismatch of modern, low-rise apartment blocks. It was hard to believe an area of such outstanding natural beauty could look so ugly.

After lunch we drove along the coast, stopping every now and then to admire the scenery and take photos. By 4:30 pm we arrived in the village of Santa Mariña.

'There,' said Melanie, pointing at a sign for Casa de Trillo.

I turned into the driveway and parked. The house looked exactly as it had in the online photos, a large, stone-built farmhouse with a barn conversion opposite. The renovation work was outstanding. The owner had seen us arrive and came to greet us.

Our pet-friendly room was on the ground floor.

'What time would you like dinner?' asked the owner.

'Would half past nine be OK?'

'That's fine. You are our only guests tonight so whatever time suits you best.'

It seemed we had the run of the place.

'My husband and I live across the courtyard in the barn. If there's anything you need just knock on the door,' she said before leaving.

The bedroom was enormous with a king-sized bed to match.

'Let's see if we can buy a bottle of wine and sit in the garden,' I suggested.

I tapped on the door and our host obliged.

The gardens were beautifully landscaped with hidden treasures around every corner. We took a seat, sipped a delicious Albariño wine and watched the sun slip behind a distant hill.

'Let's take Jazz for a walk,' suggested Melanie.

The village of Santa Mariña is little more than a hamlet. We wandered along the narrow lanes, encouraging Jazz to keep up. Late summer twilight provided a stunning palette of pastel shades.

A raging log fire greeted our arrival for dinner, which was traditional Galician fare made from locally sourced ingredients. We started with *huevos revueltos*, scrambled eggs with mushrooms, served with a mixed salad. The main course was *estofado de ternera gallega con patatas*, beef hotpot with potatoes; for desert we had *filloas con miel y nata*, pancakes served with cream and honey. It wasn't fine dining but everything was delicious and we had more than enough. After dinner we relaxed in front of the fire and finished the wine before turning in.

An excellent breakfast set us up for the day. Once again, the forecasters of inclement weather were proved wrong. We left the hotel and headed for Finisterre, the most westerly point on mainland Spain. Roughly translated it means Land's End. There's a lighthouse perched at the tip of the Cabo de Finisterre. Looking down from the clifftop it's easy to see how this stretch of coastline has claimed the lives of so many mariners. Perhaps its name is justified. Like swirls of cream in a mug of coffee, underwater reefs create patterns on the sea as bubbles of air rise to the surface. Venture too close to shore and disaster lies in wait.

The coastline is characterised by *rias* or inlets. They make a road trip along the coast long and winding but stunningly picturesque. Around every bend nestles a quiet beach or small fishing village. We left Finisterre and drove through Cee and on to the village of O Pindo where we stopped to stretch our legs and enjoy a mid-morning coffee. The air felt comfortably warm in the sunshine but cool and crisp in the shade. The next place of note was the seaside town of Muros.

'Let's stop for lunch,' I suggested.

Our trip along the coast was drawing to a close.

'OK,' said Melanie.

From Muros we drove to Noia where we headed inland towards Santiago de Compostela and back home. Three hours after leaving Muros we were driving through Canabal. From the beautiful coastline to the traditional cuisine, we couldn't have asked for a better autumn break.

The house felt noticeably cooler on our return.

'It's warmer outside,' remarked Melanie.

Winter was on its way.

'In that case, let's sit outside for a Teatime Taster.'

'Great idea,' she replied.

It felt quite pleasant sitting in the afternoon sun but as soon as it dipped below the horizon the temperature plummeted. That evening we lit the gas fire in the lounge, the first time since early spring.

'I think we might have to switch on the heating,' I commented.

'I think you're right and I'll dig out the winter duvet.'

Our reluctance to submit to the changing weather had nothing to do with cost and everything to do with the loss of summer. That evening, I turned on the heating and Melanie changed the duvet. Winter had officially begun.

Dragging ourselves out of bed was all the more difficult given the warm embrace of a heavy winter duvet.

'We'd better get up,' said Melanie. 'Roy will be here in half an hour.'

Another downside of employing people.

By the time we arrived at Vilatán, Manolo had been there for two hours. Alfonso was conspicuous by his absence.

'*Buenos días*,' I said to Manolo.

'*Muy buenas.*'

'Did Alfonso turn up yesterday?' I asked.

'No.'

That was disappointing. I rang to find out why.

'Something came up but I will definitely start next Monday,' he said.

Manolo had been waiting for me to finish the call.

'I've got a bit of a problem,' he said.

That wasn't like him; he usually brings solutions, not problems.

'What's matter?' I asked.

'It's the staircase, it doesn't fit.'

We were having an internal staircase built from the *bodega* to the first floor. It would run the width of the house and be cast in reinforced concrete with granite steps. On paper, everything fitted perfectly, but in reality the landing at the top of the stairs would be too narrow to open the door. Once Manolo poured the concrete, there was no turning back. We had one shot to get it right.

'What do you think we should do?' I asked.

'We could run it horizontally down the length of the house,' he replied.

Manolo's suggestion would mean shortening the second bedroom, leaving space for only one single bed instead of two. The impact on rental revenue would be considerable. There had to be another way.

'Can you run through the problem again?' I asked.

'The first floor is three metres and forty centimetres above the ground floor. A standard step rises twenty centimetres every twenty centimetres. That means it will take seventeen steps to reach the first floor.'

I nodded my understanding.

'Seventeen steps equate to a total run of three metres forty centimetres.'

'But the house is five metres twenty wide,' I replied.

'That's true but the landing at the bottom of the steps needs to be at least one metre which leaves eighty centimetres at the top.'

How on earth had I made such a fundamental error?

I racked my brain for an answer; then the penny dropped. The new concrete floor would be twenty centimetres thicker than the old wooden floorboards. I'd accounted for sixteen steps not seventeen. Identifying the reason didn't solve the problem.

'Do you need an answer right now?' I asked.

'No, but soon. Once the concrete ramp is poured my cousin and his labourer will be coming to help me build the new floor,' he said.

'Let me have a think about it.'

Cladding the terrace wall gave me lots of time to mull it over. It didn't take long to figure out a possible solution.

'I know,' I blurted out.

'You know what?' asked Melanie.

'I know what we can do about the stairs.'

I dropped my trowel into the cement bucket and went to speak to Manolo, and Melanie followed.

'I've got an idea,' I said.

Manolo stopped what he was doing and came to see what I had in mind.

'Instead of having a metre-wide landing at the foot of the stairs, can we build one step at a right angle to the main staircase and then a metre diameter bend of three steps before the run to the top?'

Manolo stared at the floor, contemplating my suggestion. I turned to Melanie for support, but she hadn't a clue what I was rambling on about.

'You mean have one step leading to three curved steps, instead of a metre-wide landing?'

'Exactly.'

I could tell from Manolo's expression my idea had legs. Melanie looked none the wiser.

'What difference will it make?' she asked.

'Well, instead of the staircase rising twenty centimetres in the space of a metre, it'll rise eighty.'

'And that means we won't have to shorten the bedroom,' she added.

The penny had dropped.

'It might work,' said Manolo. 'I'll nip into town after lunch and see if the wholesaler can cut the granite to the required shape.'

Manolo got the assurances he needed. Building the interior staircase could now begin.

10

Midnight Moonshine

The 21st of October marked a change in the weather. A light frost left us with a sugar-coated car. Our decision to switch on the heating hadn't come a moment too soon. Frosty mornings in Galicia are often followed by bright sunny days. By 10:00 am the ice had melted and the mercury was on the rise.

'I'm going to clean the wine this morning,' I said.

'Will you need any help?'

'Probably, I'll give you a shout when I do.'

The primary fermentation had taken longer than usual. Changeable summer weather resulted in a late harvest, followed by cooler temperatures which had resulted in a slower fermentation.

My skills as a vintner are in their infancy. Our neighbour Meli had shown me the basics but my education had stalled. Results to date had been disappointing. A trainee sommelier might describe my wine as having a distinctive pale colour with a unique flavour, bursting with fruity tones, low tannins and a long finish. His tutor would probably say it was watery and unappetising with an unpleasant aftertaste.

'Are you going to try it?' asked Melanie, as I tipped the last bucketful of clean wine into the vat.

'I am not,' I replied.

Good wine requires a winter of cold stabilisation. Trying it before was out of the question.

'But you can if you like,' I added.

'No thanks.'

My wine is nothing if not consistent. Every year it has the same off flavour and every year I fail to understand why. The most likely culprit is one of the many different grape varieties we use. Without making a separate batch for each one, I'm unlikely to find the offending fruit. On the plus side, if the wine is too bad to drink I can always distil it into *aguardiente*.

Aguardiente is the local firewater. It's distilled from the remnants of the winemaking process. Last year we bought a potbellied still and made our own.

'I'm going to make a start on the *aguardiente* tomorrow,' I said, as we strolled back to the house.

'What about Roy?'

Melanie's question jolted my memory. Last Friday, Roy had asked if we could work Monday afternoon instead of the morning. He had a doctor's appointment and didn't want to miss it. I'd agreed.

'I'll have to start when we get back,' I said.

'Will you have enough time?'

I'd have to make time; the grape must wouldn't last forever.

Once prepared, the sixty litre *pote* (potbellied still) takes about seven hours to produce four litres of spirit. As well as the grape must I had the leftovers of last year's wine and forty litres a friend had given me in exchange for a litre of *aguardiente*. If I was lucky, two *potes* would do the trick.

The following afternoon, Roy called as arranged and the three of us drove to Vilatán. At 6:30 pm we headed home.

'See you in the morning,' said Roy, as he left.

'OK.'

And off he went.

'I'm going to make a start on the *aguardiente*,' I said.

'I'll give you a shout when dinner is ready.'

The morning had been icy cold but it quickly warmed. Later in the day it clouded over and now looked like rain.

'Dinner's ready,' called Melanie.

Time flies when you're cobbling together a potbellied still. It didn't seem two minutes since I'd started. I hurried inside and wolfed my meal down.

'Delicious,' I said, getting to my feet.

'Give it chance to settle.'

A curious expression I've never quite understood. Unlike the saying 'Time, tide and a potbellied still wait for no man'.

'I'm fine,' I replied.

'Don't you want any pudding?'

'No thanks but I wouldn't say no to a coffee in a few minutes.'

In the short time it had taken me to eat dinner the temperature had dropped another few degrees. The sooner I fired up the still the warmer I'd be. Ten minutes later Melanie knocked on the shed door.

'How's it going?' she asked, handing me a mug of steaming coffee.

'I'm nearly there. I've just got the joints to cement.'

I mixed up some fire cement in a small bowl and used a butter knife and my fingers to seal all the joints between the various copper components. By the time I lit the burner, the clock had ticked around to 8:45 pm.

'It's off,' I announced as I stepped into the lounge.

'You look frozen.'

'I am.'

Melanie popped the kettle on and I thawed out. An hour later I checked on progress. When I pushed open the shed door a curtain of warm air brushed past my cheeks. Inside the air felt toasty warm. The gas burner was on its lowest setting ensuring the contents of the *pote* didn't overheat and burn. Experience had taught me to leave the door slightly ajar, allowing deadly carbon monoxide to escape. A cold-water hosepipe attached to the inlet tube on the condenser prevented the water tank from overheating and the shed filling with condensation. Everything was working perfectly.

'Well?' asked Melanie, on my return.

'Nothing yet,' I replied.

'You're joking. It's gone ten o'clock.'

'It shouldn't be long now.'

An hour later I checked again. There was a real chill in the air as I stepped outside and walked across to the shed. As I pushed open the door a breath of warm air greeted me. I stepped inside and closed it. Still nothing to show for my efforts. I pulled up a garden chair, took a seat and stared at the outlet spout on the condenser, willing it to start dripping. Within minutes of sitting down, a droplet of clear liquid formed on the end of the spout. Before long it fell into the glass measuring jug I'd placed underneath. I waited for a second drop to fall before reporting the news.

'It's started,' I announced.

'Not before time. How long do you think it'll take?'

'Put it this way, I've got a long night ahead of me.'

By midnight we had our first bottle. A quick measurement using the Gay-Lussac alcoholmeter registered an alcohol content of eighty-nine percent proof. We'd certainly have to water that down before drinking it.

When I returned to the house, Melanie had fallen asleep in her chair. I nudged her gently.

'I think it's time you went to bed,' I said quietly.

'Are you coming?'

'Not yet.'

Melanie gave me a kiss and wandered into the bedroom. By the time my head hit the pillow the clock had ticked around to 3:45 am.

Beep, beep, beep, beep!

Melanie rolled over and hit the snooze button. Five minutes later, *beep, beep, beep, beep!* This time she switched it off and got up. A few minutes later the bedroom door opened and Jazz jumped onto the bed.

'Watch where you're putting your feet,' I squealed.

'Good morning,' said Melanie.

'Is it?'

'What time did you get to bed?'

I rolled over and squinted at the clock. The digital display read 08:25.

'About four and a half hours ago.'

'Here,' she said, perching a mug of coffee on the bedside table, 'you'd better drink this. Roy will be here in less than an hour.'

By the time he pulled into the driveway, I'd rejoined the land of the living and was ready for a morning of cement mixing and stone cladding. When we arrived at Vilatán, Manolo was standing in the lane chatting to a smartly dressed man holding a clipboard. Two other men were waiting in the meadow. By the look of their clothing they were Manolo's cousin and his workmate.

'*Hola*,' I said as we walked past.

Roy and I had only just started when Manolo came to have a word.

'That was the building inspector,' he said.

'What did he want?' I asked.

Permissions and permits are part and parcel of any Spanish building project but here in rural Galicia there's the official way of doing things and the recognised way. We'd taken the recognised approach.

'He's fined me for not having any hard hats.'

'Oh,' I replied, 'I'm sorry about that.'

Manolo's misfortune was a setback but at least it wasn't anything more serious.

'It's not your fault,' he replied.

'Was it much?' I asked.

'Two hundred euros.'

'Crikey! That sounds expensive.'

Manolo looked at me.

'Two hundred euros for each of us, six hundred in total.'

His oversight had cost him a week's wage. My mind drifted back to the renovations on our house. The first thing the builder did was mount a laminated health and safety notice to the front gate and make a coat stand out of three pieces of wood and three six-inch nails. One nail for each brother. The next thing he did was hook a brand-new bright yellow hard hat on each nail. Six months later, he unhooked the unused hard hats and put them back in his van.

'How did he know you were here?' I asked.

'He said he was in the area looking at another property.'

I couldn't help thinking that Manolo was either very unlucky or darker forces were at work. Why had the building inspector turned up on the very day he had two assistants?

During the tendering process Manolo had been our preferred choice but his price was also the lowest. Perhaps his competitors hadn't taken kindly to an outsider muscling in on their patch. I don't suppose we'll ever know.

By the time Manolo and his team left for lunch, they'd removed two of the five chestnut floor bearers. The bearers spanned the width of the house and supported the old wooden floor joists. Each one was five and a half metres long and honed from a single tree trunk. They ranged in diameter from forty-five centimetres at one end to thirty at the other and weighed the best part of a ton.

'Do you have a chainsaw?' I asked Roy, as we headed home for lunch.

'I've got two,' he replied.

'Can you bring one tomorrow and we'll get those bearers sawn into manageable pieces?'

'No problem.'

That evening my sister rang.

'Can you ring me back?' she asked. 'I'm at Dad's and the phone company have stopped outgoing calls.'

I rang straight back.

'I think we should reduce the asking price,' she said.

We'd put Dad's house on the market before Melanie and I returned to Spain. The government were introducing some costly new legislation for sellers which we were keen to avoid.

'That's fine by me,' I replied.

We'd sold our home in England six months after moving here and weren't interested in owning another, inherited or otherwise.

Clang, clang, clang, clang!

That sounded exactly like the bell on our front gate.

Clang, clang, clang, clang!

There it went again.

'Craig.' Melanie nudged me in the back.

'What?' I moaned.

'Roy's here,' she said, jumping out of bed.

I wasn't dreaming; that was our brass bell.

'What time is it?' I asked as Melanie tugged on her dressing gown.

'It's twenty to ten.'

We'd both slept in.

Melanie asked Roy to take Jazz for a walk while we readied ourselves. By 9:50 am, we were on our way to Vilatán. Halfway there we drove past Otero's delivery wagon. It was parked at the side of the highway with the hazard warning lights flashing.

'I hope they're not delivering to us,' I joked.

The wagon was laden with reinforced concrete joists. One of the straps securing the load had snapped and they were hanging over the side of the wagon. Fortunately, the driver had noticed and was trying to slide them back into position.

When we arrived at Vilatán, Manolo was on the phone, pacing up and down. His cousin and the other lad were standing around idle.

'What's the matter?' I asked, when Manolo ended his call.

'Otero's haven't delivered the floor joists. They tell me the driver left an hour ago but he can't have done.'

The load we'd just passed was bound for us.

I told Manolo what we'd seen. The three of them jumped in his van and drove off.

'Right then,' said Roy, chainsaw at the ready, 'what size do you want them?'

'About that long,' I said, holding my hands about forty centimetres apart.

Once the bearers had been sawn into manageable lengths I could split them for firewood but that was a job for another day.

'They're as hard as iron,' said Roy as the chainsaw tore at the chestnut timber.

Three cuts into the first beam, Manolo's van pulled into the driveway followed by Otero's delivery wagon. The four of them had manhandled the heavy concrete joists back into position and secured them to the flatbed.

While Roy continued sawing the beams, Melanie and I mixed some cement and continued cladding the wall.

'We're going to run out of stone,' I commented.

'You'd better call Moncho and see if he's got any in stock yet,' said Melanie.

Moncho was having supply problems. I'd phoned around but there seemed to be a general shortage.

'Still haven't got any,' he said, 'I'll let you know as soon as I have.'

Without materials we had little choice but to lay Roy off.

By the time we left for lunch, Roy had managed to saw his way through three of the five beams. Melanie and I had used the last of the stone cladding and Manolo and company had lifted half a dozen floor joists into position.

On the drive home I gave Roy the bad news.

'No problem,' he said. 'Just give me a call when you want me to start again.'

We hadn't had a lie-in for weeks and on the one morning we could, we were up with the larks.

'We might as well go up to Vilatán and see how the floor is coming along,' I suggested.

Completing the floor would signify a turning point in the renovation and bring to an end the major structural work.

When we arrived at the house, we were delighted to see Alfonso.

'*Buenos dias,*' I said.

Alfonso is one of those happy-go-lucky characters who always wear a smile. He greeted us warmly and continued working. The floor was progressing well. Since yesterday lunchtime they'd installed all the concrete joists and started laying the blocks.

Building a concrete floor is a simple process. The tee shaped floor joists span the width of the house at equal intervals along its length. Hollow blocks, with a lip on both sides, sit in equidistant gaps between the joists. A mesh of reinforcing steel is laid over that and the whole lot is covered with a layer of concrete. It takes between twenty-four and forty-eight hours for it to harden and twenty-eight days until it's fully cured.

Happy that everything was going to plan, we left.

The following morning, we couldn't wait to see how things had progressed. Everyone was busy when we arrived. To our amazement, all the blocks were in place. For the first time in months, the underside of the roof couldn't be seen from the *bodega*.

'Wow! Look at that,' said Melanie.

'Come on,' I said, striding towards the back door. I couldn't wait to take a closer look.

I skipped up the side steps, across the terrace and around the corner of the house. The back door was wide open. I couldn't believe my eyes. Laid out in front of me was a wide expanse of uniform concrete floor joists and row upon row of grey blocks. Manolo and his two workmates were on their knees at the far end of the house wiring together steel reinforcing rods in a crisscross pattern. Without saying a word, I wandered inside. Five metres from the door, Manolo spotted me.

'Stop right there,' he called.

I froze to the spot, wondering what I'd done wrong. Manolo jumped to his feet and walked towards me.

'Stand on the joists,' he instructed.

Quickly I moved my feet and straddled two joists.

'The blocks are hollow, if they crack you'll end up in the *bodega*.'

'I'll leave you to it,' I said sheepishly, stepping carefully back to the open door.

'One of these days…' said Melanie.

Before leaving I checked to see if Moncho had made a delivery; unfortunately not.

That evening we sat out on the back terrace. Every day our Teatime Taster started that little bit earlier, but autumn evenings do have some compensations.

'Chestnuts?' I asked.

'Yes please.'

Roasted chestnuts are a seasonal delicacy. A few years ago, we bought a chestnut roasting pan. It fits perfectly on top of the paella burner. We tried roasting them in the oven but Melanie tired of cleaning exploded nuts off the inside. The pan is similar to a deep frying pan with ten-millimetre holes drilled in the base. Flames hop through the holes, cook the nuts and crisp the husks. Twenty minutes and two explosions later, they were ready.

'Ow, ow, ow!'

'Just wait,' I said.

I couldn't blame her; the smell of freshly roasted chestnuts is irresistible.

'These are delicious,' she said.

For someone who hated them before we moved to Spain, she can't get enough of them now. Red wine and roast chestnuts, what better way to end an autumn day.

11

Dognapped

Gone are the days of unlimited luggage and in-flight meals. Nowadays, discount airlines compete in a race to the bottom on price and service. Weight restricted carry-ons are the modern way to travel.

'Have you got any room in your case?' asked Melanie.

'You've got to be joking.'

This trip to England was meant to be a quick in and out. Get everything boxed up, labelled and ready for Elite-European to collect from Richard and Yvonne's.

We'd arranged to go out for lunch before our midnight flit. The idea being a full meal and a few glasses of wine would help induce an afternoon siesta and take the edge off the drive to Madrid.

Everything was going to plan until, *ring, ring … ring, ring!*

I dragged myself out of bed and raced to pick up phone.

'Hello.'

'It's me,' said my sister Julie.

I'm sure older sisters are only created to annoy younger brothers.

'What do you want?'

'Charming. I've lost my phone charger and think it's at Dad's. Can you have a look when you get there?'

'OK.'

'If you do find it can you post it back to me along with any mail there might be?'

'OK.'

'And I've arranged for an auctioneer to come and give us an idea how much the house might fetch at auction.'

'When?'

'Thursday at 10:30 am.'

'OK.'

She said goodbye and I went back to bed. Nodding off during the day is difficult enough at the best of times; managing it a second time proved elusive. The thought of speeding through the Spanish countryside at midnight kept me awake.

On the stroke of twelve our journey began. A full moon illuminated the night sky. An hour into the trip the glare of oncoming headlights started to take the edge off my excitement. By the end of the second hour, the strain was taking its toll. Only when we reached the well-lit suburbs of Madrid did I get some respite. By the time we pulled into the airport carpark I'd had enough. Night driving on unlit roads is not romantic or mysterious; it's not even fun.

The time had ticked around to 4:45 am. The early morning temperature was icy cold. Thankfully, the wait for the airport service bus was short.

We've been in a few airports in our time but never one as quiet as this. The departures hall was deserted. All the shops were closed and shuttered, so too the bars and restaurants.

'Where is everyone?' whispered Melanie.

'I've no idea.'

I half-expected a ragtag army of bloodthirsty zombies to emerge from the shadows.

'There,' said Melanie, pointing at a cleaner.

I gave her the once-over to make sure she had all her limbs. You can't be too careful when zombies are on the prowl.

'At least we're not on our own,' I replied.

The check-in desks in the departure lounge were abandoned. We followed the information screen to the allotted gate number and took a seat.

'Would you like a drink?' I asked, pointing at a vending machine across the hallway.

'Yes please. I could murder some water.'

The floor tiles were squeaky clean. I turned to Melanie and smiled, and she responded by putting a finger to her lips. Two euros for a bottle of water seemed a bit steep but beggars can't be choosers. I pushed a coin into the slot. It rattled through the machine and dropped into the return tray. That was all I needed. I tried again and again, each time with the same result. That's when I noticed the plug lying on the floor. Even the vending machine was closed for business. I considered plugging it in but resisted the temptation and mooched back to Melanie empty-handed.

Half an hour passed before the next passengers arrived. They too tried the vending machine.

'Go on,' I whispered.

They noticed the plug on the floor, picked it up and then decided against it.

From then on, a steady stream of people wandered towards the departure gate. It opened half an hour before take-off and a half-full plane departed on time.

The flight time was two hours and fifteen minutes. In all that time I didn't sleep a wink. All I could see when I closed my eyes were oncoming headlights. The plane landed ten minutes early. By the time we'd picked up the hire car and driven to Melanie's mum's, the clock had ticked around to 10:30 am.

'How are you feeling?' asked Melanie, as she unlocked the back door.

Jennifer had left us a key under the doormat. She was out at work.

'I feel better now than I have done in hours.'

'Me too.'

We'd caught our second wind. That raised the question of what to do now.

'Let's nip up to the butcher's in the village and get some pork pies,' I suggested.

'For breakfast?'

'Why not?'

'OK, I bet Rusty could do with a walk.'

Rusty is Jennifer's middle-aged Cairn Terrier with a short temper and an attitude problem. She acquired him by accident when a short-term adoption turned into a lifelong inheritance.

'Come on lad,' I said, clipping him to his lead.

The icy temperature in Madrid did nothing to prepare us for the windswept drizzle howling off the Pennines. We leaned into the wind and trudged the half mile into Golcar village. Occupying pride of place on the main street is H. Copley Family Butchers, the perfect place to buy freshly baked pies.

'You can't bring him in,' said Melanie.

'Well I'm not standing out there with him.'

The high street felt like a wind tunnel, funnelling the inclement weather into something approaching a power washer.

'Tie him to those railings.'

'Are you sure?'

'We'll only be two minutes.'

'Good morning. What can I get you?' asked the butcher.

'Have you got any pork pies?'

'They'll be out of the oven in two minutes if you'd like to wait.'

I'd waited months for some proper pork pies; another two minutes wouldn't make any difference. Five minutes later he brought a tray of steaming pies out from the back and placed them on the counter.

'How many would you like?'

I glanced at Melanie.

'No,' she said. 'You can't have them all.'

'Half a dozen will be fine for now,' I replied.

'Let them cool before you eat them,' cautioned the butcher. 'They're piping hot.'

He wasn't kidding; holding the bag was hot enough.

'Bye for now,' said Melanie as she pulled open the door.

'What's matter?'

Melanie was frozen to the top step.

'Where's Rusty?'

My heart sank. Surely he hadn't been dognapped. I stared at the railings. His lead was hanging down with the collar still attached.

'The little bugger,' I said. 'He's slipped his collar.'

'But where is he?'

Melanie's voice cracked.

'Don't worry,' I said, in a vain attempt to calm her down, 'he can't have gone far.'

'Mum's going to kill us.'

'What do you mean us? It was your idea to tie him up,' I joked.

Melanie was not in the mood.

'You go that way and I'll go this,' I added.

Dividing our efforts gave us a better chance of finding him.

'You haven't seen a Cairn Terrier running loose have you?' Melanie asked a passer-by.

'Have you lost one?' asked the old man.

Why else would she be asking, I thought to myself.

'He's slipped his collar and run away,' she said.

'Sorry love, I haven't seen a thing.'

'I'll look this way,' I said, walking off across the road.

'Rusty!' I called. 'Rusty!'

Melanie walked off in the opposite direction.

Rusty's name echoed through the village, fading into silence as the distance between us lengthened.

Five minutes later I saw Melanie strutting towards me with Rusty in tow. Thank heavens for that.

Throughout my search the aroma of warm pies had brought me to the edge of distraction. Now he was back, I had one thing on my mind.

'Would you like a pie?' I asked, as we walked back.

'Are they cool enough?'

'They should be by now,' I replied, dipping my hand inside the paper bag and handing her one.

'Be careful,' she said, as I nibbled the crust around the edge of my pie.

The gelatine was still hot, and when I bit into the crust it leaked over my fingers. Freshly baked pork pies for breakfast: this is the life. This one moment of ecstasy made our night-time manoeuvres all worthwhile.

What was billed as a working trip turned into a holiday. Melanie visited her granny every day and we both spent time with friends. I got to watch my beloved Huddersfield Town – twice. Saturday's match against Port Vale finished three, one to Town with club legend Andy Booth scoring the opener and a Tuesday night match saw us beat Hartlepool United, two goals to nil. We also found time to enjoy our favourite foods: Indian takeaways, sticky vanilla slices from the supermarket, fish and chips, and more pork pies.

Before we knew it, we were heading home. Ten hours door to door, not bad considering the drive from Madrid took five. Jazz was pleased to see us but reluctant to leave Roy's. She'd clearly been spoilt for a week.

'See you in the morning at a quarter to ten,' said Roy, as Jazz jumped into the back of the car.

Had we really been away for a week?

The following morning, we readied ourselves as usual, overalls and working boots. When Roy said he'd see us tomorrow, I'd forgotten all about the lack of material. I could only hope Moncho had delivered some stone while we'd been away.

'Look at that,' said Melanie, as I pulled into the driveway.

Alfonso had finished the drystone wall running along the bottom of the meadow and it looked stunning.

'That looks fantastic,' I remarked, and that wasn't all.

Manolo was working inside the house, standing on the new floor, pointing the wall in what would be the lounge.

'*Buenos dias.*'

He looked up and smiled.

'*Hola*, Moncho has left you some stone at the top of the track.'

More good news. I went to tell Roy.

'That's not going to last long,' he said.

He was right; half a pallet wouldn't go far.

Manolo left for lunch at his usual time and we left an hour later. That afternoon we drove up to Escairón to order some more stone from Moncho.

'I haven't got any,' he said, 'and I'm not sure when I will.'

That was the last thing I wanted to hear. We were one pallet short of finishing the job.

'What's the problem?' I asked.

He said the stone originated in the high hills and the authorities were concerned too much was going missing.

'They're on the lookout for thieves,' he said.

'Does that mean you won't be able to get any more?'

'No, but it could be twenty days before I do.'

'As soon as you get some we'll need another pallet.'

'No problem,' he replied.

We didn't know what to make of Moncho's high hills story but whatever the reason for the shortage, we would have to wait. My attention turned to the paving for the terrace. We'd decided to use the same type of material we have at home. It's basically waste, offcuts of marble and granite from kitchen worktops, fire surrounds and even headstones. Shiny side down, the rough surface on the reverse creates an attractive natural surface. The only exception to this was under the new porch. Moncho had shown us some sandstone flags which were ideal.

That afternoon I went to speak with Emilio at Marmoles Grande, suppliers of the marble offcuts. If ever a man's stature suited his occupation, Emilio was the perfect example. At well over six foot tall and built like the side of a house, he could lift lumps of marble mere mortals could only dream of.

'I'd like to order two pallets of offcuts,' I said.

'No problem, where are they going?'

'Could you deliver them to Moncho's in Escairón?' I asked.

Moncho didn't know it yet but I was going to get him to deliver them on his URO. That way we'd get them dropped exactly where they were needed.

'No problem.'

'How soon can you deliver?'

'Some time this week.'

'The sooner the better,' I said.

All I needed to do now was let Moncho in on the arrangement.

Later that day Melanie reminded me of an upcoming social event.

'You haven't forgotten about Gerry's sixtieth birthday party, have you?'

It had completely slipped my mind. Gerry's partner Carol had surprised him by booking flights to their holiday home here in Galicia. What she hadn't told him was his three kids were joining them. Melanie and I were delighted to be part of the family celebrations.

'Of course not, when is it exactly?' I replied.

'Tsk, tomorrow.'

'Ah yes, that sixtieth birthday party.'
'What have you got him?'
Melanie was teasing, or at least I hoped she was.
'I'm not sure; what have I bought him?'
'Don't look at me! I haven't got him anything.'
She wasn't joking. I thought for a moment.
'Let's go to Bazar Isa this afternoon. They're bound to have something.'

Bazar Isa is aptly named; most of their stock is extremely bizarre. It's a typically Spanish emporium filled with unusual gift ideas. Imagine a shop packed with outrageously expensive unwanted wedding gifts and you won't be far off the mark. We stumbled across it a few years ago completely by accident. I suspect certain individuals with undeclared income are happy to exchange black money for sparkling trinkets. Hidden within this upmarket outlet are a few precious gems waiting to be discovered.

'That's a good idea,' said Melanie.

And so it proved: a tasteful *licor café* decanter and six *chupito* (shot) glasses made by Porcelana Galos, a prestigious Galician porcelain maker.

The party was being held in Monforte de Lemos, at the restaurant La Maja. Melanie and I arrived early to hang the 60th celebration bunting. After dinner the party continued at Mulligans, an Irish themed bar just around the corner, and carried on into the early hours.

The following morning I felt dreadful. Spanish red wine, French champagne, Galician liqueurs and Irish beer. We'd drunk our way around the world and I wasn't quite sure which country I'd ended up in.

'Are you getting up?' asked Melanie.

I had neither the will nor inclination to respond.

'Everyone will be there in an hour,' she added.

I hadn't the faintest idea what she was talking about.

'Don't you remember?'

At this point I wasn't even sure of my name.

'I told you not to invite them.'

That sounded familiar. What had I done?

'What?' I groaned.

'You invited everyone to Vilatán for some roast chestnuts.'

What was she going on about?

'What?' I moaned.

I tried to lift my head off the pillow but it weighed a ton.

'Last night at Mulligans, just after the landlord had treated everyone to a round of drinks on the house, you invited Gerry, Carol and his three kids to Vilatán for roast chestnuts.'

'Are you sure?'

'I'm certain. Now get up.'

What choice did I have?

Eventually I managed to drag myself out of bed without throwing up. I hadn't felt this bad in years.

'What about the chestnuts?' asked Melanie.

Just the thought of them brought a lump to my throat.

'You're not serious, are you?'

'You offered to roast them.'

Roasting chestnuts was a step too far.

'Don't worry,' said Melanie, 'I don't think anyone was that bothered.'

Thanks heavens for that.

By the time we got to Vilatán, Gerry, Carol and the kids were already there.

'You look a bit fragile,' remarked Carol.

Fragile was an understatement. What made it worse was Gerry looked as fresh as a daisy.

'So, where are these roast chestnuts you promised?' he asked.

Trust him to remember.

'You don't really want any, do you?'

'Don't tell me you've forgotten them. I was really looking forward to some.'

Now he was rubbing it in. I wouldn't hear the last of this.

'Sorry Gerry, no nuts.'

I handed Melanie the keys to the house.

'Would you mind?'

Melanie gave our guests a guided tour while I perched my bum on the wall outside, trying my best to keep the contents of my stomach where they were.

Comments about the house were encouraging if somewhat reserved. Understandable given the amount of work still to do. As soon as we got home, I went straight to bed.

What remained of the weekend passed in a semi-conscious blur. By Monday morning I was raring to go. I'd phoned Roy over the weekend and asked him not to work. As soon as the paving was delivered, I'd give him a call.

'Let's nip into town this morning and get some money for Moncho,' I said.

His payment terms were regular but flexible. Every four to six weeks he'd give us an invoice and we'd pay it. It suited us both.

'We can call at that new central heating shop while we're there,' said Melanie.

Last winter a shop selling electric radiators opened in Monforte. Our original plan was to install storage heaters but we decided their lack of flexibility wouldn't suit a rental property. Standard radiators would be a better option.

The shop was closed so I scribbled down their phone number to call later.

Moncho was pleased to see us. He always is when we're paying him.

'I've asked Emilio at Marmoles Grande to drop a couple of pallets of paving off here. Could you deliver them to the house for us?'

'No problem.'

'Do you know when the paving slabs will be delivered?'

'It might be later in the week.'

His reply was so vague we'd just have to wait.

Over lunch we discussed the windows. Hardwood was the obvious choice but we'd opted for white aluminium. They'd be quick and easy to clean, require very little maintenance, and most importantly, would match many of the other houses in the village. Livestock were also an issue. At least four of our neighbours have sheep, cattle, chickens or all three. During the hot summer months, animals attract flies. A fly screen on every window was a must and although screen surrounds are available in various colours, we didn't see the sense in buying expensive hardwood window frames only to cover them with a fly screen.

After lunch we drove to the village of Vilaescura to ask José Metal if he would come to the house and measure up.

Of course, José Metal isn't his real name but with so many Spaniards taking their name from Catholic saints and such a small pool to choose from, repetition is common. As well as José Metal, we also have José Well, José Builder, José Kitchen, and José Digger logged into our phone.

Fortunately, José Metal was at home when we called.

'When do you want me to come?' he asked.

'Whenever suits you.'

'I'll give you a call when I'm available,' he replied.

Pinning him down to a specific day was pointless. If we hadn't heard from him in a week, we could give him a polite nudge.

'Let's call at Javier's while we're sorting out the windows,' I suggested, on the drive home.

Javier SL supplied the windows for our house. They aren't the best in the world but they were cheap. They too would call when they had time to measure up.

Our day off had been anything but. Tomorrow we'd be back to the grindstone but before then there was time for a Teatime Taster and some roasted chestnuts.

12

The Office Party

A long soak in a warm bathtub has spawned many eureka moments. Nowadays, I prefer showers and rely on our Teatime Taster for inspiration.

'What about a Christmas party?'
'What?' asked Melanie.

I'd been so engrossed in my thoughts I'd forgotten to share them with Melanie.

'What do you think to the idea of organising a Christmas party?'
'What's brought that on?'

Copious glasses of wine but I wasn't about to admit it.

'I was just thinking about work.'
'Work!'
'Not work as such, more about the old business.'

Melanie looked at me as if I'd gone mad.

'What are you going on about?'
'It was about this time of year I started looking for a suitable venue.'

'A suitable venue for what?'

'The works Christmas party.'

The smooth running of a small business relies on the goodwill of its staff and their spouses. Paying for a Christmas party had been my way of saying thank you.

'But we don't have a business,' said Melanie.

'I know but we could still organise a Christmas party.'

'For who?'

'Our friends.'

'You weren't thinking of having it here, were you?'

'After the last fiasco, definitely not.'

Nightmare memories of hosting an expat party for our village fiesta a few years back still haunted us.

'Where then?'

My seed of an idea hadn't grown as far as a venue. I thought for a moment.

'I know,' I said.

'Where?'

'The Jing Huà.'

'In Chaves! That's a bit far, isn't it?'

'We could stay in a hotel overnight.'

'And who exactly is we?'

That was something else I hadn't thought about.

'I bet Roy and Maria would be up for it.'

'And Bill and Di,' said Melanie.

My suggestion was gaining momentum.

'We'll have to invite Penelope,' I said.

'And what about that new couple, Peter and Veronica?'

'We could ask them.'

'Hang on a minute, who's going to pay for all this?' asked Melanie.

'Everyone can pay for themselves.'

'What about presents?' asked Melanie.

'Don't get carried away. Buying something for everyone would cost a small fortune.'

'That's true.' Melanie paused for a moment. 'I know what we can do.'

'What?'
'We could have a Secret Santa.'
'What's that?'
'Everyone's name goes into a hat and lots are drawn to determine who buys a present for who.'
'That's a great idea.'
'We ought to set a spending limit as well.'
'How much?'
'Shall we say five euros?'

I topped up our glasses and we fleshed out the plan. We even came up with a name for our little soirée: The Office Party.

In the cold light of day, The Office Party had lost none of its appeal. The following afternoon I searched the internet for a suitable place to stay. One establishment stood out from the crowd, Residencial Bem Estar.

'How much is it?' asked Melanie.
'Twenty-five euros a night for a double room.'
'What's wrong with it?'
'Nothing's wrong with it. They even accept pets. Come and take a look.'

The photos were great and its central location, perfect.
'What about Penelope? How much is a single?'
'Twenty euros.'
'That sounds alright.'
'And breakfast is included.'
'You're kidding.'
'Nope.'
'What are you waiting for? Get it booked.'
'Perhaps we ought to find out who's coming first.'
'Oh yes. That's a good idea.'

Melanie phoned around. Everyone was keen to be involved.

'Let's go to Chaves next week, check out the hotel and make the bookings,' I suggested.

To date, the autumn weather had been kind to us. If the rain held off and Moncho could get his hands on some stone, Roy and I would soon be finished.

'Do you need me today?' asked Melanie. 'It's just there's a mountain of ironing to catch up with.'

'No problem, you stay here. If you get a minute, can you give the central heating shop in Monforte a ring and ask them for a quote?'

'OK.'

Halfway through the morning an unannounced visitor called to see me at Vilatán.

'*Hola. Eres señor Bricks* (Hello. Are you Mr Briggs)?' he asked.

'That's right.'

He introduced himself as Diego from the central heating shop.

'Your wife asked me to call in,' he said.

I led him inside, gave him a copy of the floor plan, and explained what we wanted. He studied the drawing.

'Give me a few days and I'll get back to you with a price.'

He was just about to leave when I heard '*Hola*'. I recognised the voice instantly.

'*Hola* Carmen, how are you?'

Carmen owns the house directly behind us.

'You're busy, I'll call back later.'

'Don't go on my behalf,' said Diego, 'I'm just leaving.'

I thanked him for calling and said I hoped to hear from him soon. Carmen seemed fascinated with the new floor.

'We're going to tile it,' I said.

She nodded her approval.

'When are you going to start building the wall?' she asked.

Carmen was referring to the boundary wall between the meadow and her orchard.

'I'm not sure,' I admitted.

We hadn't seen Alfonso since he finished the bottom wall.

'The stonemason is on another job at the moment but as soon as he's back he'll make a start.'

I half-expected her to moan about the delay but she didn't seem bothered. Instead she asked, 'Where will he build it?'

The wording of her question rang alarm bells. The existing wall was in a ruinous state but it wasn't difficult to see where it had once been. Surely she wasn't going to argue over a few inches this way or that, especially as we were paying for it.

'Along the line of the old one,' I said.

'Show me,' she replied, and turned to leave.

I followed her out the back door, around the side of the house, along the front and into the meadow.

'Exactly where it is now,' I said, using a sweeping arm movement to allow room for manoeuvre.

'Hmm.' Carmen paused for thought. Something was bothering her.

'What about here?' she said, pointing at the end nearest the house.

The wall ran in a straight line from the driveway to a point about three metres from the house. Here it turned at a right angle until it met the corner of Carmen's barn. Alfonso said it would look much better without the dog leg but as we didn't own the land, that was out of the question.

'Don't worry,' I said, 'we'll rebuild it exactly as it is now.'

'Wouldn't it be easier to build it in a straight line?'

I sensed her question had an ulterior motive.

'It would,' I replied.

'I'll sell you this corner if you like and then you can build a straight wall,' she said.

Carmen had sprung her trap but the question was, how much would this neighbourly gesture cost us?

'How much do you want for it?'

'Only 500 euros.'

Carmen had it all worked out. Whether by design or coincidence, her asking price was exactly the same as we'd paid her sister for the narrow strip of land to widen the driveway. Before I had a chance to reply she continued.

'There's no rush. Have a chat with your wife and let me know.'

Unlike our dealings with her sister Maruja, Carmen was giving us the choice. Her asking price was undoubtedly exorbitant but the saving we'd make building a straight wall would far outweigh the cost of the land. We would be fools to turn her down.

That lunchtime I discussed her offer with Melanie.

'She's got a cheek,' she said.

'I know but it's bound to save us money in the long run.'

'I suppose we'd better buy it then.'

'In that case let's nip up this afternoon and tell her.'

'What's the rush?'

'I don't want her to change her mind.'

Melanie agreed.

That afternoon we called to see her.

'If you give us your NIE number (National Identity Number) I'll have a contract drawn up,' I told her.

'I can't afford to pay for that,' replied Carmen.

Now there's a surprise.

'Don't worry, we'll sort it out.'

We were becoming quite adept at organising private sale contracts. Carmen gave us everything we needed and Melanie and I measured up the land. That afternoon I sketched out the new boundary on the computer and printed a copy.

The day after that, we were up with the larks, a wholly inaccurate expression for what turned out to be almost nine o'clock. I'd asked Roy to take the day off so Melanie and I could go to Chaves and finalise the arrangements for The Office Party. Before then, we wanted to nip into town and get a *gestor* (administrator) to draw up the contract for Carmen's land.

The *gestor* had it done in no time.

'Can we go to Portugal now?' asked Melanie.

'Yep.'

Even when it's overcast, the drive to Chaves is a pleasure. The A-52, Autovía de las Rías Bajas, runs from Pontevedra, on the west coast of Galicia, to Benavente in the province of Zamora. We joined the two-lane highway in Ourense and journeyed south east to the town of Verin. From there we headed west into Portugal.

The hotel was tucked away down a one-way street in the centre of town. The manager was happy to show us a room and even happier when we booked three doubles and a single. I glanced at my watch; lunchtime was beckoning.

As usual the Jing Huà Chinese restaurant was relatively quiet. After lunch we booked a table for nine on the evening of the 12th of December. Things couldn't have gone smoother. Everything was set. All we had to do now was draw lots for the Secret Santa.

The weather had improved throughout the day but by the time we got home it was too late to sit outside for a Teatime Taster. Oh well, tomorrow is another day.

The morning brought a blanket of mist. It clung to the surrounding countryside like a wet towel. If we were lucky, the sun would burn it away by lunchtime. Roy arrived on schedule. The drive to Vilatán takes us out of the Val de Lemos and up into the surrounding hills. As we climbed out of the valley we punched through the clouds into a world of bright sunshine and powder blue sky.

In an effort to crack on, I left the sale contract at home. Melanie and I could call tomorrow; Carmen was bound to be in over the weekend.

By the time we drove home for lunch, there was no trace of the earlier mist.

'You forgot the contract,' said Melanie, on my return.

'I thought we could go with it tomorrow morning.'

'You did, did you?'

'Yes, and on the way back we can call to see everyone with the names for the Secret Santa.'

'That's a good idea.'

'I have my moments.'

'Of course darling,' she replied, with more than a hint of sarcasm.

Day-long sunshine is a real bonus in November and one we were determined to take full advantage of.

'Teatime Taster?' I asked.

Melanie glanced at the clock.

'Why not?'

'Chestnuts?'

'Yes please.'

Our stockpile of nuts was dwindling. The sunshine felt comfortably warm and the nuts smelled tantalisingly delicious. No sooner had the evening sun dropped below the woody knoll than the temperature plummeted. We braved the chill for an hour or so before surrendering and heading inside.

'It's going to be a cold one tonight,' I said.

My prediction proved spectacularly correct. When I flung open the bedroom shutters, the car, the garden and the whole of the surrounding countryside was blanketed with a thick layer of frost. Quickly, I closed the window and jumped back under the duvet.

'It's freezing out there,' said Melanie, as she nudged open the bedroom door carrying our morning cuppa.

Jazz ran past her and leapt onto the bed.

'The washer's frozen,' she added.

The washing machine is housed in the laundry room attached to the shed, neither of which are heated. As a consequence, when the temperature drops below zero, the water pipes freeze.

'Oh dear, you'll have to wait for it to thaw.'

Within the hour we were ready for off. When I stepped outside my face tightened. It felt as if a thousand needles had pierced my epidermis. It wasn't just cold, it was extremely cold. I started the engine, switched the fan on full and hopped out to scrape the windscreen. Scraping ice off the car is a rare occurrence. Tiny shards of ice found their way down the top of my glove, burning my wrist like liquid nitrogen.

'I'm frozen,' I said, as I stepped back indoors.

Melanie was nowhere to be seen. Seconds later she pushed open the back door and stepped inside.

'The washer's still frozen,' she said.

'I'm not surprised, it's absolutely freezing out there.'

'Are you ready for off?'

I looked out of the dining room window. The windscreen was almost clear.

'Yes. Come on. Let's go.'

Melanie grabbed the bag containing the names for the Secret Santa and picked up the sale contract, both of which were lying on the dining table. I stepped outside and opened the gates.

'Chuff me!' said Melanie, as we drove down the lane into the village.

'What?'

'Look at the temperature.'

I glanced at the digital display on the dashboard.

'Crikey! Minus eleven degrees.'

In the time it had taken us to drive the 100 metres into the village, our warm breath had misted up the windscreen. I had to bend lower and squint through a small semicircle of clear glass at the bottom. By the time we reached the main road, the fan had cleared it again.

When we arrived in Vilatán, Manolo was standing in the meadow staring at the expansion tank on top of the borehole. Since returning from his summer break he'd started working Saturday mornings. The advantage of a fixed price contract was the quicker he finished the more he'd earn.

'*Buenos días*,' I said as we stepped from the car.

'Not really,' he replied.

The pipe at the top of the borehole had frozen. Manolo had been on site for an hour and a half and still didn't have any water. Without it, he couldn't mix cement and without cement, he might as well have stayed at home.

'Leave it with me,' I said, before hopping back in the car.

Twenty minutes later I was back. I'd nipped to the builder's merchant in Escairón for some rockwool insulation. When Moncho found out how little I wanted, he gave me a piece. I wrapped it around the pipe and the expansion tank. Manolo secured it with a length of twine. At least now there was a chance it might thaw out.

We left Manolo and walked around to Carmen's house. I knocked on the door and she shouted down from the upstairs kitchen.

'Come in, it's open.'

We climbed the steps to the first-floor accommodation. Carmen was waiting by the kitchen door.

'Quickly, come in,' she said, gesturing us to enter.

Inside felt toasty warm. The wood burning stove was radiating heat.

'Sit down,' she said. 'Would you like a coffee?'

At times like this I wish Spanish coffee making wasn't such a protracted ritual. Whatever happened to tipping a teaspoon of instant coffee into a mug and filling it with boiling water.

'Thank you, but no. We can't stop, we have to visit some friends.'

Melanie and I huddled together on a long bench at the back of the stove. For the first time since getting out of bed, my knees began to warm up.

'This is the contract,' I said, sliding two copies across the kitchen table. 'They're both the same, one for you and a copy for us.'

She flicked through it.

'We've already signed them. They just need your signature,' I said, pointing at the spot.

Melanie pulled ten fifty-euro notes out of her bag and handed them to me.

'And this is for you,' I said, handing her the cash.

Carmen counted it and signed the forms.

With the deal done, we shook hands and said goodbye.

'Who first?' asked Melanie, as we sped away.

'I thought we could call at Penelope's and then Peter and Veronica's. If there's time we'll go to Roy and Maria's on the way back.'

'What about Bill and Di?'

'They're in England at the moment. We'll have to see them later.'

'Oh yes, I'd forgotten. Penelope's it is then.'

When we left Vilatán, the temperature read three degrees but if felt much warmer. Bright sunshine angled in through the windscreen and the only clouds were wispy vapour trails left by high flying airliners. We couldn't have wished for a better autumn day. Penelope dipped her hand in the cotton bag and pulled out a name.

'Don't look at it until we've gone,' said Melanie, 'and don't tell a soul who you've got.'

Next stop, Peter and Veronica, who lived nearby. They'd bought a restoration project and were in the early stages of fixing it up. Unlike us, they were doing all the work themselves and living on site. They'd tolerated the inconvenience during the summer months but the onset of winter brought new challenges.

Peter had built a small shed in the garden, approximately eight foot wide by twelve foot long, and divided it in two. They were using the largest section to store their belongings and were sleeping on an elevated mezzanine, inches from the roof. Rudimentary bathroom facilities filled the other part. Their sitting and dining room came courtesy of a two-berth caravan Peter had dragged here from the UK. Cooking facilities were al fresco. As things stood, no one could accuse them of lacking fortitude.

From the roadside, the house looked abandoned. Peter had started the renovation work by building an extension on the back. I parked at the front and we walked around to the side entrance. I could see a light on through a glass-panelled door so knocked. Veronica opened it, carrying a butcher's knife and covered in blood.

'Hello,' she said chirpily, 'come in.'

We hesitated.

'Don't worry, I haven't killed him,' she added.

Conscious of letting the heat escape, we stepped inside. Nothing could have been further from the truth; the room felt like a freezer. What greeted us was like a scene from a horror movie. In the centre of the room was a large makeshift table with a sheet of plastic covering the top. Scattered on that were numerous body parts in various stages of butchering.

'Hello,' said Peter. 'What brings you out this way?'

We were lost for words.

'I won't shake your hands,' he added, holding out his bloody palms.

'Are we interrupting something?'

I couldn't believe I'd asked such a stupid question.

'We're butchering the pig our neighbour reared for us.'

Peter explained that earlier in the year, one of their neighbours had asked if they wanted him to rear a pig for them. Apparently he does it for a number of people. They'd said yes and after months of waiting collected the carcass the previous evening.

'He asked us if we wanted the head, trotters and numerous internal organs but we just chose the best bits,' explained Veronica.

Neither of them had any butchering skills. Instead they were following instructions from a book Peter had found in a secondhand bookshop in Lancashire. As fascinating as it looked, I couldn't help thinking their time would be better spent putting a permanent roof over their heads.

'We've brought the lots for the Secret Santa,' I said.

In the midst of their homemade abattoir, drawing lots seemed quite surreal.

'Don't lose them,' cautioned Melanie.

We chatted for a while about the hotel and Chinese restaurant.

'Anyway, we'll let you get on,' I said.

'Would you like some ribs?' asked Veronica.

'We couldn't,' replied Melanie.

'If you don't take them we'll probably throw them away,' she replied.

'In that case, we'd be delighted to.'

Veronica wrapped them in cling film.

'Thank you.'

Back in the car we headed towards Roy and Maria's, a fifteen-minute drive away.

'Come in,' said Roy. 'Drink?'

Their house felt lovely and warm.

'That would be nice,' replied Melanie.

'Coffee, tea, or can I tempt you with a glass of wine?' he asked.

Roy and Maria had recently renovated a house on the banks of the river Sil with the intention of letting it to tourists. A small vineyard came with the house and, like us, they'd started making their own wine.

'A glass of red would be lovely,' said Melanie.

I glanced at my watch.

'It's a bit early for me, Roy,' I said, before winking at him.

Maria brought four glasses and Roy fetched a jug of wine from the *bodega*.

'We've brought the names for the Secret Santa,' I said on his return.

They each drew a lot and we whiled away an hour or so, sipping wine and chewing the cud.

'We must get off,' said Melanie, having finished her drink. 'Jazz will think we've deserted her.'

'Roy, get some wine for them before they go,' said Maria.

Minutes later, Roy returned carrying a ten-litre box.

'Are you sure?' I asked.

'We don't drink much,' said Roy.

We thanked them for their generosity and headed home.

We'd set out on an errand of goodwill and arrived home with tomorrow night's dinner and enough red wine to last a fortnight. What a wonderful life indeed.

13

Are You Pedro?

The start of the week brought a change in the weather. Thick frost and icy temperatures gave way to milder, wetter conditions. As a result, rain stopped play and work was called off.

'At least the pipes in the laundry room have defrosted,' I said.

The pipes had remained frozen all weekend.

'A fat lot of good that is. How am I supposed to get it dry?'

She had a point. We have a dryer but limit its use to towels and socks, both of which come out soft and fluffy.

Dong, dong, dong … Dong … Dong … Dong … Dong, dong, dong … Dong … Dong … Dong …

The distinctive chimes of the death knell rang out across the village. During the night, someone had passed from this world to the next.

'Oh no,' said Melanie.

'What?'

'I think they might be for Mr Meli.'

Meli is our nearest neighbour and a good friend. Her husband, who we affectionately called Mr Meli, had been very poorly for a long time. He had suffered a number of severe strokes which impaired his mobility and left him unable to speak. Since then, Meli had dedicated her life to taking care of him.

Melanie walked to the end of the driveway and looked down the lane.

'I'm sure they're for him,' she said on her return. 'All her *persianas* (window blinds) are closed and there are cars parked outside.'

His suffering was over; Meli's had only just begun.

The rain continued throughout the week, intermittent showers of varying severity. On Thursday morning Manolo rang.

'There's a problem with the walls,' he said. 'They're not square. Can you come and take a look?'

'We'll be right there,' I replied.

I wasn't quite sure what he was referring to but he seemed anxious for us to see. At the moment the upstairs was a blank canvas of 118m². Manolo's next job was to build the internal walls.

By the time we arrived, Manolo had marked out each room on the floor with a line of bricks. We wandered around our virtual house, imagining how it would look.

'This is perfect,' I said.

Manolo's main concern was the unevenness of the original walls in areas that would be tiled. Rather than trying to level the existing walls, his suggestion was to build new ones with very thin bricks.

'Whatever you think is best,' I said.

Having allayed his fears, we turned to leave.

'*Buenos dias*.' José Metal was standing in the doorway. 'I've come to measure up for the new windows.'

What happened to giving us a call, I thought to myself.

We said goodbye and left Manolo and José to get on with their work.

'Hang on a minute,' I said, as we walked back to the car, 'before we leave I want to see if Moncho has delivered the paving.'

Melanie waited while I checked.

'There's nothing,' I said on my return. 'Let's call to see him while we're out this way.'

Moncho knew exactly why we'd called.

'I've been really busy this week but I'll definitely deliver the paving slabs first thing in the morning,' he promised.

'And don't forget the drainage channels.'

Moncho nodded.

'Have Marmoles Grande delivered the other paving?' I asked.

'Not yet.'

That was something else I needed to chase up.

A break in the weather gave Roy and me the opportunity to get back to work. While he readied the cement mixer I made sure Moncho had kept his word.

'Well?' asked Roy.

'The paving slabs are here but he's forgotten the drainage channels.'

'We're going to need them,' said Roy.

The channels would divert rainwater from the back of the house into the track outside. Without them, the porch would flood every time it rained.

'Bugger!'

'What's matter?'

'I've forgotten my phone.'

'Use mine,' said Roy.

I rang Melanie and asked her to call Moncho. Twenty minutes later she rang back.

'It's taken me ages to get hold of him,' she said.

'And?'

'He's forgotten them.'

'I know that but how soon can he come back?'

'He can't, not today.'

Delays are only important when you're paying others to stand around idle.

'He said you can pick them up if you want,' she added.

Moncho's yard was nothing more than a badly secured field at the back of a warehouse. Building materials were scattered haphazardly all over the place. It might take me ages to find them, but what choice did I have?

'OK, I'll do that.'

When I arrived, the place was deserted save for one elderly man.

'*Buenos días,*' I said.

The old man reciprocated my greeting.

'I'm the Englishman from Vilatán. I've come to collect the drainage channels.'

He looked me up and down as if I'd dropped in from outer space. Perhaps he was a customer and not an employee.

'Are you Pedro?' he asked.

'No, my name's Craig,' I replied.

'Oh, there must be two Englishmen living in Vilatán.'

I can't imagine there's another blond haired, blue eyed Englishman going by the name of Pedro living in the whole of Spain, never mind the tiny village of Vilatán. I didn't have the heart to shatter his delusion so left him with his thoughts and began my search. Before long I found exactly what we needed.

'Can you tell Moncho I've taken these?' I said, as I loaded them into the back of the van.

Roy had been busy in my absence and the results looked great. At three o'clock we headed home, porch paved and drainage sorted. Little by little, this side of the house was starting to take shape.

'You haven't forgotten that Maria and I are in England next week, have you?' asked Roy, when he dropped me off.

'No,' I said, which wasn't exactly true. 'Have a safe trip and enjoy your break.'

That afternoon, Diego called with the quote for the central heating. At first glance the price looked good.

'What do you think?' asked Melanie, after he'd left.

'It looks pretty good,' I replied.

Melanie looked surprised.

'I don't,' she said unequivocally. 'You do know it doesn't include the wiring?'

'I thought he said the sockets were included.'

'No, he said installation was included but we would have to fit the sockets.'

At times like this a second pair of ears is invaluable. Given the complexity of Spanish verbs, it was an easy mistake to make.

'Are you sure?' I asked.

'Positive.'

'In that case it's pants.'

I spent the rest of the afternoon searching the internet for electric radiator suppliers and found the perfect solution.

'Come and look at these,' I said.

Melanie was reading a book her mum had sent through the post. How it got here is anyone's guess. She has a habit of sticking two second class stamps to every package, regardless of weight or size. Amazingly, they always find their way here.

'What is it?'

'I've found identical radiators online for a fraction of the cost.'

My time on the internet would save us a fortune.

That evening we drove into Monforte for our Teatime Taster. On cold autumn evenings we occasionally treat ourselves to a *pinta de* Murphy's and tapas at Mulligans. For those living on the Mediterranean coast, Irish themed bars are commonplace. Here in Monforte, its opening was akin to the second coming.

'What are we going to do for Christmas?' I asked.

The waiter had just brought our order, a pint of Murphy's, a glass of Mencia red wine, and two mouth-watering tapas of Spanish tortilla.

'I hadn't really thought about it.'

'You know it's only four weeks away?'

'You're kidding. What do you think we should do?' she asked.

Christmas in Galicia is a family affair. Most restaurants and bars are closed on Christmas Eve and New Year is not much better. Eating out can cost a small fortune. Had it not been for our upcoming trip to Australia, we would probably have gone away.

'We could go off,' I said, longingly.

'That would be nice, but seriously, what are we going to do?'

'What about a quiet Christmas at home and dinner out on New Year's Eve?'

'Where?'

'I don't know, O Grelo perhaps, or the Parador?'

O Grelo is regarded as one of the best restaurants in Monforte. As for the Parador, the dining room décor is outstanding, the food less so.

'They might be expensive,' she replied.

'There's only one way to find out.'

'OK, I'll have a ring round next week.'

Roy's absence gave me the opportunity to finish pointing the boundary wall at the back of the house. After that, I turned my attention to varnishing the porch timbers and the soffits.

'I rang O Grelo this morning,' said Melanie, on my return.

'How much?' I asked.

'Nothing.'

'Nothing?'

'That's right. They're closed from the 22nd of December until the 3rd of January.'

Imagine my surprise. One of the busiest times in the catering calendar and Monforte's top restaurant was closed.

'What about the Parador?' I asked.

'They're open and they have a menu for both Christmas Eve and New Year.'

Melanie paused. I sensed a but coming.

'But they haven't got any prices yet.'

'And what about the menu?'

'We can call in and pick one up.'

'That's generous of them,' I quipped.

Clang, clang, clang, clang!

Jazz jumped to her feet and sprinted to the French doors.

'It's José Metal,' I said, opening the door.

She darted out and sprinted to the gate, barking furiously and wagging her tail.

'*Hola*,' I called as I walked down the drive.

'I've got your quote,' he said, handing it to me. 'Just let me know if you want to go ahead.'

On that note he climbed back into his 4 x 4 and drove off.

'That was quick,' said Melanie, as I stepped back inside.

The price was more or less what we'd expected. Providing Javier SL weren't a lot cheaper, José was our man.

'That reminds me, Manolo has finished the new walls in the kitchen so we need to ask José Kitchen to come and measure up.'

'I'll phone him after lunch,' said Melanie.

'I've been thinking about the radiators.'

Mind-numbing varnishing leaves ample time to ruminate.

'What about them?'

'Perhaps towel radiators would be better in the bathrooms.'

'That's a great idea. They'll look much nicer and be far more practical.'

'That's what I thought. When you get a minute, can you phone the supplier and ask how much it would cost to swap them over?' I asked.

'No problem.'

Melanie had prepared chicken and vegetable soup for lunch and homemade bread rolls.

'I think we ought to go to Ourense this afternoon and have a look at some tiles.'

The tile warehouse in Ourense offers a much wider selection than local suppliers. We didn't buy anything but the shop displays gave us some great ideas. We headed home bubbling with excitement.

The next morning, José Kitchen turned up as arranged.

'*Hola Crife*,' he said.

I was busy giving the porch timbers a second coat of varnish.

'*Hola*, come in,' I said.

I explained what we had in mind and asked his advice. We were keen to have the sink directly under the window but to do so would require bespoke units running down one wall.

'Will that be expensive?' I asked.

'Not really,' he replied. 'The carcasses will need shortening but the doors and drawer fronts will be a standard size.'

That was good news.

'What colour were you thinking of having?' he asked.

'I'm not sure, do you have anything that looks like wood but isn't?'

'I've got a few different finishes like that. Why don't you come to the shop this afternoon and see which you prefer?' he said.

'OK.'

While José finished measuring up, I continued varnishing. A few minutes later he said goodbye.

'See you later,' he said.

The second coat gave the woodwork a rich satin finish and was definitely worth the effort.

'I rang the Parador again this morning,' said Melanie on my return.

'What did they have to say?'

'Their New Year's Eve menu is 150 euros.'

'You're kidding, seventy-five euros each.'

'No, 150 each.'

'That's ridiculous! We're not paying that.'

'What are we going to do now?' she asked.

I had no idea. Perhaps going away wasn't such a bad idea after all.

That afternoon we called to see José Kitchen. We were amazed how realistic the wood effect laminate looked. Needless to say, the design we favoured was also the most expensive.

There's nothing quite like the pitter-patter of raindrops on terracotta roof tiles to discourage one from leaving the warm embrace of a twenty-tog duvet.

'Look what we've got,' said Melanie, as she pushed open the bedroom door.

Jazz jumped onto the bed and sat to attention, waiting for her morning treats.

'What?'

'If I'm not mistaken this is a Christmas card from Ray and Lesley,' she replied.

When Melanie was growing up, Ray and Lesley were her next-door neighbours. Since she left home, they've kept in touch by exchanging Christmas cards.

'What's the date today?' I asked.

'The first.'

'They get earlier every year,' I joked. 'Have you written any cards?'

'Not yet.'

Melanie ripped open the envelope; her prediction proved correct.

Later that morning we visited Bill and Di. They were the only ones yet to draw their Secret Santa names. On our return, we drew the remaining lots.

'Go on then,' I said, offering Melanie the bag.

'You first.'

'Ladies before gents.'

Melanie drew a name from the bag and I tipped the last one out onto the palm of my hand. Who would it be? Carefully, I unfolded the paper: Penelope. All I had to do now was think of something to buy, without exceeding the five-euro budget.

'Who've you got?' I asked.

'I'm not telling you. Why, who've you got?'

'Mind your own business.'

Sunday's weather mirrored Saturday's, grey, wet, and miserable. The cost of New Year's dinner was playing on my mind. Finding a local venue at an affordable price looked decidedly unlikely. The thought of spending the festive period holed up at home with nothing but Scrabble and backgammon to entertain ourselves wasn't particularly appealing. Last year we spent Christmas and New Year on the Costa del Sol and really enjoyed it. If it wasn't for our upcoming trip to Australia, I'm sure we would have done the same this year.

That said, what did a trip to Australia have to do with Christmas? Why couldn't we do both?

In the absence of a valid reason, I emailed Maria at Just Mijas to enquire about availability. Within the hour she'd replied. The apartment we'd stayed in last year was available and she was happy to let us have it for the same price as last year.

Time to find out what Melanie thought.

'I've been thinking about Christmas,' I announced, as I entered the lounge.

'Really.'

Melanie knew there was more to my statement than an idle thought.

'Yes.'

'And what have you been thinking?'

'Perhaps we should go away.'

'I thought we'd decided not to.'

'We had, but why?'

Melanie paused before answering.

'Because we're going to Australia at the beginning of February.'

'And what difference does that make?'

Like me, Melanie was struggling to come up with a reason.

'It's a bit late to be booking now, isn't it?' she asked.

'It's funny you should say that.'

'Why?'

'I emailed Maria at Just Mijas to see if she had any availability.'

'You did, did you?'

'Yes.'

'And what did Maria say?'

'The place we stayed in last year is available.'

'That sounds alright. How much will it cost?'

I could tell she was warming to the idea but sidestepped the question.

'There's one more thing.'

'What?'

'If we do decide to go, we can call at the Chinese embassy in Madrid on our way south and apply for our visas.'

We needed a tourist visa for our stay in Shanghai and unlike Australia, the Chinese authorities insist applicants apply in person at a Chinese embassy. The only one in Spain is in Madrid.

'But what about collecting it?'

'I've checked on the embassy website and they quote a turnaround time of ten days. If everything goes to plan we can pick it up on the way back.'

'And if not?'

'We'll cross that bridge when we come to it.'

'OK, so tell me, how much will all this cost?'

I couldn't put it off any longer.

'Four hundred and eighty euros.'

'For the fortnight?'

'Yep. What do you think?'

'I think we ought to book it before Maria changes her mind.'

14

Bounce

Buying Christmas gifts is difficult enough at the best of times; with a budget of five euros it becomes mission impossible. My Secret Santa recipient was Penelope, an independent woman of retirement age who arrived in the area a couple of years after us.

As a young woman she married an army officer. When he resigned his commission, they went into business producing military insignia. In her fifties a divorce encouraged her to travel the world. On her return she went into business, growing hemp, but hard work and enthusiasm failed to prevent its premature demise. Pending retirement prompted her move to Spain.

Penelope is an interesting and articulate woman with a passion for the environment and a unique spirituality. For someone who lives on her own, she has a wide circle of friends, a testament to her kind and generous nature.

If anyone deserved a little personal pampering it was her but an overnight stay at a luxury spa was out of the question. Five euros wouldn't buy a drink from the minibar.

Think Craig, think.

My first challenge was to identify possible retailers. Local markets sprang to mind. On second thoughts, Bridget Jones knickers and agricultural tools didn't quite resonate with the theme of self-indulgence. That left Chinese bazaars and the local supermarket.

Think Craig, think.

What about soothing melodies, relaxing aromas, fine wine and Belgian chocolates? Now we were getting somewhere.

Think Craig, think.

Soothing melodies?

I know, pirated panpipes. I could download some haunting tunes off the internet and create a CD. Best of all, it wouldn't cost a bean.

Relaxing aromas?

A couple of scented candles from the Chinese bazaar would set the mood.

Fine wine?

A tasty bottle of ninety-nine-cent Rioja from the supermarket and a wine glass from the Chinese bazaar.

Finally, Belgian chocolates?

Overpriced and overrated. A ninety-nine-cent box of truffles would fit the bill.

Armed with my shopping list, I drove into town. It's amazing what you can achieve with some big ideas and a small budget.

Manolo was making swift progress building the internal walls. We would soon need an electrician.

'What are we going to do about an electrician?' I asked one evening.

Our trade contacts in this area were few and far between.

'What about Mr Bean?' suggested Melanie.

Mr Bean, aka José Manuel, had rewired *El Sueño*. The architect christened him Mr Bean due to his uncanny resemblance to Rowan Atkinson. He had the skills we needed but would he want the work? The last time we'd asked him to quote for a job, we hadn't heard back from him.

'It can't do any harm to ask,' I replied.

Melanie made the call.

'What did he say?'

'He didn't sound interested. He said he was busy at the moment and didn't know when he'd have time to take a look.'

That didn't sound promising.

'Perhaps Ramon knows someone,' suggested Melanie.

Ramon is a plumber but it was likely he would have other trade contacts.

'It's worth a try.'

Ramon recommended a chap called Felix. When we rang him, he agreed to meet us at the house on Tuesday evening at 8:00 pm.

We both took an instant liking to Felix. He had a smile that lit up the room but he did have one confession to make.

'We can only work Saturday afternoons and the occasional night during the week,' he said.

Felix worked with two others and all three had full-time jobs. It wasn't ideal but it couldn't harm to get a price.

'Can you prepare a quote for us?' I asked.

Felix smiled.

'I'll need to come back when it's light,' he replied.

We agreed to meet again the coming Saturday.

On the morning of The Office Party a thick frost blanketed the countryside. At 10:30 am the thermometer still hadn't risen above -2°C. Arranging transport for nine proved challenging. In the end we agreed to take Peter and

Veronica, Penelope would go with Bill and Di, and Roy and Maria would travel in their own car. All that was about to change.

Ring, ring … Ring, ring.

'I'll get it,' called Melanie.

Seconds later she came back into the bedroom.

'That was Di. She's not coming.'

'Why?'

'She picked up a bug during their trip to England and doesn't want to pass it on.'

This wasn't the start we were hoping for.

'Bill's going to take Pen and Peter and Veronica,' she added.

'In that case, we'll take Roy and Maria.'

When we arrived at the hotel, Bill and party were already there.

'It's very nice,' commented Veronica.

We started the celebrations with a tour of the old town. For some, this was their first visit to Chaves.

'Right then, who's up for a drink?' I asked.

Everyone was keen. By the time we returned to the hotel to get ready for our evening of Eastern promise, we were all in the Christmas spirit.

'We'll meet back here in an hour,' I said.

'What about the Secret Santa?' asked Maria.

'Let's do it before we go out,' I suggested.

An hour later we gathered in the hotel lounge. Bill popped the cork on a bottle of bubbly.

'Cheers,' he said.

'Merry Christmas everyone,' I added.

One by one the gifts were handed out. Penelope seemed delighted with her selection and couldn't believe so many things could be bought with a fiver. I received a head torch; your guess is as good as mine.

Throughout the day, the temperature hadn't risen above 10°C. Everyone wrapped up warm for the short stroll to the restaurant. The air felt crisp and cold. The narrow streets had a real Dickensian feel. Seasonal window displays reflected images of passers-by.

Since our last visit, the proprietors of the Jing Huà had dressed the restaurant for a Western Christmas. We were guided to a large round table set for nine. I explained we were only eight.

'No problem, no problem,' said the owner, as she cleared away a place setting.

Dinner was a great success. We started with spring rolls and ended with flambéed ice cream. In between we shared seven different dishes as well as fried rice and Chinese bread. Portuguese wine kept the mood lively and copious amounts of port brought our dining experience to a fitting conclusion. At twenty-two euros per head, everyone left happy.

'For you,' said the owner, handing me a bottle of Chinese rice wine. '*Feliz Natal* (Merry Christmas).'

The stroll back to the hotel was punctuated with visits to some of the town's liveliest bars, a nightcap here and one for the road there.

Jazz had spent the evening snuggled up in the hotel room. By the time we returned from taking her out, the clock had ticked around to 3:00 am. The Office Party had been a great success. Twelve hours from start to finish but everyone had stayed the course.

Breakfast revealed the extent of the walking wounded. By the time I showed my face everyone except Penelope was already in the dining room. Roy, Maria and Bill were on top form and couldn't resist a few wisecracks at my expense. I managed two cups of strong coffee but couldn't face the food. My fellow revellers tucked into a selection of cold meats, cheeses, bread, cakes, cereals, and fruit juice.

The drive home passed without incident.

'I'm going to have a lay down,' said Melanie.

By mid-afternoon my stomach started grumbling. Melanie was fast asleep so I warmed a tin of baked beans and toasted two slices of bread. No sooner had I sat at the table than Melanie showed her face.

'Do you want some?' I asked.

Melanie looked worse now than she had first thing that morning.

'No thanks,' she replied, slumping into the chair.

Ring, ring ... Ring, ring!

Partying during the week had thrown my body clock out of kilter. Brain said Sunday, calendar read Thursday.

'Hello.'

'*Hola*, this is José, I've done the drawings for the kitchen. Can you come and take a look?' he asked.

'We'll call in tomorrow,' I replied.

Two minutes after replacing the receiver, it rang again. This time it was Javier SL with a quote for the new windows.

'How much is it?' asked Melanie.

'More than José Metal.'

'That's good,' she replied.

Not really, but I knew what she meant. We could now ask José to start, confident we'd get a good job at the right price.

That evening we managed to keep our eyes open until 10:30 pm before retiring for some much-needed sleep.

A lazy start finalised our recuperation.

'I thought we could go into town this morning and sort out a few things,' I said over breakfast.

'What things?'

'We need to find out if Emilio has delivered the paving; then there's the kitchen designs to approve and I'd like to get my hair cut.'

Melanie looked at me quizzically.

'You haven't forgotten about the photos for the visa, have you?' I added.

With less than a week until our trip to the Costa del Sol, time was running out.

For a giant of a man, Emilio looked decidedly sheepish when we entered the office.

'Today,' he said, 'I'll definitely deliver it today.'

A ver (We'll see).

Our next stop was far more interesting. José Kitchen had worked his design magic and transformed our ideas into a three-dimensional image. A tweak here and there and his design was good to go.

'I'll email you a copy of the amendments and the final quote. If you're happy with everything let me know and I'll order the doors and drawer fronts,' he said.

Next stop, Salon 2000. Wash, cut, and blow dry for me at the remarkably low price of seven euros.

Looking spick and span we wandered down the street to the photographic studio.

'Let's have a look,' I said to Melanie.

'They're awful.'

Be it passport, driving licence, or in this case travel visa, official photos always are.

Reluctantly, Melanie handed them over.

'If you think they're bad, look at these.'

'They're not that bad.'

Beauty is in the eye of the beholder.

Over the weekend the temperature continued to fall and the pipes in the laundry room froze again. On Sunday morning the phone rang.

'Is that Mr Briggs?' asked the caller.

'It is.'

'Good morning Mr Briggs, Linda here from Elite-European.'

Were we finally going to get our stuff delivered?

'Good morning Linda, how are you?'

'I'm fine but we have a problem.'

Not more delays?

'The cheque you sent for the deposit payment. It's been returned unpaid.'

I didn't know what to say. There must be a mistake.

'Mr Briggs, are you still there?'

'Yes, I'm sorry, I don't understand.'

'Are you sure there are enough funds in the account?' she asked.

'I'm certain. I'll have to speak with the bank on Monday and find out what's happened.'

'If you could let me know, I'd be grateful,' she replied.

'I'll ring you as soon as I've sorted it out.'

'You realise I can't send anything until we have the payment,' she added.

A polite if somewhat uncompromising statement.

'I completely understand and please accept my apology. I can't imagine what's gone wrong.'

I'd never felt so embarrassed. Someone was going to pay for this.

'What's the matter?' asked Melanie.

'The cheque I sent to Elite-European has bounced.'

'You're joking.'

'I wish I was.'

I spent the rest of the morning checking my balance and searching through records to find out what might have gone wrong. Nowadays, I rarely write cheques. That led me to a possible answer. Months ago, I had misplaced my cheque book and ordered a replacement. Not long after that I found it again. The cheque I sent to Elite-European was from that book. Perhaps when the bank issued the new book, they cancelled the other. If that was the case, they could have let me know.

Later that day Felix rang.

'I'm on my way to the house,' he said.

'We'll be there in twenty minutes.'

We jumped into the car and sped up to Vilatán. Within minutes of our arrival, Felix drove into the driveway.

It had been chilly all day and the house felt like a cold store. We showed him where we wanted the sockets, switches, and light fittings. He noted everything down.

'I'll let you know when I've prepared the quote and we'll take it from there,' he said.

Before leaving I checked if Moncho had delivered.

'We still don't have any paving,' I said to Melanie.

'I'll give Moncho a ring on Monday,' she replied.

Monday morning provided no respite from the freezing temperatures.

'The washing machine is still frozen,' said Melanie.

'I can put the gas fire in there if you want,' I suggested.

'If it's still frozen tomorrow, we're going to have to do something. There's loads of washing to do before we go away.'

A fortnight in the sun seemed more appealing than ever.

'I almost forgot, the pool is frozen as well,' she added.

I went outside to take look. About a third of the pool was covered with a thin layer of ice. Using a garden fork, I smashed it into pieces. The last thing we needed was a skating rink in the back garden.

Phoning the bank was my next job. My suspicions proved correct. I spoke to Linda and explained. She was very understanding but suggested a bank transfer might be more appropriate. As a sign of goodwill, I agreed to pay the full amount prior to delivery.

Melanie rang Moncho about the granite.

'I can't deliver what I haven't got,' he said.

Moncho sounded almost as frustrated as we were. Melanie was straight on the phone to Emilio.

'I'll definitely deliver it later today,' he said.

Without camping outside his office, there was very little we could do but keep pestering him.

As promised, José Kitchen emailed the revised plan along with the final quote.

'What do you think?' I asked Melanie.

'It looks OK.'

'What about the white goods?'

'What about them?'

'We can probably save money if we buy them ourselves.'

Melanie agreed. I rang José to asked if he'd mind if we bought them.

'No problem,' he replied.

His profit was in building and fitting the kitchen. Supplying the white goods was often more hassle than it was worth.

That afternoon we drove into Ourense to price up appliances. The place is much bigger than Monforte and has a wider choice of retailers. The savings were quite considerable.

'What do you think?' I asked.

We'd stumbled across an end of line oven, hob and extractor hood from a top manufacturer that were heavily discounted. We knew from experience that if we dithered, we could lose out.

'I think we ought to get them,' said Melanie.

'Can you deliver them in the new year?' I asked the sales assistant.

'Certainly sir.'

The dishwasher and fridge-freezer could wait until the January sales.

From Ourense we drove the 115 kilometres to Santiago de Compostela, end point of the Camino de Santiago and home to Leroy Merlin, one of the largest DIY superstores in Galicia. Before making a final decision on the tiles, we wanted to see what they had to offer. We left, confident that Santiago wasn't the tile Mecca others had suggested, but we didn't leave empty-handed.

While browsing we found a very nice antique style vanity unit complete with sink and brass effect mixer tap. It was exactly what we'd been looking for. It came in two different sizes. Unfortunately, the larger one was out of stock.

'These will look lovely in the shower rooms,' said Melanie.

I had to agree.

'It's a pity the larger one is out of stock.'

'Let's get the small one anyway and come back later for the other.'

'OK.'

All in all, we'd had a very productive day.

The longest cold snap since we'd moved to Spain continued. Defrosting the laundry room was now a priority. We had three days to wash, dry, and iron anything we wanted to take to the Costa del Sol.

'I'm going to put the gas fire on in the laundry room and see if that makes any difference,' I said.

By lunchtime the pipes were still frozen. Coincidentally, I received an email from the radiator supplier detailing the final price for the radiators.

'We might as well order these for delivery in the new year,' I suggested.

'OK.'

Melanie had been checking the laundry room at regular intervals throughout the day. By 3:00 pm water began to flow.

'At least we'll have some clean clothes for the holiday,' said Melanie. 'Mind you, they might not be dry.'

She was teasing.

Isn't it always the case? We'd gone to the effort and expense to defrost the pipes only for the temperature to jump ten degrees the following morning.

Melanie rang Emilio to check on the paving.

'The driver's left,' he said.

What happened to delivering it yesterday afternoon?

After lunch I drove to Vilatán to make sure he'd kept his word. Melanie stayed at home to make a start on the ironing. After several weeks of badgering, the paving had been delivered. As soon as we got back from our break, Roy and I could make a start.

One of these days we'll pack exactly what we need for a holiday. Until then, we'll take far too much. By the time I'd finished coercing everything into the back of the car, there was just enough space for Jazz. That said, she much prefers being squashed in than sliding around.

'Is that everything?' I asked.

'There's just toothbrushes, hairbrushes and the picnic.'

'In that case, we're ready for off.'

15

Visa Visit

I felt like I'd been awake for hours when the alarm clock shattered the silence. It's always the case the night before a holiday. Instinctively I checked the time: 6:00 am. I leant over and switched on the bedside lamp. Within the hour we were ready for off.

It was pitch black when we left Canabal. An hour later the heavens began to lighten. On quiet roads we made swift progress. By 11:00 am, we'd reached the outskirts of Madrid.

'Right then, you'd better have a look at the directions,' I said.

A few days earlier, I'd asked Google Maps for directions to the Chinese embassy.

'Where are we?' asked Melanie. She was staring at the map.

I glanced across.

'I think you'll find it's upside down.'

'Tsk.'

It was clearly my fault she didn't know her north from her south.

'Oh, I don't know where we are.'

When it comes to map reading, Melanie's patience is limited only by her inaptitude. I took another peek.

'About there,' I said, pointing at the spot.

'Just watch where you're going.'

If I didn't have to read the map I would. A comment better thought than said.

'We've just passed junction thirteen on the A-6 and we need to join the M-40 at junction eleven,' I said.

As soon as Melanie found where we were, she confidently guided me to the embassy. She's hopeless at map reading but excellent at narrating driving instructions.

'It's down here, number forty,' she said.

We'd reached our destination without a glitch.

'There,' she said, pointing at a fairly nondescript office block, 'number forty.'

I'd expected to find an old palace or stately home with tall gates, barbed wire and a multitude of CCTV cameras. This looked more like the offices of a city stockbroker than a foreign embassy.

Kerbside parking was busy but I managed to find a space within easy walking distance. We entered the building without so much as a by-your-leave. Even the council offices in Lugo have metal detectors. The only visible sign of security was a bored-looking *vigilante* (security guard) leant against the wall.

'Over there,' said Melanie, pointing at the building directory fixed to the wall.

Passport and visa applications, third floor. We took the lift to a brightly lit and busy office. The queue for visa applications was on our left.

I'd downloaded the English version of the application form from the consulate website and we'd completed them prior to travelling. All we needed to do was hand them in along with our passports and mug shots.

Chinese conversation appears boisterous and argumentative at the best of times; today was no different. Six staff members were handling applications. They were sitting on one side of a long counter. Opposite them were six applicants all of whom seemed to be having problems. Between them was a glass screen.

Completing the online application had been fairly straightforward which begged the question, why were these six struggling? The wait fostered doubt. I opened the file and pulled out the forms.

'What's matter?' asked Melanie.

'I just want to check we've filled them in correctly.'

Carefully, I read each one.

'Well?' asked Melanie.

'As far as I can tell, everything looks OK.'

The commotion at the counter hadn't let up. The queue was going nowhere.

'You don't think we should have printed off the Spanish forms, do you?' I asked.

Melanie's facial expression changed from frustration to panic.

'I don't know.'

'After all, this is the Chinese embassy in Spain.'

'Perhaps we ought to fill them out in Spanish as well, just in case,' she replied.

Melanie kept our place in the queue while I grabbed two forms from a stationery rack near the doorway. By the time we'd filled them in, we were next up. As soon as a position became available we stepped up to the counter.

'*Buenos días,*' I said, sliding the English version of the forms under the glass along with the photos and passports.

After the briefest examination the clerk handed me a receipt and that was that.

'Your visa will be ready to collect in ten days,' he said.

'I don't believe it, we waited all that time and he hardly looked at them.' I said as we left.

'I hope everything is alright,' said Melanie.

So did I but it was too late now. One way or another, we'd find out on our return.

The rest of the journey went smoothly. We'd covered 1,100 kilometres in twelve hours including a two-hour interlude in Madrid. As we approached Malaga, droplets of rain bounced off the windscreen. We consoled ourselves in the knowledge that it's not called the Costa del Sol (Coast of Sun) for nothing.

After unpacking the car, we went out for dinner. We drove round and round for what seemed like hours in search of our favourite Indian restaurant before realising it had closed down.

'Chinese?' suggested Melanie.

'Why not?'

The village of Puebla Aida had lost none of its charm, a beautiful complex of houses and apartments built in the style of an Andalucian hilltop village. The apartment was exactly how we remembered it. From our lofty position we looked out across rooftops to the two championship golf courses of Mijas Golf. In the distance, the holiday resort of Fuengirola and beyond that, the turquoise tones of the Mediterranean Sea.

Despite changeable weather, we quickly settled in to our opulent surroundings. Most mornings we enjoyed breakfast on the terrace. Sausage butties and strong coffee – what better way to start the day?

Some say that a change is as good as a rest but when it comes to Christmas lunch, I'm not sure. For the past ten years we've abandoned a traditional turkey dinner in favour of a barbecue; this year would be different. Friends had invited us to dine with them and while Christmas dinner with all the trimmings made a pleasant change, it didn't quite compare to sitting in the sunshine enjoying flame grilled treats.

Between Christmas and New Year, Melanie caught a cold but nothing was going to stop us from visiting our favourite places and adding new ones.

We particularly liked Ronda, a city divided in two by the El Tajo gorge. On one side sits the 15th century new town and on the other the Moorish old town. Spanning the 300-foot-deep gorge is an impressive stone-built bridge. Built between 1751 and 1793, Puente Nuevo (New Bridge) seems a wholly inappropriate name. If it wasn't for traffic noise, wandering through the narrow city streets with their whitewashed buildings would be like travelling back in time.

It took until New Year's Eve for Melanie to share her cold. The following morning, her gift had mutated into full blown man-flu. If only women could appreciate how debilitating this man-only condition can be, I'm sure they'd be more sympathetic.

I spent the final few days of the holiday cooped up in the apartment flitting between bed and sofa. The last thing I needed was a 6:00 am alarm call and a 1,100-kilometre drive, to say nothing of the detour through Madrid to collect our visas.

'Look at the time,' said Melanie, as we sped toward Madrid.

I'd been keeping an eye on the clock for the past hour and a half. The embassy closed for lunch at one o'clock. Time was running out. If we didn't get there before one, we'd have three hours to kill in Madrid and all I wanted to do was curl up and go to sleep.

'Will we make it in time?' she added.

'I hope so.'

The driving instructions for the return trip were very different to those coming. Melanie followed them to the letter and we arrived outside the embassy with eight minutes to spare.

'Jump out and get inside before someone locks the door,' I said.

Unlike a fortnight ago, every parking space was occupied. Melanie hopped out.

One o'clock came and went and still I waited. By twenty past I was becoming a little concerned. Surely she hadn't got herself locked in.

Suddenly the car door opened and Melanie jumped in.

'Thank heavens for that! I thought they'd kidnapped you.'

'I only just made it. I'd hardly walked through the door when the security guard locked it.'

'Have you got them?'

'Yep.'

Melanie opened her passport and showed me the official visa stamp. Our trip of a lifetime could now go ahead.

As festive breaks go, this wasn't the best we'd ever had. Nevertheless, warm temperatures and patches of winter sun seldom go amiss.

The journey home had taken its toll. A damp and miserable morning did little to lift our spirits. Fatigue and flu conspired to shackle me to the bed but there were urgent matters to attend to and very little time. In less than a month the first leg of our voyage to the far side of the world would begin. Between now and then we had to make sure everything was in place to allow work to continue uninterrupted during our absence.

The clock had ticked around to 11:15 am when we eventually dragged ourselves out of bed.

'Let's find out what's been happening since we've been away,' I suggested.

Melanie's lack of enthusiasm mirrored my mood. The worst of her symptoms had passed but mine remained unchanged.

'OK,' she said halfheartedly.

When we arrived at the house, Manolo was busy fitting the new ceilings. We'd chosen tongue and groove pine floorboards as they were much thicker than typical ceiling cladding. Manolo had treated them to protect against woodworm. Once he'd finished, I would stain them a traditional chestnut colour.

'*Feliz año nuevo* (Happy New Year),' I announced as we entered.

Manolo reciprocated.

We had hoped to see Ramon the plumber but no such luck. He was tasked with bringing the water supply from the borehole into the house, installing all the plumbing, and fitting the furniture in the shower rooms. Manolo would then tile them.

'Can you spare a moment to tell us how many tiles we'll need?' I asked.

'No problem.'

Manolo brought a tape measure and calculated the areas.

'Has Ramon been in touch?' I asked.

'He's hoping to start on Thursday.'

Little by little, our dream of providing luxury accommodation for the discerning traveller was becoming a reality.

We hadn't been home a week when a lorry pulled up outside the house.

Clang, clang, clang, clang!

Jazz leapt to her feet and ran to the French doors, barking excitedly.

'Who is it, lass?' I asked, as I went to take a look.

'Who is it?' asked Melanie.

'I've no idea.'

As soon as I opened the door Jazz raced to the gate. On seeing me, the lorry driver went back to his vehicle and opened the side door. He lifted out a long narrow box and walked back to the gate.

'*¿Señor Bricks?*' he asked.

'Yes.'

'I have some radiators for you,' he said, handing me the paperwork. 'Where would you like them?'

'Through here,' I said, leading him into the back bedroom.

Back and forth he walked. After the fifth package he asked me to sign the delivery note.

'Is that all?' I asked.

'Yes.'

'There should be two towel radiators as well.'

'That's all I've got,' he replied.

As soon as he left I rang the supplier. They assured me the towel radiators would arrive in due course.

'They're held in a different depot,' he said.

That evening, we were just about to sit down to dinner when someone rang the bell on the gate.

'Who's that at this time of night?' asked Melanie.

I flicked on the outside lights and unlocked the front door. Felix was striding towards me.

'*Hola*,' he said, with a broad smile.

'*Hola*,' I replied, 'come in.'

'I've brought the quote,' he said, handing me a blue cardboard folder.

Inside were two sheets of A4 listing every item including the labour cost. The important figure was at the bottom of page two. We'd been expecting something in the region of 6,000 euros. This was less than half that. Without hesitation we accepted.

'How soon can you start?' I asked.

We pencilled in the 19th of the month.

The day after the radiators arrived another lorry pulled up outside. This time they'd brought the stove, hob, and extractor hood.

'Down there will be fine,' I said to the driver, pointing at a space next to the radiators.

The day after that, the towel radiators turned up.

'Just there will do,' I said.

The back bedroom was filling up nicely.

Our priority shifted to ordering the tiles. Without them, the interior renovations would grind to a halt.

'You know what we've forgotten?' I said, as we readied to head off to Ourense.

'What?'

'The kitchen tiles.'

We'd decided to have the same floor tiles throughout and seen exactly what we wanted in Monforte. Manolo had given us the meterage for the shower rooms, but what we didn't have was the figure for the kitchen.

'We'll have to speak to José Kitchen,' I added.

As usual, something that should have taken two minutes ended up taking all morning. Our trip to Ourense would have to wait until the afternoon.

The price of tiles varies widely depending on style and design. Skirting and border tiles are particularly expensive. Because the surface areas of the shower rooms and kitchen were relatively small, preference took priority over price.

'This one's lovely,' said Melanie, pointing at a pastel blue shade.

The surface of the tiles was slightly uneven, giving the impression of being handmade.

'They would look lovely in the en suite,' I replied.

'Chuff me! Look at the price of the matching border tile.'

Nine euros, ninety cents each. To put that in perspective, the floor tiles we'd ordered that morning in Monforte were less than five euros per square metre.

'Excuse me,' I said, calling over the shop owner. 'Is this correct?' I asked, pointing at the price ticket.

'That's a good price,' he replied.

'No, it's too much.'

'Too much?'

'What's your best price?'

'One minute.'

The bartering had begun. He walked across to his desk, picked up a calculator and returned. He looked again at the ticket and tapped on his machine.

'I can do them for €7.48,' he said.

A saving of almost €2.50. On thirty-six tiles that was an amount worth saving.

Negotiations continued with each tile we chose. By the time we left, we'd ordered everything we needed and saved more than 300 euros on the marked prices.

On the way back, we called in to BricoKing, Spain's interpretation of a DIY superstore. We weren't looking for anything specific but as we were passing thought we'd call in.

'Look,' said Melanie, pointing at a vanity unit, 'that's the same design as the small one we bought in Santiago.'

'It's more expensive here,' I replied.

'Five euros. The fuel to Santiago and back will cost more than that.'

She was right. Buying it here made better sense.

Over the weekend I rang Roy.

'Can you start work again on Monday?' I asked.

'No problem, as long as the weather holds up.'

If the weather turned against us, I could varnish the new ceilings, but if not, Roy and I would crack on with paving the terrace.

16

Fireplace Overload

Monday morning brought a mixed bag of short-lived showers interspersed with bright sunshine. Roy turned up as usual so we made our way to Vilatán. Once again, Ramon was conspicuous by his absence. If he didn't start work tomorrow, I'd have to chase him up.

During one of the heaviest showers, Roy and I took refuge in the house.

'What do you think?' I asked, raising my eyes to the ceiling.

'It looks great,' he said. 'Are you going to stain it?'

'We've decided to go for chestnut,' I replied.

Roy nodded his approval.

Laying irregular shaped pieces of granite wasn't as difficult as I'd imagined. By the end of the first day, we'd completed the path running along the back of the house and a small section of the terrace. The hard work would begin when we cemented between the gaps.

On Tuesday morning, bad weather stopped play. I gave Roy the day off and made a start on varnishing the ceilings. The metre-thick stone walls ensured working inside the house was colder than working out.

Before leaving for lunch, Manolo asked about the fireplace.

'I'll have to install it before I tile the floor,' he said.

'How soon will you need it?'

'As soon as possible.'

'I'll see what I can do.'

After lunch I struck a deal with Melanie.

'If I give Ramon a call will you ring Amelia?' I asked.

Conversations over the phone are difficult enough in Spanish without attempting them in Portuguese.

'Why do I have to ring Amelia?'

'Because your Portuguese is better than mine.'

'My Portuguese is rubbish.'

True, but it was still better than mine. Reluctantly she agreed.

'We can pick it up tomorrow afternoon,' said Melanie. 'At least I think that's what she said.'

My turn now.

As with the use of please and thank you, Spaniards don't apologise out of politeness. Ramon agreed to meet me at the house the following morning.

The sound of rain ushered in a new day. Within ten minutes of arriving at Vilatán, Ramon pulled into the muddy driveway.

'I can't stop, I've got another job to finish,' he said.

Hardly the greeting I was hoping for.

'Show me where you want the pipes and I'll make a start later in the week,' he added.

Renovating a ruinous property throws up many unexpected issues, and this was one of them.

'Me, you want me to tell you where to put the pipes?'

Ramon helped me out. He proposed that grey water from the showers and sinks would run into a soakaway at the edge of the garden along with rainwater from the gutters. Waste from the soil pipes would go into a new septic tank. The route of the water pipe from the wellhead into the house was the most difficult to decide. That would be dictated by our future plans for the meadow, plans we hadn't yet finalised.

In the main, I took his advice. By the time he left, we'd more or less decided where all the pipes and tubes would go and the position of the electric water heater in the *bodega*. The new septic tank would be buried in front of the house with the soakaway behind that.

As soon as he'd gone, I continue varnishing the ceilings. By the time I left for lunch, I'd finished the first coat in the twin bedroom and varnished half of the shower room.

After lunch I hitched up the trailer and we set off to Portugal. Before collecting the fireplace, we went to Almacenes Europa, a large department store on the outskirts of town. We'd spent months pricing up ceiling lights and decided to buy them here. For some inexplicable reason, light fittings in Spain cost a small fortune. Buying them here would save us over 1,000 euros, a staggering amount for household essentials.

'Have you got enough money to pay for the fireplace?' I asked, as we left Almacenes Europa.

Melanie totted up.

'Just.'

When we arrived at Amelia's there wasn't a soul in sight.

'Are you sure she said this afternoon?' I asked.

'Of course I am.'

'Perhaps you ought to phone her.'

Melanie took out her mobile and made the call.

'Well?' I asked.

'She's coming now.'

No sooner had Melanie put her phone away than the front door of the adjacent property opened. Amelia stepped out, followed by a man I presumed to be her husband.

'I was just having a coffee,' she said.

At least I think that's what she said.

'Jaime will give us a hand to load up.'

The fireplace hadn't moved since the first time we'd seen it. Hardly surprising given its size. One by one, we carried each piece to the trailer, twenty in total. It wasn't until we were halfway through loading that I began to doubt the wisdom of our decision.

'Is it safe?' asked Melanie.

I wasn't the only one having second thoughts.

'Perhaps we should put some of the smaller pieces in the back of the car,' I suggested.

Amelia and Jaime shrugged off our concerns but they didn't have to haul it 160 kilometres to Vilatán.

I opened the tailgate and folded down the back seats.

'Be careful with the lights,' said Melanie.

On reflection, getting them today had not been a good idea.

I moved some of the smaller lumps of granite into the car, sliding them over the back axle to distribute the weight more evenly.

By the time we'd finished, the rear suspension was almost touching the ground and the tyres on the trailer looked like a cartoon animation. Melanie went inside to settle the bill and I took a peek at the trailer's logbook. Load capacity 450kg. I could only hope that was enough.

Out of Melanie's earshot I asked Jaime how much it weighed. He shrugged his shoulders. I wasn't sure if he hadn't understood the question or didn't know the answer. I forced a polite smile and went to ask Amelia.

When I entered the shop, Melanie and Amelia seemed to be at odds.

'What's the matter?' I asked.

'I've given her our last 560 euros and she seems to think we still owe 100.'

'Have you told her about the deposit?'

'I'm trying to.'

'You owe me 100 euros more,' she said, directing her claim at me.

'We paid you a deposit of 100 euros,' said Melanie. 'One minute.'

She opened her handbag and rifled through. By the time she'd found the receipt, half of the bag's contents were strewn over the sales counter.

'Look,' said Melanie, handing her the receipt.

'Ahh.' Amelia smiled and began counting the money again. 'OK, all correct.'

'No, it's not,' said Melanie, 'you owe me ten euros.'

Starting with the 100-euro receipt she recounted.

'Ahh,' she said, 'I owe you ten euros.'

Finally, we'd come to an agreement and I was able to ask my question.

'Amelia, how much does the fireplace weigh?'

She hadn't a clue.

I had a sneaking suspicion we were slightly overweight but kept it to myself. I checked the trailer's anchor point once last time, filed my visual risk assessment under proceed with caution and carefully lowered myself into the driver's seat.

'Ready?' I asked.

'As I'll ever be.'

I pushed the start button on the ignition, engaged first gear and increased the revs. Slowly, I lifted my foot off the clutch. The car crept forward. Early indications were good. At the junction with the main road I looked left and right and pulled out. The first gear change didn't go exactly to plan. The load was so heavy that by the time I'd pushed the clutch down, slipped her into second and put my foot back on the accelerator, the car was at a standstill. Quickly, I stamped on the clutch and dropped back into first gear.

In my eagerness to gain momentum the car started bunny hopping down the road.

'What's happening?' screamed Melanie.

'Whoops, sorry.'

I had two options, lift off or floor it. Given the circumstances, I floored it.

Along the flat roads of the river valley the car coped admirably. The real test was yet to come. Having crossed the border into Spain we joined the A-52 heading towards Ourense. From here the highway climbs steeply into the aptly named Massif mountains. So far, I hadn't used sixth gear and I wasn't about to risk it now. She climbed the foothills without too much grumbling. Confidence was high as we reached the steepest climb. Halfway up our speed began to slow. With lightning precision, I changed from fifth gear to fourth and floored the accelerator. It's surprising how minor blemishes in the tarmac pass unnoticed under normal driving conditions. Dragging this heavy load up the mountainside highlighted every imperfection.

We held our breath, willing our trusty Renault to reach the summit. The speed of deceleration accelerated as we neared the top. My knuckles turned white as I tightened my grip on the steering wheel.

Come on my beauty, you're almost there.

The road began to level out. We breathed a sigh of relief as the incline swung in our favour. We'd made it.

An hour and a half later we pulled gingerly into the meadow at Vilatán. Most of the journey had passed in silence, neither of us wanting to tempt fate.

'There we go, piece of cake,' I said.

'Really!'

One by one we carried the pieces into the house and assembled the granite jigsaw in the middle of the lounge.

'Manolo can figure it out from that,' I said.

By the time we'd finished, daylight had succumbed to darkness and the clock had ticked around to 8:00 pm.

'Pint and a tapa?' I asked.

'That's the best idea you've had all day.'

We suffered no ill effects from manhandling heavy lumps of granite, and I hoped the same would be true for the car. Melanie phoned Otero's first thing to find out when the floor tiles would be delivered.

'They'll be there in two hours,' she said.

'In that case, can you come with us this morning and give me a hand moving them into the house?'

I wanted Roy to continue paving the terrace. Time was running out and I was determined to get it finished before we left for Australia.

'No problem.'

When we arrived at Vilatán, Ramon was there, knocking holes in the bathroom wall. I doubt I'll ever understand why Spanish plumbers and electricians install pipes and conduit after the walls are built rather than during their construction.

Manolo was standing in the lounge, staring at the fireplace.

'*Buenos días*,' I said, 'what do you think?'

'It's beautiful,' he replied.

High praise indeed.

The tiles turned up on time and Melanie and I carried the heavy cartons upstairs. By the time we headed home for lunch, Roy had set the final pieces of granite paving on the terrace. All we had to do now was cement between the gaps. Manolo had made a start on building the fireplace and Ramon had chiselled a series of channels into the wall in the en suite bathroom and drilled holes in the floor for the waste and water pipes. We even had two pipes protruding from the ceiling in the *bodega*.

Over the weekend, Melanie caught up with some household chores and I pruned the trees in the front garden. The project had taken some time to get going but lately we hadn't had a minute to ourselves.

Monday morning continued apace. Our focus turned to the doors. All but one of the internal doors were included in Manolo's quote. We had something special in mind for the other. The door between the kitchen/dining room and lounge marked the mid-point of the house. We felt a half-panelled door topped with nine panes of mirrored glass with a clear bevelled edge would hint at what lay beyond. The front, back, and two *bodega* doors would be crafted from solid chestnut. They'd be expensive but the house deserved them.

Two tenders would guarantee quality and price. Carlos from Ferreira had supplied the doors for *El Sueño* and we'd been very happy with the work and the price. Despite losing several fingers during his apprenticeship, Carlos was a skilled craftsman and well respected in the area. We hoped a neighbour could recommend another. Every day, on our drive through the village, we pass their beautiful *bodega* doors. We were determined to find out who'd made them.

'Carpinteros Licin,' said the neighbour.

'Are they local?' I asked.

His bewildered expression hinted at my ignorance.

'They're in Licin,' he replied.

I was none the wiser.

'And how do we get there?'

Wild arm gestures and a rapid narrative gave us a general idea.

His directions were excellent but in a hamlet of a dozen properties the carpenter proved elusive.

'There's someone,' said Melanie, pointing at an old man tending a small flock of sheep.

I pulled up alongside and lowered the window.

'*Buenos días*, can you tell me where Carpinteros Licin is?' I asked.

'This is Licin,' he replied.

If at first…

'Where is the *carpintero*?'

'José Manuel?' he asked.

I hadn't a clue who he was referring to but agreed anyway.

How many carpenters could there be in Licin?

'That's right,' I replied.

'Down there,' he said, pointing at an unmade track to our left, 'last house.'

I thanked him and headed down the track.

In common with many Galician country tracks, within metres of leaving the village road it narrowed to within a whisker of the width of the car. We proceeded slowly, weaving between ruinous properties. After 200 metres it came to an end. On the right were two houses. The nearest was old but in reasonable condition. Further back was another in the early stages of restoration. Directly in front was what Spaniards call a *taller* or workshop. The doors were closed. Curiosity greeted our arrival. No sooner had we stepped from the car than a window opened on the first floor of the old house.

'*Hola*,' called an elderly woman, 'can I help you?'

'We're looking for the *carpintero*,' I replied.

'One minute,' she said, before closing the window.

Moments later she appeared at the front door.

'What do you want?' she asked.

'We're looking for the *carpintero*.'

'José Manuel?'

In for a penny...

'That's right.'

'He's out at the moment but he'll be back for lunch.'

I glanced at my watch. If we waited, there was a good chance we'd miss Carlos. The old woman sensed our urgency.

'I'm his mother,' she said with a broad smile. 'Let me get you his phone number and you can give him a call.'

We thanked her and headed off.

Carlos was getting ready to leave when we arrived. We explained what we were looking for.

'I'm very busy at the moment but if you bring me the dimensions, I'll do a quote as soon as I can,' he said.

His lack of enthusiasm didn't bode well.

That afternoon someone from the tile shop in Ourense rang.

'We'll be delivering your order between 10:00 am and 2:00 pm tomorrow,' they said.

That was great news.

In the evening Melanie phoned Felix to make sure everything was on schedule for him to start tomorrow.

'We'll be there between eight and half past in the evening,' he said.

The joys of managing your own building project: start at the crack of dawn and finish in the middle of the night.

17

Bequests Addressed

As the clock ticked down to our departure, unresolved issues took on a new urgency. We would be away from home for seven weeks and two days. Between now and then, we had to do everything we could to ensure the project remained on track.

My obsession with writing lists didn't help. It's a habit I picked up as a small business owner. Back then it was a daily ritual; now it's less frequent. I've christened my reminders Infinity Lists. They ebb and flow depending on the workload but never end. At the moment, a tsunami of entries threatened to drown me in a sea of jobs.

'I must get my hair cut before we go off,' I said, over morning coffee.

One more thing to add to the list.

'And don't forget those trousers you want dry cleaning.'

Make that two.

'We need to sort out some shower screens as well.'

We'd ordered the toilets and shower trays from Otero's. They would be delivered on request. We'd sourced the sinks, vanity units, taps, shower heads and other bathroom accessories from various shops. They were in the back bedroom waiting to be taken to Vilatán. The only items still to buy were shower screens.

'Let's go into town this afternoon and see if BricoKing have got any,' suggested Melanie.

BricoKing had recently opened a store in Monforte which was great news for us.

'We can call at the vet's while we're in town and sort out Jazz's passport,' she added.

PETS (Pet Travel Scheme) was introduced in 2001. It allows animals to avoid quarantine when travelling between participating EU countries. To qualify, each pet is required to hold a passport detailing their vaccination history. Immediately prior to travelling a registered vet must certify the records.

'That's a good idea and don't forget to ring your mum and ask her to get us some yuan.'

'Some what?'

'Yuan, the currency in China.'

'How much?'

'Two hundred quid's worth should be enough.'

We would only be there three days and I'd already paid for the hotel and sightseeing trip.

'And don't forget, you have to prune the grapevines before we go.'

How could I? We hadn't yet got out of bed and my list had grown by six jobs.

Roy arrived at his usual time and the three of us drove to Vilatán. The morning was bitterly cold. Roy and I quickly found our rhythm and Melanie kept us busy with buckets of cement. The tiles didn't arrive until 1:00 pm. Before leaving we moved them into the house. By the time we got home, the earlier mist had disappeared and the temperature had risen to a very respectable 17°C.

BricoKing didn't open until 4:30 pm, just as well given our late lunch.

'Are you ready?' I asked.

'Ready when you are.'

Their range of shower screens was quite extensive. After much deliberation we whittled it down to two. A cheap opaque plastic cubicle or a more expensive glass one.

'We're not having that,' said, Melanie, pointing at the plastic screen.

'You won't be using it,' I replied.

'I don't care, we're not having it.'

'Glass it is then.'

I took the point of sale ticket to the checkout.

'I'm sorry but we're out of stock of that one at the moment. We can order them for you.'

'How soon will they be here?' I asked.

'It could be any time.'

Her reply didn't fill us with confidence but we ordered them anyway.

'We'll ring you as soon as they arrive,' she said.

Our next stop was the veterinary surgery.

When it comes to administering the PETS scheme, the UK authorities are sticklers for accuracy. Failure to dot an i or cross a t and Jazz could face months in quarantine or, worse still, be refused entry. Thankfully, this wasn't her first trip to the UK and the staff were familiar with the process.

The regulations state that only registered practitioners can certify compliance. It's their responsibility to ensure that Jazz's vaccination record is up to date and that prior to departure she's been treated to prevent ticks and fleas and taken a worming tablet. The only problem is that both treatments must be administered between twenty-four and forty-eight hours before entering the UK. On a journey that starts long before the clinic opens and takes thirty-three hours to complete, the mechanics of abiding by the rules become almost impossible. Fortunately, we have an understanding vet.

'What date are you travelling?' he asked.

'We sail from Calais on Sunday the 3rd at about 3:00 pm.'

'What date and time would you like me to put on the certificate?

'Saturday the 2nd at 9:00 am would be ideal.'

'Come back tomorrow and I'll have everything ready for you.'

The afternoon had gone smoother than expected. We now faced a dilemma. If we went home, we wouldn't be there two minutes before we had to set off to meet Felix but if we went to Vilatán now, we might have a lengthy wait in the freezing cold.

'We'd better go straight to Vilatán,' I suggested.

'It's a bit early?'

'We can wait in the car.'

Reluctantly, Melanie agreed.

Manolo had left by the time we arrived.

'I'm going to have a look around,' I said, keen to see what he'd been doing.

'I'll wait here.'

Eight o'clock came and went. By 8:30 pm we were frozen stiff.

'How much longer?' moaned Melanie.

'Give him a call and find out where he is.'

Within two minutes of speaking to him, a van pulled into the driveway. Felix and two others jumped out. While his workmates unloaded tools from the van, Felix and I wandered around the house making sure he knew exactly where to put the sockets and switches.

'We'll leave you to it,' I said.

Besides being freezing cold and starving, Melanie and I were surplus to requirements.

Roy arrived the following morning at his usual time. A thick layer of frost covered the surrounding countryside. The thermometer in the car read -1°C.

'Can you ring Carpintero Licin this morning and see if we can call up this afternoon?' I asked Melanie.

'No problem.'

Manolo was spitting feathers when we arrived at the house.

'Look at the mess,' he said, pointing at lumps of red brick and chips of plaster.

Felix and his workmates had drilled channels in the internal walls for the conduit and left their mess for someone else to sweep up.

'I'm sorry Manolo, I'll have a word with them. Leave this with me, I'll sweep it up.'

At our current rate of progress, cementing between the gaps was going to be a long job but providing the weather held, I was confident we would finish before we left for Australia.

Before heading home for lunch Roy gave me a hand to measure the doorways.

'How's it going?' asked Melanie on my return.

'Slowly. Did you speak to the carpenter?' I asked.

'Yes, he'll be at the workshop all afternoon.'

I told her about the mess Felix had left and asked her to call him. He apologised and promised to clean up in future.

On the way to Licin we called to see Carlos in Ferreira with the measurements for the doors. The noise of a circular saw echoed through the workshop as we arrived.

'*Buenas tardes*,' I shouted over the racket.

A worker switched off the machine.

'Is Carlos here?' I asked.

'He'll be out all afternoon. Can you call back tomorrow?'

I explained who we were and why we'd called.

'Can you give him these measurements?' I asked,

handing them to him.

'No problem, I'll see he gets them.'

Fifteen minutes later we were creeping down the narrow track leading to the workshop of Carpintero Licin. Parked at the bottom was a white panel van.

'Someone's home,' commented Melanie.

I pulled up alongside and we made our way to the workshop. There were three men inside, all working on different machines. On seeing us, one man switched off his machine and came to greet us.

'*Hola*, Melanie. *Que tal* (How are you)?' he asked.

Melanie and I were gobsmacked. How on earth did he know her name?

'You don't recognise me, do you?' he added.

When people are removed from the environment you expect to see them in, it's often difficult to remember who they are.

'No,' she admitted.

'I'm José Manuel.'

Melanie looked none the wiser.

'José Manuel, from physiotherapy,' he added.

All of a sudden, the penny dropped. Two and a half years earlier, Melanie had undergone a course of physiotherapy at the hospital in Monforte. José Manuel had been a patient at the same time.

'Ah yes, now I remember.'

The two were like long-lost siblings.

'How are you?' she asked.

'Much better, and you?'

'It took surgery to sort my knee out but I'm fine now.'

Reminiscences shared, we explained why we'd called and who had recommended him.

'I have some rough dimensions,' I said.

'I'll need to come and measure up properly,' he replied.

This was the professional response I'd expected from Carlos.

'What type of wood do you want?' he asked.

'Chestnut.'

'And what style?'

Describing what we had in mind proved difficult.

'Come with me,' he said, leading us outside.

All the doors on his mother's home were crafted in different styles.

'This is exactly what we're looking for,' I said, pointing at the *bodega* doors.

'And what type of hinges would you like?'

I hadn't imagined we'd have a choice.

'Come and take a look,' he said, leading us back into the workshop.

José Manuel showed us a range of samples. With his guidance we chose hinges, handles, and locks.

'I'll call tomorrow morning and measure up,' he said.

José Manuel was much keener to do the work than Carlos. We hoped his price reflected his enthusiasm.

On the way home, we collected Jazz's paperwork.

'Here you go,' said the vet, handing Melanie the validated certificate.

'And the drugs?' she asked.

'Oh, you want the drugs?'

Bending the rules to accommodate a lengthy drive was one thing; breaking them to save a few bob was quite another.

'Yes please, we'll give them to her on the journey,' replied Melanie.

That was Jazz sorted; all we had to do now was sort ourselves out.

Spain is a member of the European Health Card scheme which entitles residents of one EU country to receive medical treatment in another, free of charge or at heavily discounted rates. Our route back to the UK took us through France and even though we had holiday insurance, it seemed prudent to make sure we were covered under the state scheme. The application process is painless. Within half an hour of entering the offices of the social security department, they'd issued the necessary travel certificate.

'Do we need to do anything else?' asked Melanie, on the way home.

The car had been serviced within the last 10,000 kilometres. We had state health cover for France and the UK, and worldwide insurance while we were away. The return ferry to the UK was booked. Airline tickets had arrived and our passports didn't expire for four years. The only thing left to do was choose the beneficiaries of our estate should the holiday of a lifetime end a lifetime of holidays.

'We need to sort out who's getting the money.'

'What money?'

'The insurance money.'

'Nothing's going to happen.'

'That's besides the point. If something does we'll be worth a fortune.'

Melanie said nothing.

That evening I broached the subject again.

'Right,' I said, pen and paper at the ready. 'First things first. Who do we want to look after Jazz?'

Starting with the dog garnered some enthusiasm.

'What about Roy and Maria?' she suggested.

They've looked after her on a number of occasions and Jazz loves Roy.

'That's a good idea.'

'OK. To Roy and Maria, we bequeath 100,000 euros on the proviso they adopt Jazz.'

'One hundred thousand euros! Don't you think that's a bit much?'

'If we both cop it, there'll be over three million to give away. Unless there's someone else you've got in mind, I suggest we start off big and work our way down.'

Over the next hour we gifted money to everyone we'd ever met, no matter how fleetingly. Giving away three million euros is a lot harder than it sounds.

'That should do it,' I said.

'And what are you going to do with the list?'

'I thought I'd give it to Jeremy for safekeeping.'

Besides being our brother-in-law, he's also a Methodist lay preacher. If you can't trust a man of the cloth, who can you trust?

'Whatever you do, don't mention it to anyone,' I added.

Melanie looked at me quizzically.

'People have killed for less.'

A wry smile was followed by a period of contemplation. Who were the potential suspects?

The cold snap continued for the rest of the week. Manolo knocked the fireplace up in no time, but the chimney took a bit longer. Once finished he continued pointing the internal stone walls. Roy and I soldiered on with the terrace.

On Thursday afternoon I pruned the vines at the back of our house. The morning after I did those in the front.

On Saturday evening, I checked the weather in Shanghai.

'Crikey!'

'What?' asked Melanie.

'If you think it's cold here you ought to see the forecast for Shanghai.'

'Why, what is it?'

'Snow and ice, and according to the BBC website, there are over 170,000 people stranded.'

'Stranded?'

'The heavy snow has caused travel chaos for those heading home for the Chinese New Year.'

'Will it be gone by the time we get there?'

'Probably.'

I hadn't a clue but saw no reason to concern her.

With a week to go everything was falling into place. Roy and I finished the terrace with four days to spare. Carlos and José Manuel had tendered their quotes for the doors. There was very little between their prices but a gulf between start dates. On that basis José Manuel got the job. Felix would finish the upstairs electrics that weekend. Alfonso had promised to restart work on the boundary walls but we weren't holding our breath, and Ramon would crack on with the plumbing. Manolo had plenty to keep him occupied and we surprised him with a 6,000-euro payment before leaving.

'I've got some bad news,' he said, when we called to see him. 'I've got a date for my operation.'

Manolo had been waiting for corrective surgery on a leg break he'd suffered eighteen months ago while working for us on Bob and Janet's house.

'When is it?' I asked.

'It's while you're away but I shouldn't be off work long.'

Manolo was as keen as us to keep things moving along.

'That's fine, you take as long as you need.'

His accident was nothing to do with us but nevertheless, we felt a level of responsibility.

All we had to do now was buy Melanie's mum a few bottles of cheap spirits and find a winter coat for me.

After much consideration I chose a three-quarter length leather coat with a detachable fur collar. If that didn't keep me warm, nothing would. The night before leaving we locked all the window shutters and security grills, packed the car and had an early night. Almost a year after agreeing to a house swap, our Australian adventure was about to begin.

18

Dinner Time

What could be worse than a 6:00 am start to the day? One that involves scraping a thick layer of ice off the windscreen. By the time I'd finished, the ends of my fingers were numb.

'It's freezing,' said Melanie, as she jumped into the car.

She wasn't kidding. The dashboard temperature display read -6°C. As we drove through the village, it fell to -7°C. The fan was on full speed, belting out icy cold air like an Arctic wind tunnel. Fifteen minutes later the interior temperature finally began to rise.

Our destination today was the town of Saintes in the Nouvelle-Aquitaine region of southwest France, a drive of just over 1,000 kilometres. It's roughly halfway between home and the UK.

The scenery across northern Spain is outstanding: green fields, picturesque villages and rugged mountains. It's the perfect antidote to the tedium of traffic-free highways. After six hours on the road the snow-capped peaks of the Pyrenees came into view.

'I'm going to fill up with fuel before we cross the border,' I said.

'Good, I'm dying for a pee.'

'You should have gone to the loo before we left home,' I joked.

'That was six hours ago, and I did.'

Fuel in Spain is much cheaper than in France and the UK. Filling up at the border would allow us to cover the 1,100 kilometres to Calais without having to refuel. Tolls on French roads are expensive enough without having to buy their overpriced diesel.

Driving through France is very different to northern Spain: mile after mile of straight roads and flat scenery. The highway around Bordeaux provided some welcome relief from the motorway monotony. After eight hours behind the wheel, madcap Bordelais drivers kept me on my toes.

One of the challenges of a brief stay in another country is communication. The compulsion is to speak Spanish when logic requires French. *Si* gets confused with *oui* and *gracias* with *merci*. I'm in awe of people who are not only multilingual but can interchange languages mid-sentence. Not one for resting on my laurels, I'd asked Melanie to pack a French phrasebook.

'Right then, let's have a go at learning some French,' I suggested.

If nothing else it would keep me alert for the remaining 100 kilometres.

'What would you like to say?' asked Melanie.

'I don't know.'

Melanie flicked through the book.

'What about "Where is the railway station?"'

'Why on earth would I want to know where the railway station is?'

'Well what then?'

I thought for a moment. The last time we'd stayed in Saintes, we turned up late for dinner and almost missed out.

'I know.'

'What?'

'What about "What time is dinner?"'

Melanie saw the logic and searched through the book.

'That's not in.'

Typical.

'Is there a dictionary in the back?'

Melanie had a look.

'Here we go, *A quelle heure…*'

'Is that it?'

'Give me a chance.'

She flicked through a few more pages.

'*…est le dîner.*'

To my mind, a good French accent requires an acute blockage of one's nasal sinuses. Melanie's broad Yorkshire accent didn't quite cut it.

'Say it again, in full.'

'*A quelle heure est le dîner.*'

'*A quelle heure est le dîner,*' I repeated.

'That's it,' she said encouragingly.

'*A quelle heure est le dîner. A quelle heure est le dîner. A quelle heure est le dîner.*'

'You've got it.'

'*A quelle heure est le dîner. A quelle heure est le dîner. A quelle heure es* dinner.

'It's *est le dîner,*' Melanie corrected me.

'That's what I said.'

'No it isn't.'

'*A quelle heure est le dîner.*'

'That right.'

I repeated the sentence over and over again.

'Only twenty-six to go,' said Melanie, as we sped past another road sign.

'*A que hora es la diner.*'

'That's not it.'

'What do you mean that's not it?'

'It's *à quelle heure est le dîner.*'

'That's what I said.'

'No you didn't.'

'I'm no chuffing good at French,' I replied.

'It's only one sentence. Try it again, *A quelle heure est le dîner.*'

Time and time again I repeated the phrase.

'What was that?' I asked.

'What?'

'That exit?'

I'd been concentrating so much on chuffing *dîner*, I'd driven straight past the exit for Saintes.

'I don't know.'

'Just have a look at the sign on the other carriageway.'

Melanie swivelled in her seat.

'Saintes,' she said.

'Bugger!'

The next exit was seventeen kilometres away. After driving over 1,000 kilometres, the last thing I needed was a thirty-four-kilometre detour. Thankfully, we saw the funny side of it.

We arrived at the Kyriad Hotel, Saintes in a confident mood. The additional thirty-four kilometres had given me the opportunity to perfect my newly learnt French phrase. The formalities of checking in passed seamlessly with the question of dinner repeating in my head. The receptionist handed me the room key and I seized the moment.

'*A quelle heure est le dîner?*'

The sentence flowed off my tongue like a native Parisienne. I waited proudly for her response.

'The restaurant's not open this evening,' she replied.

I couldn't believe it. I'd spent the best part of two hours perfecting a phrase that had no value whatsoever. I was devastated. She showed us how to get to the nearest eatery but it didn't quite compensate for my disappointment. As we strolled through the corridors of the hotel, Melanie and I could hardly contain our laughter.

Later that evening, we found the restaurant she'd recommended, a Bernie Inn-style establishment serving posh microwaved meals at exorbitant prices. One of these days I'm going to discover why France has such a marvellous reputation for great cuisine, but until then I stick with my claim that it's nothing to write home about.

On our return to the hotel, we ordered a gin and tonic before turning in. One thousand kilometres down; only one thousand two hundred to go.

Melanie's alarm clock shattered the silence. I opened my eyes and thought I'd gone blind. I turned over and fumbled in the darkness for the bedside lamp but switched on the ceiling light by mistake.

'Must you?' complained Melanie.

'Sorry, wrong switch.'

After a brief lie-in we rolled out of bed. My back was killing me. Today's road trip was going to be challenging.

'How did you sleep?' asked Melanie as we made our way to the dining room for breakfast.

'Terrible, all I could think about was *à quelle heure est le dîner.*'

Melanie laughed.

'It's not funny.'

By 7:00 am we were speeding towards Paris on the E5. Four hundred and seventy kilometres later we hit the Périphérique (Paris ring road). Weaving in and out of traffic at breakneck speed highlighted exactly why Alain Prost was such a good racing driver. We reached the port of Calais at 3:00 pm. Jazz's paperwork passed muster and we boarded the ferry. An hour and a half later we disembarked in Dover.

The volume of traffic in England was extraordinary. We passed more cars in half an hour than in the previous two days. Forty hours after leaving home we arrived in Huddersfield, a bit stiff but none the worse for wear.

Our two-day stay passed in a haze of catching up with friends and takeaway food. Saying goodbye to Jazz brought a tear to Melanie's eye.

'She'll be fine,' I reassured her.

From Huddersfield we drove to Grove Park in south east London to stay overnight with my sister Julie. That evening Jeremy treated us to a meal at one of my favourite London restaurants, Chapter Two in Blackheath. When we got back, I handed him the list of beneficiaries, sealed in an envelope with my signature across the flap.

'If we don't make it back, can you see our wishes are fulfilled?' I asked, handing him the envelope.

'I hope I'm on it,' said Julie.

'No chance,' I joked.

The day after, we left the car in their driveway and Jeremy took us to Heathrow Airport. We set off early to allow for hold-ups on the M25, the London Orbital Motorway. Halfway to the airport I realised I had forgotten something.

'Oh no!'

'What?' asked Melanie.

'I've forgotten my sunglasses.'

After months of careful planning I'd left my prescription sunglasses in the car. Without them I couldn't see a thing.

'It's too late to go back,' said Jeremy, 'and anyway, you won't need sunglasses.'

Jeremy doesn't wear sunglasses. He believes that using a filter to protect your eyes from the sun's harmful rays hampers vision. For a Cambridge graduate he has some strange ideas.

I racked my brains for a solution. Sunglasses aside, I'd packed two pairs of spectacles, one for Sunday best and the other for daily use. As soon as we touched down in Oz, I would find an optician and get them to tint one pair.

Given Jeremy's passion for clear lenses, I decided to keep this cunning plan to myself.

The journey proved less problematic than anticipated and by 3:45 pm we were hauling our suitcases out of the car.

'Thanks Jem. We get back on the 15th of March at 8:00 pm.'

'OK, have a good time and I'll see you then.'

My dislike of air travel is well documented. Some say the only way to enjoy a flight is to turn left after boarding. Maybe one day I'll find out; until then I'll suffer the cheap seats. To make matters worse, we had over five hours to wait for the gate to open.

The plane took off from Heathrow at 9:00 pm and landed eleven hours later in Shanghai, local time 4:00 pm. In-flight services lived up to my low expectations. There's always a price to pay for budget airfares.

The flight landed a little later than scheduled, throwing our hotel transfer plans into question. We'd hoped to catch the last Maglev train into Shanghai and make our way to the hotel from there. Most of our fellow travellers turned right after disembarking, and followed an airline rep to a waiting coach. We turned left, following signs to baggage handling. That's when it dawned on me: we were on our own.

'If the luggage doesn't come soon we'll miss the train,' I said.

The vast baggage handling hall was deserted and the luggage conveyor was at a standstill.

'What time does it leave?'

I looked at my watch.

'In about ten minutes.'

'How far away is the station?'

Without warning the conveyor lurched into action.

'Your guess is as good as mine.'

As usual, the first item to appear was a cardboard box. Our luggage had to be next; there was no one else here.

We watched as the box did a lap of honour. Eventually, the first of our cases punched its way through the rubber curtain followed in close succession by the others.

When packing for multiple stopovers it's important to be organised. We'd already had an overnight stay in France and three nights at two separate locations in the UK. We were here for two nights before travelling on to Australia. Without careful planning, we would have ended up packing and unpacking more times than a travelling circus. In the end, we'd managed to squeeze everything into two carry-ons and two large suitcases.

Next stop, customs and immigration.

We slalomed our way through miles of retractable barriers to the passport control desk. Contact with officialdom made me inexplicably nervous. I slid my passport across the counter. The customs officer stared at the photo and then at me. It's natural to want to smile but I resisted the urge. His attention shifted back to the passport. He flicked through the crisp, unblemished pages until he found the visa and pondered its authenticity. If I didn't breathe soon, I was in danger of collapsing. Without cracking his solemn glare, he slid it back across the counter and waved me through. I'd done it; I'd officially entered the People's Republic of China.

Melanie tried smiling but fared no better.

Having cleared passport control we found ourselves in an eerily quiet arrivals hall. We stared at the information signs. The word Maglev didn't appear on any.

'It's all in Chinese,' whispered Melanie.

'Let's ask over there,' I said, pointing at the one place that resembled an information desk.

'Hello, we're looking for the Maglev,' I said.

A smartly dressed young woman smiled back reassuringly and then spoke. East collided with West and the legal aliens came off worse. To the best of our understanding, the train service had closed early due to a public holiday.

Before embarking on this epic adventure, it seemed prudent to learn a few Chinese words. Please and thank you never go amiss. The owner of the Jing Huà Chinese restaurant in Chaves was a great help.

'*Faz favor* (please) *es qîng y obrigado* (thank you) *es xièxiè*,' she'd said.

We hadn't yet left the airport and they were already coming in handy.

'*Xièxiè*,' I said, with a broad smile and a slight bow.

Only when we turned to leave did I wonder if my reply was as polite as I'd intended.

'Is it the Japanese who bow?' I asked in a hushed tone.

'I think it is,' replied Melanie.

It's easy to see how people get themselves into trouble on holidays to far-flung places.

Our only choice now was to get a taxi.

When we stepped outside, the air was icy cold and twilight was surrendering to darkness. I looked around for a taxi rank.

'Over there,' I said, pointing at a queue across the road.

For a city of over twenty-four million inhabitants, the drop-off area in front of the terminal was near-deserted. We walked across the road and made our way to the back of the queue. At the front, a uniformed official directed proceedings. Waiting taxis were parked on the opposite side of the road, fifty metres away. As soon as one party boarded a taxi, the officer blew a whistle and another came racing across the road. It seemed a bit unnecessary but I guess that's communism.

The taxis were doing a brisk trade. As our turn neared I readied the hotel paperwork. The man in front was carrying a briefcase. When his ride pulled up, he jumped in and they were off in a flash. The officer whistled a cab for us. I was still trying to shuffle our luggage along when the vehicle ground to a halt and the driver leapt out. In one continuous movement he opened the boot, picked up Melanie's suitcase and flung it in. The officer seemed agitated with our slow progress and shouted at the driver. We were holding up the queue.

'You get in,' I said to Melanie, doing my best to speed things up.

I wasn't going anywhere until I'd seen everything loaded and the boot closed. The driver tossed the last case in, slammed the boot lid and we were ready for off. I leapt into the back and closed the door.

The driver hit the accelerator like a would-be racing driver, pinning us to the seat. Next came a tirade of incoherent narrative. I presumed he was asking where we wanted to go.

'The Bund Riverside Hotel,' I said.

My request caused the taxi to grind to a halt. Melanie's early entry had given her time to fasten her safety belt. I wasn't so fortunate and lurched forward, bumping into the front seat. The driver turned to face me. Another tirade followed.

'English, do you speak English?' I asked.

The driver shook his head and yelled something else at me. I unfolded the booking form and offered it to him. Repeated high pitched whistles drew my attention to the taxi rank. Our actions hadn't gone unnoticed. If he wasn't careful, the red-faced officer would blow a gasket. Anxiety levels rose.

I turned back to the driver. He was staring at the printed sheet, shaking his head. The confirmation included a photo of the entrance. It was a long shot but if we didn't move soon we were in danger of spending a night behind bars. The whistling continued. I turned around. The officer was marching towards us, gesticulating with wild arm movements. Melanie looked terrified. Any minute now, she'd throw her toys out of the pram and someone would cop an earful. Just when everything seemed lost, the driver thrust the paper back at me, engaged gear and sped away. Melanie and I breathed a sigh of relief.

We had no idea if he'd driven off to evade officialdom or knew where we wanted to go. We had little choice but to sit back and hope for the best.

The highways into the city were busy but free flowing. The fare meter flicked over at an alarming rate; providing we ended up at our destination, we could argue over the cost later. Twenty minutes into the journey the driver swerved across eight lanes of speeding traffic and headed back in the direction we'd just come. Five minutes later, he made a similar manoeuvre. We were completely at his mercy; even the Chinese road signs gave no hint of our whereabouts.

Fifty minutes after leaving the airport, the taxi pulled up outside a hotel and the driver leapt out. We've learnt from experience to check the destination before leaving the vehicle. I looked out of the window. To my relief the sign above the entrance read The Bund Riverside Hotel. We'd made it. Now for the bad news. The meter registered ninety-two yuan.

'How much is that in real money?' whispered Melanie.

I thought for a moment.

'Ninety euros.'

'Chuff me!'

'Hang on a minute.' I recalculated. 'No, it's nine euros not ninety.'

'Are you sure?'

'Positive.'

Before I'd had a chance to pay the driver, a bellboy skipped down the hotel steps. He was wearing a starched purple tunic with polished brass buttons. He smiled politely, picked up our luggage and carried it inside: at last, civilisation.

By the time we'd completed a stress-free registration and been guided to our room, the trials of our trip from the airport were a source of amusement. A story to share with friends over a glass of wine.

The room was everything I'd expect of a five-star hotel and the views of the Pudong Business District were outstanding. We couldn't have chosen a better location. What struck me most about the panorama was the low intensity of the lighting. It was almost as if there wasn't enough electricity to power the city.

Our time in Shanghai was short and despite feeling tired we had no intention of wasting it. After a brief nap and a soothing shower, we headed for dinner on the eighteenth floor. If we thought the vista from our bedroom was outstanding, we hadn't seen anything yet. From the restaurant we had a near 270-degree view over the city. It's said that Shanghai has more skyscrapers than New York City, and standing here it was easy to see why. We'd never seen anything like it. The population of one of these cloud-kissing monoliths was probably greater than the number of residents in the entire municipality of Sober.

Dinner wasn't bad but nothing to write home about, unlike the wine. We decided to go native and try a bottle of Chinese red. The taste was surprisingly good, the price less so.

'We can buy a case at home for that price,' I said.

'Well we're not at home, we're on holiday.'

That told me.

After dinner we strolled the 800 metres to the Huangpu River for a night-time cruise. I'd made the reservations online. The streets were eerily quiet, and dim streetlighting added to the Victorian ambience. That said, we didn't once feel uneasy. The quayside was very quiet. Dock workers slipped in and out of the shadows. There were a number of operators to choose from, each with their own ticket office. We found ours, handed in the tickets and stepped aboard. The low passenger numbers reflected the lateness of the hour and the off-peak season.

The cruise took about an hour, down one side and up the other. The temperature outside on the observation deck was freezing, exaggerated by a stiff breeze. Inside wasn't much warmer. We resisted the urge to order a brandy, opting instead for a locally brewed beer.

By the time we'd strolled back to the hotel we were shattered. We'd managed to catch forty winks on the plane but nothing compares to a comfy king-size and a heavy duvet.

19

Shanghai Surprise

'Craig, Craig, I forgot to set the alarm,' said Melanie, rocking me back and forth.

'What?' I groaned.

'I forgot to set the alarm. If we don't make a move we're going to be late.'

Slowly, I opened my eyes. The heavy curtains obscured the brightness of a new day.

Melanie rolled out of bed and flicked on the kettle on her way to the bathroom. On her return, she pulled opened the curtains.

'Coffee?' she asked.

'Yes please.'

In the distance, the silhouette of the Oriental Pearl Tower took centre stage, flanked on both sides by tall skyscrapers.

The Pudong Financial District was less than a kilometre away but a veil of air pollution turned the urban landscape into a collage of grey. We'd never seen anything like it. At this time of year in Galicia, the colours are at their most vivid.

'Here you go,' she said, handing me a cuppa.

I hauled myself into a seated position.

'Thanks.'

After a quick shower we hot-footed it to the eighteenth floor for breakfast. Melanie chose from the buffet; I opted for a full English. A valiant effort but China is not the place to experience one of England's finest culinary creations.

Before going down to the lobby, we nipped back to the room, brushed our teeth and collected our coats.

'Have you got the camera?' asked Melanie.

I knew I had but checked anyway.

At exactly 9:00 am, a young man entered the lobby and walked up to reception. He spoke briefly with the receptionist. Her response was to point at us.

'Hello,' said the young man. 'My name is Bernie and I'm your tour guide for the day.'

Of all the names he could have chosen.

Bernie was in his early twenties, about five foot seven and, despite his bright quilted jacket and woolly scarf, a wisp of a man. His command of the English language was very good and his campness added to his charm.

'You're my only clients today,' he said, as he led us outside.

I'd spent hours agonising over whether to book a private or group tour. In the end, cost determined my decision yet here we were, on a private tour at group rates. Now that's what I call a Shanghai Surprise.

Parked outside was a small minibus. Bernie tugged open the sliding door and Melanie and I hopped in. The driver turned to face us and tipped his head. Bernie followed us in and away we went.

'The first stop is the Yuyuan Garden,' said Bernie.

Melanie and I were none the wiser. The driver clearly knew his way around the city. Ten minutes after leaving the hotel we stopped and Bernie slid open the door.

'This way,' he said, before giving the driver new instructions.

Yuyuan Garden is one of the city's most famous classical gardens. During the Ming Dynasty, a government officer by the name of Pan Yunduan commissioned its construction to enable his parents to enjoy a peaceful life in their old age. Today, it provides that same tranquillity to tourists and locals alike. Given the cost of city centre real estate, it's refreshing to know that China has spared this five-acre site for future generations.

Bernie seemed thrilled at the prospect of becoming our official photographer for the day and his knowledge kept our attention.

'You see this,' he said, pointing at the entrance to a pavilion, 'every doorway in the world has one of these and the Chinese invented it over one thousand years ago.'

Bernie was referring to the threshold. This particular one was twelve inches high. I joked about the strength required to carry a bride over it but my satirical remark was lost in a clash of cultures.

'Stand there and I'll take your photo,' he said.

The morning air was icy cold and remnants of earlier snowfall covered the rooftops of the garden's halls and pavilions. Bernie kept us moving along. He had a timetable to stick to and dawdling was not on the agenda.

We left the garden and walked straight into Yuyuan Old Street, second destination on the tour. The street was crowded with people. We were mesmerised by the traditional architecture of red columns, pink panelled walls, black roof tiles, and upturned eaves. Back in the Ming and Qing dynasties the arrival of banks, jewellery stores, teahouses, and wine shops helped establish this area as Shanghai's first commercial district.

Every time I lifted my camera to take a snap, Bernie insisted on taking a second with Melanie and I in the frame.

'This way, this way,' he said, scuttling along in front.

Getting lost in this crowd was unthinkable.

'Look,' he said, pointing at a strange looking animated character standing three metres tall and crafted in powder blue plastic, 'this is Haibao.'

His tone suggested we should be familiar with it.

'You know, Haibao.'

Melanie and I hadn't a clue.

'It's the mascot for the 2010 Shanghai Expo,' he said.

If we didn't acknowledge its existence soon, we were in danger of upsetting our host.

'Oh yes, Haribo. Nice shade of blue,' I added.

Melanie elbowed me in the ribs.

'It's Haibao,' he replied, before marching off.

We walked out of the pedestrianised streets onto an adjacent road. He leaned forward and waved, and seconds later the minibus pulled up alongside. We stepped inside and the driver raced away.

'Would you like to stop for a drink?' asked Bernie.

The tour included a traditional tea tasting ceremony.

'Sure.'

'There's a Starbucks in the French Concession,' he said.

Not exactly what we were expecting but Bernie seemed thrilled at the prospect.

Foreign concessions are associated with colonialism. They're areas of territory conceded to a foreign power. The concessions were occupied and governed by that nation. In effect, sovereign territory within another country. Similar to an embassy but on a much larger scale. The French Concession was established in 1849. At its height, it covered an area of almost 1,000 hectares. Over time the concession became the city's main retail area and its most prestigious residential zone. The contrast in architectural styles between here and Yuyuan Old Street was unbelievable. It felt as if we were back in Europe.

'This way,' said Bernie, guiding us towards a bright shopfront bearing the famous Starbucks logo.

No sooner had we entered than his mood changed and his confidence waned. Perhaps this was his Forbidden City.

Bernie had downed his latte before we were halfway through ours. Despite efforts to the contrary he couldn't hide his impatience. I asked for the bill. Bernie's hand moved towards his pocket.

'I'll get these,' I said.

Given his reaction you would think I'd offered him my wallet.

'The next place on the tour is the Jade Buddha Temple,' he said. 'Make sure you look after your valuables. The place is a den of thieves.'

Hardly the best advertisement for a religious building. He needn't have worried; I'd hidden my wallet in the lining of my coat and Melanie's handbag was looped around her neck. If anyone wanted that, they'd have to take her with them.

The streets around the temple were heaving. The driver thumped the horn with increasing frustration but to little effect. As we approached a narrow yet busy crossroads, I caught sight of my first real taste of communist China. Until then, Shanghai had seemed like any other bustling metropolis, but the appearance of a uniformed soldier changed that.

He looked as if he'd stepped off the set of a Hollywood movie. His winter fatigues consisted of a thick quilted jacket and matching pants. He wore a trademark leather cap, fur lined with lolloping ear protectors and a menacing-looking red star embroidered on the front. His attempts at directing traffic went ignored. Given his age, I wondered if his role was self-appointed: an ageing warrior seeking a purpose.

We drove past him and stopped outside the temple. Crowds circled the bus.

'OK, are you ready?' asked Bernie.

We nodded.

'Stay close and follow me and whatever you do, don't stop,' he cautioned.

Bernie flung open the door and hopped out, and Melanie and I followed. Quickly, he slammed it shut and hurried across the street to the temple entrance. Melanie grabbed my hand and we raced after him. Seconds later we were safely inside. Bernie's relief was tangible.

The current temple was built in 1928 on the site of an earlier one. The traditional architecture and ancient artefacts made it look much older. My biggest surprise were the two statues of Buddha, one seated and the other reclining.

'I thought they were made out of jade,' I whispered to Melanie.

Bernie overheard.

'They are,' he replied.

'But they're white.'

Bernie looked confused.

'I thought jade was green,' I added.

'This is white jade,' he replied.

I didn't know such a material existed but no one could argue with their craftsmanship.

'Now we go for the traditional tea ceremony,' said Bernie, gesturing us to climb a flight of stairs.

At the top of the stairs the space opened out into a large square hall. Occupying the centre of the rooms was a long, highly polished dining table with seating for twenty or more. White translucent roller blinds covered all the windows and Chinese lanterns were hanging from the ceiling. Oriental dressers were positioned along three sides of the room, each one containing an array of tea making paraphernalia. The dressers resembled display shelves associated with 19th century alchemists' shops. Along the other wall was a low counter with carefully arranged tea caddies sporting traditional marketing logos.

'Take a seat,' said Bernie, directing us to two chairs placed centrally in front of the counter.

Sitting across from us was the presenter of our tea ceremony, dressed in a brightly coloured silk kimono.

The mechanics of preparing tea are complicated and time-consuming and drinking it is as much about self-medication as enjoyment. Our host gave us a list of two dozen different leaves each with its own miraculous quality: stress relief, heart attack prevention, and bowel movements, to name but a few. We were asked to choose three to taste. Needless to say, we passed on the bowel movement.

With the exception of one called Breakfast Tea, the others weren't to our taste. When asked if we'd like to buy some, we couldn't resist showing our appreciation by purchasing a small caddy of the Breakfast variety.

'Xièxiè,' we said as we left.

Bernie looked surprised with our reply.

The clock had ticked around to lunchtime. The first half of our tour was drawing to a close.

'Would you like to see some watches before lunch?' asked Bernie.

This wasn't part of the official itinerary but sounded interesting. The shop was tucked away down a narrow alley. All the premium brands were represented, if the names on the faces were anything to go by. The copies, more commonly referred to as fakes, were manufactured to a high standard.

'That one's nice,' I said to Melanie, pointing at a particularly fine example of a ladies' Bulgari.

The watch had a pearlised pink face, diamond encrusted bezel and stainless steel band.

'Try it on,' I added.
'I do good price,' said the salesman.
Melanie tried it on; the band was on the large side.
'No problem. I shorten. No problem. Very good price.'
'Do you like it?' I asked.
'It's lovely.'
'How much?' I asked.
'For you I do very good price.'
'But how much?'
'Cheaper for two. You choose one more.'
'I don't want another. How much for this one?'
'Cheaper with two. Look, look, this very nice watch.'

Rolex Submariners are undoubtedly fine timepieces but I wasn't in the market for a new watch, fake or otherwise.

'It's very nice but we only want this one. How much for this one?'

The salesman quoted a price.

'No, no, that's too much,' I replied.

It was a bargain but he wasn't getting away that easy.

'That good price, very good price.'

'No, too much.' I placed the watch back on the display and we turned to leave.

'OK, no problem. I give you best price.'

With very little persuasion he halved his original price. I was preparing for round two of the negotiations when Melanie gave me one of those 'I don't like haggling' looks, so I conceded defeat.

'OK we'll take it.'

Melanie breathed a sigh of relief and the salesman removed a link. He wrapped the watch up and handed it to Melanie with a polite smile.

'And the link,' I said.

'What?'

'The link,' I repeated, pointing at the one he'd just removed.

Reluctantly, he handed it over and we left.

Bernie had been watching through the shop window. He led us back to the minibus and moments later we were pulling up outside another narrow alleyway.

'Come with me,' he said.

At the end of this one was the entrance to our lunchtime eatery.

'One beverage is included in the price,' warned Bernie.

The restaurant was packed with diners and the noise was deafening. Our table had been reserved. Surprisingly, not one person lifted their head as we took a seat. Even in Galicia diners stop and stare at foreigners.

The set menu consisted of one lukewarm dish after another, none of which were recognisable as food.

'I think that's meant to be boiled rice,' I suggested.

I stabbed my fork into the rice bowl and lifted out every grain in one congealed mass. The half an hour break was more than enough to pick at our plates. If this restaurant was representative of food served in China, the dishes bore no resemblance to the wonderful food we're served in the West.

Bernie collected us as promised and whisked us back to the waiting minibus.

As well as tea, Shanghai is famous for silks and pearls. Within minutes of leaving the restaurant we were grinding to a stop outside a commercial centre that specialised in both.

'This is where they make pearl jewellery,' said Bernie.

We were standing in a bright and airy lobby. Directly in front of us was a flight of stairs; to our left, a long shallow tank contained oysters. Bernie pressed a buzzer and a smartly dressed woman appeared at the top of the stairs and made her way towards us.

'Good afternoon, my name is Chen and I am your guide this afternoon,' she said, in near perfect English.

Chen explained that China is the world's largest producer of pearls. Here in Shanghai, the production of freshwater cultured pearls began in 1962. Quality is attributed to size, roundness and colour, the most common being white. Pearls are also found in peach, pink, grey, black, and gold. The most prized are black and gold ones found in the South China Sea, the largest of which can sell for millions of dollars.

'Every oyster holds a secret,' she said, dipping her hand into the tank and picking out an oyster.

She handed it to me.

'Guess how many pearls are hidden inside and whoever is closest can keep them,' she said, handing me the shell.

Under normal circumstances the competition in a group tour would be stiff. As things turned out, we were guaranteed a win. Shaking it revealed nothing. Who knows, I could have been holding our financial future in the palm of my hand?

'You go first,' I said, handing it to Melanie.

'One,' she said.

Melanie was clearly hoping for that million dollar prize.

If I went one higher I had a fifty-fifty chance of winning.

'Two,' I said

Chen held out her hand and Melanie handed her the oyster. With great skill she prised open the shell and showed us the contents.

'One two three four five six seven eight,' she said.

Eight white pearls of various shapes and sizes. Chen picked out the best two and handed them to me.

'For you darling,' I said, presenting them to Melanie.

It wasn't a million dollars but it's the thought that counts. Chen and Bernie smiled.

'This way,' said Chen, leading us upstairs.

She guided us into another room where more than a dozen craftsmen were busy making various pieces of jewellery. She led us around each process, finishing in the sales area. The pieces on display were stunning.

'Which colour do you like the best?' I asked.

'Those pink ones are beautiful,' replied Melanie.

'What do you think to that?' I said, pointing at a gift set of pink pearl earrings set in gold mounts and a larger pink pearl attached to a fine gold necklace.

'It's lovely.'

'Would you like it?'

'It's gorgeous but it's a bit expensive,' she said.

The chances of us ever returning here were slim. How could we resist buying pearls from the Orient?

'You're worth it,' I replied.

After finalising our purchase, Bernie was keen to move on. We thanked Chen and followed him into reception, through a door, along a corridor and into the silk factory. As we entered, another young lady greeted us. She too spoke excellent English.

Chinese manufacturers have been producing high quality silk for 8,500 years. Today, the city of Shanghai is one of the country's largest exporters. The process involves cultivating silkworm pupae, killing the worm and unravelling the cocoon to produce one continuous thread.

Coming from Yorkshire, the spiritual home of fine worsted, the processes of spinning, dying, and weaving were familiar. Unlike Yorkshire, the Chinese government has supported its manufacturing heritage rather than laid waste to it. Thanks to Margaret Thatcher, Britain's textile industry is unlikely to shine on the global stage again.

The tour ended in the salesroom. The quality and diversity of the goods on show was mind-boggling.

'Look at these,' I said to Melanie.

'They're gorgeous,' she replied, cuddling a silk and down duvet.

The cost was similar to a standard polyester duvet but the quality was outstanding. We ummed and ahed but in the end decided against hauling a hefty quilt across three continents.

'Do you like this?' I asked, holding up a pink silk spectacle case.

'Will you use it?' asked Melanie.

'I thought you might like it for your sunglasses.'

Melanie jumped at the suggestion. We couldn't leave Shanghai without buying some silk.

Bernie led us back to the minibus and we sped off again. By now we were beginning to feel the pace. I lay back in the seat watching Shanghai's daily life flash by.

'Here we are,' announced Bernie.

The respite was short-lived.

'This is the People's Square,' he said.

The space is more like a public park. Its location has created an inner-city oasis of greenery. Surrounding the square were some of the most unusual high-rise buildings we'd ever seen. The designs were truly amazing.

'This way,' said Bernie, leading us across the square. 'This is the Shanghai Museum.'

From the outside, the building looks like a concrete warehouse topped with an enormous wheel that is lying on its side. Bernie led us up the steps and into a huge lobby. The cost of admission was included.

'I'll meet you outside in one hour,' he said, looking at his watch as if to emphasise the point.

The building's interior was far more remarkable than its exterior. The central lobby rose four storeys to a glass dome which flooded the area with natural light. At the far end of the museum, escalators formed a crisscross pattern as the descending and ascending stairways crossed. Leading off each floor were vast exhibition rooms with sparsely spaced displays.

The Shanghai Museum is considered world class. Having visited the British Museum in London, what struck me here was the limited number of artefacts and the lack of global diversity. If anything, it highlighted China's turbulent past, a nation subjugated and plundered, but if you poke a Chinese tiger, one day it will bite back. I suspect that time has come.

We'd been wandering around all day and my feet were killing me. I found a public bench and took the weight off. Melanie joined me.

'It's about time we made a move,' I said, checking my watch.

We strolled outside. Bernie was waiting for us. The final destination on our all-day tour was The Bund on the banks of the Pudong River. We boarded the minibus and endured another white-knuckle ride through the busy city streets.

The Bund stands as a testament to Shanghai's colonial past. The buildings lining the street are representative of various architectural styles including Gothic, Baroque, Romanesque, Classicism, and Renaissance, everything you'd expect to find on the streets of London. This area was part of the British Concession during the 19th and early part of the 20th century. Major financial institutions took up residency along with newspaper offices, hotels, and other prestigious commercial companies. Today it's a tourist attraction.

On the opposite side of the river is its modern equivalent, the Pudong Financial District. This makes it a great place to have a photo taken with Shanghai's iconic skyline as a backdrop, an opportunity we took full advantage of. Before heading back to the hotel, Bernie was keen to show us the Huangpu Park. Constructed in 1886, the park has become synonymous with the country's humiliation at the hands of Western powers. According to folklore, at the turn of the 20th century a sign used to hang at the entrance stating "No dogs and no Chinese". Bernie made a point of entering the gardens as if to say "Not any more".

We could have walked to the hotel from here but eight hours' touring is enough to tire anyone out. When we arrived back, we thanked Bernie for his insight and tipped both him and the driver.

That evening, after a long shower and longer rest, we ordered a taxi and went back to the French Concession for dinner. The dining experience at lunchtime had encouraged us to seek out more familiar food and despite the upmarket cost, it was a price worth paying.

20

Bunny Hop Carnival

Yesterday's organised tour missed out one very important attraction, the Oriental Pearl Tower. It's not quite in the same league as the Statue of Liberty or Eiffel Tower but it's an iconic landmark recognised throughout the world.

'How are you feeling this morning?' asked Melanie, as we lounged in bed sipping our morning coffee.

'Better than I expected,' I replied.

'And what's on the agenda for today?'

'The Oriental Pearl Tower.'

Melanie leant forward and stared out of the window at the imposing structure.

'I don't know if I'm going to like it,' she replied.

'You'll be fine.'

Melanie is neither claustrophobic nor agoraphobic except when it comes to lifts. For many years she flatly refused to step inside one. Her fear stemmed from two incidents of becoming trapped. The first happened when she was at college. Melanie and her friends thought it would be amusing to commandeer the staff lift. When it broke down, the girls got more than they'd bargained for. That experience left her traumatised to such an extent she didn't step inside another for ten years. When she did, that broke down too.

Years of gentle persuasion have coaxed her back into using them but only as a last resort. Given the choice, she still prefers stairs. Visiting the Oriental Pearl Tower would pose a considerable challenge but one I was determined she would overcome.

During yesterday's visit to The Bund I noticed a sign for The Bund Sightseeing Tunnel. It transports passengers from one side of the Huangpu River to the other. If nothing else, it was worth a look.

After a leisurely breakfast we packed our bags and made our way to reception. The hotel provided a secure place for us to leave them while we continued sightseeing. We decided to walk to The Bund and follow the signs from there. The morning air felt crisp but the sky promised a bright day.

'It must be over there,' I said, pointing at a sign for the tunnel.

The Bund was bustling with visitors, all of them Chinese. The sign took us to an underground station. The main hall was lined with street traders selling all manner of souvenirs. Ticket prices were ridiculously low, less than fifty pence for a return trip. The underground ride was like nothing we'd ever experienced. The driverless carriages ran on a monorail track. Each glass pod carried up to ten passengers. The journey under the river took about five minutes through a tunnel illuminated with animated shapes and accompanying sounds.

Finding our way to the tower was easy: look up and there it is. The queues to enter were as long as the tower is tall.

'What do you think?' I asked.

'It looks busy.'

'Let's give it half an hour and see how quickly it moves.'

Melanie agreed.

With a population of over 1.325 billion it's hardly surprising China has fine-tuned the art of moving people. From the moment we stepped out of the airport, uniformed officials had micromanaged our every move. Managing this enormous queue was a piece of cake. Within half an hour we were well on our way to gaining entry.

The Oriental Radio and TV Tower stands 468 metres (1,536 feet) high and in its day was the world's tallest structure. Its space-age design consists of three main spheres connected by tubular columns. The first (and largest) sphere is called Space City. As the tower climbs the diameter of each sphere decreases.

'I think we'll get in the next one,' I said, as the doors slid closed on one of the fifty-person capacity double-decker lifts.

Melanie looked anxious. I took her hand and squeezed.

'Don't worry, you'll be fine.'

At a rate of seven metres per second the lift returned empty before Melanie had time to dwell. As soon as the doors slid open the officials ushered us inside, the doors closed and in under thirteen seconds we'd travelled ninety metres to Space City.

'That wasn't too bad, was it?' I asked, as we shuffled out.

By the time Melanie had replied the stewards had ushered us into the next elevator. Twenty-five seconds later the doors opened at the main sightseeing floor, 263 metres above ground.

A visit to the upper sphere was optional. At a height of 351 metres, the smallest of the three spheres was appropriately named the Space Module. I thought it wise to let Melanie acclimatise herself to this level before going higher.

The views over the city and the Huangpu River were amazing, even allowing for the hazy veil of air pollution. High-rise apartment blocks stretched as far as the eye could see. The murky brown river looked less appealing. After taking in a 360-degree view of the city, I popped the question.

'Would you like to go up to the Space Module?'

'I don't know about that,' she replied.

'Come on, you'll be fine.'

'You go if you want. I'll wait here.'

Melanie was worrying unnecessarily and might live to regret her decision.

'Thirty seconds, that's all it takes. By the time the doors have closed it'll be time to get out.'

Melanie paused. She'd made it this far; it would be a shame not to go all the way.

'OK.'

Within minutes of joining the queue we were boarding the lift. Seconds later we were stepping out.

From this height, the city looked more like a toy village than a thriving metropolis.

The descent to ground level was as rapid as our rise. I glanced at the time.

'Let's see if we can find somewhere to eat,' I suggested.

Our flight didn't depart until 9:00 pm so we had plenty of time.

'OK but I don't want Chinese.'

The area around the Pudong District is reminiscent of many modern cities. A short walk from the tower we found the Blue Frog American restaurant and bar. Whether real or perceived, the burger and beer was one of the best I'd ever had.

After lunch we strolled back to the river and used the return ticket to travel back through the tunnel. By the time we'd walked to the hotel, the clock had ticked around to 4:30 pm. We collected our luggage and ordered a taxi to take us to Longyang Road Station. This time we were determined to experience the Maglev before leaving.

Once again, China's vision of futuristic design came to life in the station hall. Ticket prices seemed insanely low. Organisation and supervision were impeccable and the link between timetable and operation was uncompromisingly precise.

The train floated silently into the station and the carriage doors slid open. Inside the carriage was as impressive as out, more akin to an aircraft than a train. We took a seat and waited. At the end of the carriage was a digital clock mounted above the aisle doorway. We watched as it ticked over to departure.

The movement of the train coincided exactly with the published timetable. Its seamless acceleration was noted on a digital speedometer immediately below the clock. Within seconds the train had reached a speed of 100 kilometres per hour, and moments later we were travelling at 200 kilometres. In less than two minutes we'd reached its operational speed of 301 kilometres per hour. The only comparison I can make is with an aeroplane taking off but unlike an aircraft the Maglev is as smooth as a china cup.

The wait at the airport was torturously long but we survived. The plane departed on time and we prepared ourselves for another uncomfortably long flight. This time, sleep escaped me. For a brief moment I forgot about my aches and pains as the sun rose above the distant horizon, and hopes of landing were raised when I spotted the coast of Australia. My relief was short-lived. It soon dawned on me that there was the best part of 2,500 kilometres still to fly. A ten-hour, forty-minute flight ended with a bumpy touchdown at Sydney Airport, local time 10:00 am.

Janet had agreed to meet us and take us to her dad's home in Wollongong. British passports speeded our passage through immigration. Melanie had managed to catch some shuteye but we both felt knackered. All I wanted to do was go to bed. Unbeknown to us, Janet had other plans.

One of Janet's daughters, Rachel, had accompanied her to the airport. They greeted us like family. The weather couldn't have been more different; we'd travelled from icy cold to tropically warm. Compared to the smog filled city of Shanghai, Australia seemed warm and inviting with clear skies and vivid colours. My first impressions of suburban Australia took me back to 1976 and a holiday to Florida: large bungalows, clad in timber panels and topped with tin roofs.

In the company of others, particularly those I'm less familiar with, I find it difficult to relax. Questions and conversation kept me on my toes but exhaustion was starting to take its toll. At times I felt disconnected, as if I was watching myself interact rather than participating.

The journey from the airport to Wollongong would normally take an hour along the M1 highway. In her eagerness to share some of the area's secrets, Janet took the coastal route. Having left the main highway, we headed into the countryside.

'Coming up on the right is the entrance to the Symbio Wildlife Park. It's a great place to visit. You can also feed the young kangaroos,' she said as we sped past.

I made a mental note; how long it would survive in my frazzled grey matter was anyone's guess.

After four kilometres we reached the coast and took a detour to Bald Hill Lookout. Janet pulled into a small carpark and stopped.

'Would you like to take a look?' she asked.

My mind was screaming no. All I wanted to do was curl into a ball and sleep.

'We'd love to,' I replied.

'It's busy,' said Melanie, as we stepped from the car.

'It is the weekend,' I said.

Melanie paused for thought. 'No it's not.'

'It's Sunday.'

'No, we left Shanghai on Sunday.'

She was right. I was so tired I didn't even know what day of the week it was.

'Yes it's Monday,' said Janet, as we strolled towards the cliff edge. 'Well, what do you think?'

The view along the coast took our breath away. The Tasman Sea looked like an undulating carpet of aquamarine fringed with bright white lace where it met the land. The coastline meandered into the distance punctuated with golden sandy beaches. Cotton wool clouds floated along the coast as the cool ocean air swept over the clifftops. We weren't the only people enjoying the view. Daredevil hang glider pilots leapt from the cliff like human lemmings. If only my knees could survive the landing, I'd love to give it a go.

'It's beautiful,' replied Melanie, and I had to agree.

By the time we resumed our journey the sea breeze had put a little wind back in our sails. The picturesque route weaved in and out of small coastal villages and towns. An airport run that would usually take an hour ended up taking over two.

Waiting to greet our arrival were Janet's two other children, Melissa, twenty-one and Andrew, fifteen. Her father's house was a cosy, brick-built bungalow in a quiet residential street, close to the centre of town.

'Let me show you around,' she said.

The bungalow had two bedrooms, bathroom, attached garage and small office. A large open plan kitchen, dining room and lounge area led onto a raised deck and despite not having a sea view, the open aspect was very pleasant. We couldn't have wished for a better base from which to explore this vast country.

'So, what have you two been up to since we left Spain?' asked Janet.

Janet's hospitality was commendable but I hadn't slept for thirty hours and catching up on small talk was the last thing on my mind. However the whole family had gone to such an effort to welcome us it would have been rude not to reciprocate their warmth. They lived in Canberra, a three-hour drive away, and like us had been travelling most of the day. When Janet suggested fixing lunch, we couldn't refuse. The afternoon drifted on and we did our best to keep up with the conversation. Eventually, they decided to head home.

'Let me show you the car before we make a move,' said Janet.

I glanced at my watch: 5:30 pm.

'This is Dad's computer,' she said, as we walked through the house. 'I've written his password down so use it as and when you like.'

Their generosity had no bounds.

The three kids followed us outside. Barefoot seemed to be the way to go in Oz.

The vehicle in question was a Kia Carnival, a cross between a car, a minibus, and a van. The thing was enormous.

'We've just had it serviced so you shouldn't have any problems.'

Our ride was equipped with camping gear and a double mattress.

'It's got everything you'll need,' remarked Janet.

We didn't have the heart to tell her our camping days were behind us but the cool box might come in useful.

'Thank you so much and we'll be in touch about coming to Canberra,' I said.

As their car pulled away we waved goodbye.

'I could murder a drink,' said Melanie.

A holiday lunch without a glass of wine had seemed wrong somehow.

'Me too. Let's nip to the supermarket and get a few essentials,' I suggested.

Melanie agreed.

Since passing my driving test I've driven all kinds of vehicles from family saloons to a seven tonne lorry but I have never driven anything quite like the Kia Carnival. There seemed to be a delay between pressing the accelerator pedal and anything happening. It was as if the cable was made out of knicker elastic. From a standing start the car would either bunny hop down the road, stall, or set off like a dragster.

'Craig!'

'It's this car.'

It didn't help that the angle of pedal travel was more up and down than forward and back. For most people this wouldn't pose a problem but my right ankle is pinned in a fixed position. As a result, my knee is the fulcrum of movement rather than the ankle. If you're thinking 'So what', try driving your own car without putting your heel on the carpet. It's not as easy as you might think.

Janet had told us where the nearest shopping centre was and how to get there. To my amazement, I'd actually remembered. The Woolworths name is very familiar to us, but here in Australia it's the country's leading supermarket chain. We had a wander around and picked up a few bits.

'I can't find the wines and spirits aisle,' I said.

'You're joking.'

'No, not even a can of beer.'

'I'll ask someone.'

Melanie approached a shop assistant and asked.

'Well?'

'They don't sell alcohol.'

I was shocked.

'He said there's a shop two doors down that sells it.'

That was a relief.

We paid for the groceries and left.

'Over there.'

The sign above the shop read Liquorland. As the world's fifth largest wine producer I'd expected prices to be keen, but browsing around the store changed that perception. The wineries too were unfamiliar. Choosing a good one would be pot luck.

'That's reasonable,' I said, pointing at a bottle of Merlot.

'I'm not keen on Merlot.'

'Well, what about this?' I said, holding up a Cabernet Sauvignon.

'How much is it?'

'It's on offer, three for twenty dollars.'

'How much is that in real money?'

'About fourteen euros.'

'Fourteen!'

We're used to paying about two euros a bottle for decent stuff.

'It's the cheapest they've got.'

'We'd better try that then.'

That evening we sat outside on the decking sipping a very palatable Cabernet Sauvignon. A fitting drink to christen our first Teatime Taster on the far side of the world. As for the screw-top, the jury is still out.

21

What's in a Name?

Ten hours of unbroken sleep refreshes the parts other activities cannot reach. We enjoyed breakfast outside on the decking before making plans for the day.

'Let's nip back to the shopping centre and see if we can find an optician to tint my glasses,' I suggested.

The morning weather was dull and overcast but confidence was high that it would soon improve.

'We can try and get a SIM card while we're there,' replied Melanie.

Calculating the cost of international roaming was more complicated than quantum mechanics. The simplest solution was to use a local telecommunications provider for local calls. It meant swapping the SIM card over every time we wanted to phone someone in Australia, but better that than an enormous bill once we got back home.

The optician was very helpful.

'They'll be ready tomorrow,' she said.

Ten dollars bought a pay-as-you-go SIM. Things couldn't have gone smoother. We returned to the car and headed home. I was even getting to grips with the Kia Carnival.

'Craig!'

Almost.

Eager to explore our new surroundings, I suggested a run out after lunch.

On their visit to Spain, Janet had been very impressed with the standard of Spanish roads. As a keen driver, I couldn't wait to get here and sample theirs. Even the lower speed limits hadn't dampened my excitement. If anything, I had a driving ambition to experience life in the slow lane. What I hadn't counted on was decades of underinvestment. For one of the richest countries in the world, the road network in Australia sucks.

The main arterial route south is the A1, Princes Highway. This so-called highway is nothing more than a busy main road connecting small communities. Progress was slow, hampered by school speed zones, crossroads, traffic lights, and roundabouts. As for the village names, they seemed to have been plucked from the pages of a cosy mystery. We passed through Oak Flats, Shell Cove, and Dunmore to name but a few. Heaven only knows where Blackbutt got its name.

It took over an hour to travel sixty-two kilometres to the town of Berry. In contrast to other villages, Berry high street wouldn't have looked out of place on the set of a Hollywood Western. Considering Australia's links to Britain and the Commonwealth, I'd wrongly assumed its architecture would be more colonial but Australia has its own very distinctive style.

Given the lateness of the hour and our slow progress, we decided to turn around and head back.

That evening we ate at home and turned in early. Melanie's fidgeting woke me. I rolled over and looked at the clock: 5:30 am, far too early to get up. In the morning, the reason for her restlessness revealed itself.

'Look,' she said, staring at herself in the mirror.

'What?'

'That bloody mozzie has bitten me to death.'

'What mozzie?'

'Don't tell me you didn't hear it.'

'The only thing disturbing me was you.'

'They itch like mad,' she moaned.

Unlike Melanie, I'm one of those lucky folks who rarely get bitten. The only time I did, we were holidaying in Kenya and the damn thing gave me malaria.

By the time I got up, the clock had ticked around to 11:00 am. We drove back to the shopping centre, collected my sunglasses and picked up some insect bite cream from a chemist.

'What are we going to do this afternoon?' asked Melanie over lunch.

'Let's go for another run in the car but take the coast road this time.'

'That's a good idea.'

Progress along the coast road was even slower than the highway but the traffic was much lighter and the scenery far more interesting. Today's trip was about exploring.

'Where are you going?' asked Melanie.

The sign read Bombo Headland.

'Up here.'

A single track climbed to a headland which overlooked the coastal town of Bombo. A stiff breeze whistled through the car as we stepped outside. The town of Bombo runs the length of a long bay bordered by rocky headlands. Row upon row of white breakers crashed onto a sandy beach. Despite the wind the air felt warm. I snapped a few frames before we moved on.

'That sounds interesting,' said Melanie, as we passed a sign to Kiama Blowhole.

'Let's take a look.'

If ever there was a day to view a blowhole this was it. We parked the car and made our way towards the clifftop. From a distance, the whole cliff sounded to be grumbling, and seconds later an almighty boom sent seawater exploding out of the ground. Gusts of wind carried the sea spray fifty metres or more.

'We'd better not get too close,' suggested Melanie.

From Kiama Blowhole we drove further along the coast, stopping at a secluded beach to watch a group of surfers.

'Is that it?' asked Melanie.

We had been watching them for the best part of twenty minutes and not one had attempted to catch a wave.

'Just be patient,' I replied.

After another ten minutes, even I got fed up.

Kids in England hang out on street corners; in Australia it seems they sit on a surfboard in the middle of the ocean.

'Let's carry on along the coast,' suggested Melanie.

The next place we came across was Greenwell Point, a cosy resort established on the bank of a calm lagoon. The focal point was a short, wooden quay. Three small fishing boats were moored alongside. The scene wouldn't have looked out of place on a picture postcard. Close to the quay was a slipway and in between a number of thick wooden anchor posts. Atop each one sat a plump pelican.

Set back from the shore was a quaint café. We wandered over to take a closer look.

'I think it's closed,' I said, as we approached.

'What time is it?'

I glanced at my watch.

'Ten to six.'

It had taken the best part of forty-eight hours to recover from our frenetic time in Shanghai. Adjusting to Australia's opening hours would take a little longer.

'Where is everyone?' asked Melanie.

'I've no idea. Perhaps it's busier at the weekend.'

Walking back to the car I spotted an advertising board hanging in a shop window.

'Look at that,' I said, pointing at the sign.

The notice read 'Boats for Hire'.

'Let's hire a boat,' I suggested.

'What, now?'

'No, not now.'

'When?'

'What about Friday?'

'That's a great idea. I'll make a picnic and we can have lunch on the lagoon.'

'OK, let's book it now.'

I pushed open the door and we stepped inside.

'How long would you like it for?' asked the sales assistant.

We decided two hours would be long enough.

The drive along the coast had been far more interesting than yesterday's run out but with evening drawing in, we decided to take the highway home.

That night we sat outside on the decking. The air was still and the temperature comfortably warm.

'Have you seen this?'

Melanie was reading the reverse of a till receipt from yesterday's shopping at Woolworths. It's funny how married life throws up these bizarre, rhetorical questions that cry out for a sarcastic reply but require tact and servility.

'No darling, what is it?'

'The till receipt from Woolworths.'

I bit my lip and grinned.

'There's a special offer printed on the back.'

'What kind of offer, darling?'

'A four-night midweek break to the Blue Mountains staying at the Rest Easy Motel for $179 per person including two evening meals and two breakfasts. What do you think?'

A country the size of Australia has an infinite number of must-see places. We'd decided to keep our wishlist short in the hope of uncovering a few hidden gems during our stay. One place on our list was the Blue Mountains. The others were the Hunter Valley winemaking region, for obvious reasons, Phillip Island, home to a colony of little penguins, and the Great Ocean Road.

'Why only two dinners and breakfasts?' I asked.

'I don't know, anyway, what do you think?'

Under normal circumstances, I'd spend the next twenty-four hours scouring the internet to shave five dollars off the price but these weren't normal circumstances. We'd saved a fortune on accommodation by swapping homes, I'd found an amazing deal on the flights, and Janet had been incredibly generous providing us with transport. The last thing I wanted was to miss out on something because we were trying to save a dollar. This wasn't a trip for skimping.

'Let's go for it,' I replied.

Melanie looked surprised.

'There's also a two for the price of one offer, on a week-long pass for the Explorer Bus.'

'What's that?'

'Some kind of bus tour.'

'Bus tour?'

The fact we were even considering it seemed bizarre. We love discovering new places but our approach to exploring has more in common with the chaos theory than organised excursions.

'Do we have to decide now?'

'No, we can decide when we get there,' she replied, 'and there's one other offer.'

Woolworths certainly make the most of their till receipts.

'What's that, darling?'

'Another two for one offer for entry to The Edge cinema to watch a movie about the Blue Mountains but we don't have to decide now either.'

I hadn't a clue what she was talking about but went along with it anyway.

The following morning, Melanie rang the booking agent and made the motel reservation.

'All booked. How are we going to get there?' asked Melanie.

'I assumed I'd drive.'

'I wonder if there's a train.'

Wollongong lies on the South Coast railway line. The service ends in Sydney's Central Railway Station, starting point of the Blue Mountains Line.

'Let's nip into town and pick up some timetables from the station,' I suggested.

'Do you know where it is?'

'I can soon find out.'

Having access to the internet was worth its weight in gold. I asked Google Maps and printed off directions.

'Ready when you are,' I said, handing Melanie the map.

Yesterday's wind had subsided, the temperature had risen a few degrees and the humidity had sucked the oxygen out of the air. Thankfully, the Kia's air-conditioning was in tip-top order.

'Look,' said Melanie, as we drove along Wollongong high street.

'What?' I was more concerned with the road ahead than window shopping.

'An Indian restaurant.'

'Let's call in on the way back and pick up a menu,' I suggested.

Parking at the station was pay and display so I waited in the car while Melanie dashed inside.

'Got it,' she said, as she jumped back in.

'Right, let's find that Indian restaurant.'

Once again, I waited in the car while Melanie picked up a menu.

'It looks delicious.'

'Let's book a table for this evening.'

By the time we arrived home, the morning had disappeared.

'What would you like for lunch?' asked Melanie.

'Would you like eat out?'

'Where?'

'Let's go to Symbio Wildlife Park. I'm sure I saw a café when we drove past the other day.'

'OK.'

Within an hour we were pulling into the carpark. We paid the entrance fee and bought two packets of feed for the joeys.

'That must be the most expensive rye-grass in Australia,' I overheard a woman telling her friend.

'The café's closed,' said Melanie.

Fortunately, a mobile vendor was serving a range of hot pies and cold drinks. We sat on a bench in the shade, closely monitored by a pair of roaming peacocks.

'I don't think you're meant to do that,' I said, as Melanie tossed a piece of pie crust their way.

After finishing our pies and downing our beverages we began our tour.

The term "wildlife park" conjures up images of roaming lions and herds of wildebeest. Symbio Wildlife Park was very different. A series of manmade pathways sweep guests from one enclosure to the next. Given the temperature, activity levels were limited. A pool of terrapins was one of the liveliest.

'What is that?' asked Melanie.

I hadn't a clue. It was about the length of a sheep and looked like a furry rat that had been squashed, making it fat and dumpy. I read the information board.

'It's a wombat.'

'It's lovely.'

Which is more than could be said for the occupants of the next compound.

'That is one ugly-looking bird.'

'You're not kidding.'

The bird in question was a cross between an ostrich and an emu except this species had what can only be described as an enormous tumour growing on top of its head. We walked on.

'They're not native to Australia, are they?' I asked.

The animals in question were a mob of meerkats.

'I don't know but they're cute.'

The pathway led us into a stable with animal pens on both sides.

'Oh look,' whispered Melanie, leaning over an enclosure.

I read the description board.

'It's a baby Tasmanian devil,' I whispered.

I couldn't help wondering why such a cuddly creature had been given such an evil sounding name.

Back outside we passed a large enclosure. Sleeping in the shade were a pack of dingoes with a sentry looking on. In the wild, dingoes have a fearsome reputation, and seeing them here reminded me of Jazz.

'There's a red panda in here,' I said, having read the notice. 'Apparently they're rarely seen in the wild.'

'They're not that easy to spot in captivity,' replied Melanie.

We scoured the enclosure looking for signs of life. How hard can it be to spot a panda?

'Perhaps it's on holiday,' remarked Melanie.

No sooner had the words left her lips than the tree's foliage started rustling. We stared into the leafy canopy.

'There,' I said, pointing into the tree.

The trunk of one tree had been placed at a low angle to another, creating a ramp to the floor. Slowly, the panda made its way along the trunk, seemingly oblivious to onlookers. The creature was much smaller than I expected and its long coat was more ginger than red.

Our next port of call was the aviary. The diversity of birds was amazing. Colourful cockatiels and parakeets flew from one perch to another, squawking as they went. I'd never seen such vivid colours: bright greens, reds, purples, and blues, all the colours of the rainbow and a dozen more besides. One species of bird looked like a feathered fish head.

From the aviary we moved on to the focal point of the tour. The young kangaroos, or joeys, were housed on the far side of the park. Two sets of well-spaced gates maintained security. There were about a dozen joeys in the enclosure. Some were taking an afternoon nap, and others were drinking from a water trough. As soon as we entered a few of them pricked up their ears and lifted their heads. They knew exactly why we were there.

Slowly, they ambled towards us. More a four-legged stumble than a hop. Opening the first bag of rye-grass injected some urgency into their approach. Watching Melanie feed these strange yet adorable creatures, it was easy to see how evolution had transformed this dog-like animal into such a unique species. Their mannerisms and temperament were remarkably similar to domesticated pooches but as with all pack animals, one will dominate.

'Get down,' instructed Melanie.

The leader had turned up and demanded feeding.

'Craig, it's stealing the food. Get down. Craig, help!'

I'm not sure what she expected me to do.

'Here,' I said, handing her the camera.

Melanie let out a terrified shrill as her persistent friend wouldn't take no for an answer.

'Take the camera and I'll feed them.'

Melanie grabbed the camera and I lured them away with my grass. Resting on four legs, the joeys were no taller than Jazz. I filled my hand with seed and bent down to feed them. A wet, slobbery mouth nibbled gently at them. I tried to favour the smaller ones over the dominant male but he was having none of it. He pushed them out of the way and started eating. I moved my hand towards the others; he responded by following. The quicker I moved the quicker his response. Eventually, he'd had enough. This cute, dog-like creature stretched his legs and rose from a squat position to look me square in the eyes.

Melanie let out a nervous yelp.

I wasn't sure what to do. The last thing I wanted was this oversized adolescent throwing a tantrum. I thought it wise to concede ground and make a peace offering. My unconditional surrender was accepted but not without restraint. As if to emphasise his superiority he grabbed my arm with his two front paws.

'Play nice,' I said, as his claws drew blood.

Having had his fill, he released his vicelike grip and retired to quench his thirst.

Despite his overzealous attitude, feeding the joeys had been the outstanding event of the day.

'I want one,' said Melanie as we closed the gate behind us.

'You were screaming your head off a minute ago.'

'I know but those smaller ones were lovely,' she replied.

'They do grow up, you know.'

The path we'd been following through the park had almost come full circle. We wandered through a large caged enclosure holding a number of different species of monkeys. Out of all the animals we'd seen, these seemed the least content with their confinement. They were charging around and screaming. The tour finished at the koala house where one of the wardens gave a lecture on koalas and conservation. At the end of the talk we were able to touch one of the young ones. Its coat was indescribably soft and fluffy. If ever an animal shouted 'Cuddle me', this was it.

The park had been nothing like we'd expected but in the most amazing way. Australia's creatures are truly unique.

Back home we sat out on the decking for our Teatime Taster.

'What does BYO mean?' asked Melanie.

'I've no idea, why do you ask?'

'This menu for the Indian restaurant states BYO at the bottom.'

'What's that two for the price of one acronym?'

'Bog off.'

'I beg your pardon.'

'BOGOF, buy one, get one free.'

'It's not that then.'

'It could be bring your own.'

'I bet it is.'

'Are we going to go then?'

'Why not.'

'What time would you like to eat?'

'Eight thirty?'

Melanie dialled the number on the back of the menu.

'Can we make it eight?' she whispered, holding her hand over the receiver. 'The kitchen closes at 8:30 pm.'

I nodded. It was much earlier than we were used to dining, but when in Rome…

The taxi turned up five minutes early which was just as well. Halfway into town I realised we'd forgotten our BYO. To add insult to injury the corkage fee was an outrageous five dollars. I wouldn't mind but the damn thing had a screw-top.

That first dinner in Australia was quite an eye-opener. Within five minutes of us arriving, the couple at the next table left. The manner of their departure highlighted a cultural chasm. In common with many European nationalities, Spaniards love food. Mealtimes are as much a social event as a culinary one. Long, lazy lunches are commonplace and evening meals that continue into the early hours are part of the social fabric. When the gentleman on the next table synchronised his final mouthful of food with rising to his feet, pulling out his wallet and striding toward the cash desk, we were gobsmacked. It seemed strange not to see people enjoying hours of stimulating conversation over copious amounts of coffee and after dinner liqueurs.

Dining out in Australia was a different experience than we were used to. As for the meal, that was delicious. Everything we would have expected from classic Indian cuisine. By the time we left, the main street in Wollongong was deserted. At nine in the evening, we hailed a cab and headed home.

22

Traditional Aussie

While most Australians rushed headlong into a new day, Melanie and I slept. When we finally woke, the clock read 9:20 am. Adjusting to unfamiliar eating hours was one thing; aligning our sleeping patterns to life down under was a step too far.

'What time will we have to set off?' asked Melanie.

We'd arranged to hire a boat from Greenwell Point at 12:00 pm. If we took the Princes Highway instead of the coast road, it should take about an hour and a half.

'About 10:30 am,' I replied.

The weather was a little disappointing, overcast but warm. Despite that I was feeling quite excited at the prospect of skippering my own launch. Melanie prepared a picnic and I packed a bottle of wine. Camping might not be our thing but that cool box was going to come in handy.

We arrived in good time and made a beeline for the hire shop.

'This way,' said a bronzed young man.

He led us to the edge of the lagoon where half a dozen boats were beached. Each craft was identical. The hull was made of pressed aluminium, three metres from stem to stern and a metre and a half starboard to port. A flimsy canopy provided limited shelter from the sun. It was powered by a 50cc outboard motor. The shop assistant dragged ours to the water's edge, half in and half out.

'All aboard,' he said, with an Aussie twang.

Melanie stepped in from the side and the boat keeled over.

'Take a seat in the middle,' he said.

I passed her the cool box and boarded. Once again, the boat rocked to one side. Quickly, I sat down.

'Hang on,' he said.

With an almighty push he slipped the boat into the water. I turned around and watched as we drifted from shore.

'Have you driven a boat before?' he called.

It seemed a bit late to be asking now.

'No,' I yelled.

'It's easy, just follow the instructions on the side,' he shouted, before turning around and striding back to the shop.

I turned to face Melanie. She looked terrified. It's fair to say that in some parts of Spain, health and safety is not as rigidly enforced as it ought to be but I doubt anyone would be launched into the unknown without so much as a by-your-leave. Fortunately, should anything go wrong, we're both strong swimmers.

'We're drifting back to shore,' said Melanie.

I'd taken the bloke's advice and was hurriedly familiarising myself with the operating instructions.

1. All occupants must wear a lifejacket.

I looked around. Not a jacket in sight. I thought it wise to keep quiet and move on.

'Craig, we're drifting towards the shore.'

The urgency in her voice was not helping.

'Craig!'

'Yes dear.'

When all else fails, follow your instincts. Better to be seen doing something than reading uninstructive instructions and besides, how different could it be to starting a petrol lawnmower?

I tugged on the outboard's starter cord. It replied with a lifeless grumble.

'What's wrong with it?'

'It would help if I turned the petrol tap on,' I replied.

A simple mistake to make.

'OK my little beauty, here we go.'

I summoned every ounce of strength and yanked the cord as if our life depended on it. Much to our relief, the little motor burst into life.

The throttle was integrated into the tiller and worked on a similar basis to a motorcycle. I grabbed hold of the grip and opened her up. The tiny motor screamed with joy as the boat nudged forward. Such was its lack of power, I thought the gently rippling water would be enough to beach us. Then, slowly but surely, our tiny, underpowered craft gained momentum and we began to nip along quite nicely. I headed inland, keeping clear of the shallows.

Boats are great fun, at least for the first half hour. After that, bobbing along on the waves becomes a little monotonous.

'Are you ready for lunch?' I asked.

'Why not?'

I piloted the craft to the middle of the lagoon and switched off the motor. The weather had improved throughout the morning. The wind had dropped and there was more than enough blue sky to make a herd of elephants a pair of pyjamas. The earlier swell had dropped to a gentle undulation, which was just as well. Even the shallowest ripples caused the featherlight craft to rock wildly. Melanie unpacked the sandwiches and I opened the wine. Corks might not be the most efficient way to seal a bottle but twisting a screw-top just seems wrong.

'I'd keep hold of that if I were you,' I said, passing Melanie a glass of wine.

She placed the sandwiches on the bench next to her and took the glass.

'Help yourself,' she said.

Somewhat surprisingly we suffered no ill effects from dining on the open water. Quite the contrary, we had a blast.

Confidence in my seamanship had grown throughout the morning. So much so that after lunch I pointed the craft towards the open sea and twisted the throttle. In the distance I could just about make out a line of white water where the ocean waves crashed in the shallows at the entrance to the lagoon. At our current rate of progress, we were unlikely to get anywhere near but Melanie wasn't to know that.

'Where are we going?' she asked.

'I thought we might take a look at the ocean.'

Melanie swivelled in her seat and stared into the distance.

'You've got to be joking.'

'It should be fun.'

'Don't be stupid. You'll end up drowning both of us.'

'You can swim.'

'And what about the boat?'

'Oh, alright then, I'll stay in the lagoon.'

Without warning a grating sound echoed through the flimsy metal hull.

'What's that?' asked Melanie, fear etched across her face.

I closed the throttle and the boat ground to a sudden halt. I peered over the side. If pride comes before a fall, overconfidence precedes disaster.

'We've run aground,' I replied.

'Run aground!'

An invisible sandbank had snared our tiny craft.

'Don't worry, we'll soon be free,' I said, trying to sound positive.

Unfortunately for us, we were further away from our starting point than we'd been all day. I scoured the shoreline but couldn't see a soul.

'Can you see anyone?' I asked.

Melanie scanned the horizon.

'There's no one about.'

Judging distances over open water isn't easy. The shore looked about half a mile away but it could easily have been double that. If push came to shove, one of us would have to swim for it.

'Why aren't there any oars?' asked Melanie.

I'd no idea but now seemed as good a time as any to finish reading the operating instructions. Perhaps they held the key to resolving our dilemma.

'What are you doing?'

Melanie's tone was getting more agitated with each unanswered question.

'I thought I'd read the instructions and see what they say about emergencies.'

'It's a bit late now.'

Hindsight is a wonderful thing.

'You should have been watching where you were going!' she added.

If seafaring mariners were able to spot underwater hazards, maritime history would be very different.

'Aha!'

'What?'

'Reverse.'

Given our current predicament, the one redeeming feature of our plucky little motor was a reverse gear. I flicked a switch on the tiller and twisted the throttle. Slowly but surely the whining propeller dragged us free of the hazard. Melanie let out a sigh of relief followed by a nervous chuckle.

'I told you there was nothing to worry about,' I said.

'Perhaps we ought to head back now,' she suggested.

Perhaps she was right. We'd had quite enough excitement for one day. I headed for the shore and this time beached her intentionally.

'Everything OK?' asked the assistant, on our return.

'We've had a great time,' I replied. The less said about the sandbank the better.

On the drive home, we called at Woolworths to top up our supplies.

Bing bong!

'Will all customers please make their way to the checkout,' echoed over the tannoy.

I looked at my watch. The time was 5:30 pm.

Opening times in Spain take some getting used to but closing a national supermarket at 5:30 pm on a Friday afternoon seemed ridiculous. Another time-related oddity to add to the ever-growing list.

Before dinner, Melanie and I studied the timetables we'd picked up from Wollongong railway station.

'According to this it takes almost two hours to travel from Wollongong to Sydney,' I said.

'That's about as long as it takes from Sydney to Wentworth Falls,' said Melanie. 'How long would it take in the car?'

I booted up the computer and asked Google Maps.

'Less than two hours,' I said.

Melanie was in the kitchen making a start on dinner.

'What do you want to do?'

'Let's take the car and then we can visit Hunter Valley on the way back.'

'That's a great idea.'

After eating we sat outside on the decking. I opened a bottle of red wine and we giggled about the day's activities.

'What are we going to do tomorrow?' asked Melanie.

'I thought we might venture inland.'

'Where to?'

'Let's take a look at those leaflets and plan a tour.'

Prior to our arrival, Janet's father Arnold had visited Wollongong tourist information office and collected a pile of information about local places of interest.

'OK,' she said.

A combination of sea air and Cabernet Sauvignon resulted in a great night's sleep. Over morning coffee, we made our plans. Evidence soon emerged of another cultural difference between Europe and Australia. For most Europeans, the term "local" refers to somewhere nearby, a place to walk to or a short drive away. Australians have a very different definition. To them, "local" is when you can go there and back in the same day.

With the help of Google Maps, we picked some places of interest and organised a "local" self-drive tour. The first attraction to catch my eye was the Macquarie Pass.

'This sounds interesting,' I said.

'What?'

'Macquarie Pass, the most famous road in New South Wales.'

Melanie looked decidedly unimpressed.

Macquarie Pass is an eight kilometre stretch of road, first opened in 1898. It runs through the national park of the same name. The park was established to protect one of Australia's most southerly subtropical rainforests.

'This sounds nice,' said Melanie, handing me the brochure.

Melanie had chosen Corbett Gardens. It wasn't exactly what I'd had in mind but it was en route.

'Lovely,' I replied.

'And what about Fitzroy Falls, is that anywhere near?' she asked.

I looked on the map.

'There,' I said, pointing it out.

'That looks ideal.'

She was right; from Fitzroy Falls we could drive through Kangaroo Valley to Bomaderry and then take the Princes Highway back home – perfect.

'How far is it?' she asked.

'Just over 200 kilometres.'

Now that's what you call a local tour.

Before leaving, Melanie knocked up a picnic and we set off in the Kia Carnival.

The drive took us down the Princes Highway to the intersection with the A48 Illawarra Highway. From there we headed inland. The topography of this part of the coast is like an upturned saucer with a custard tart sitting in the middle. As we drove inland the road climbed steadily until it met the custard tart or in this case the Illawarra escarpment. This impressive geological feature ranges in height from 150 to 750 metres above sea level.

The escarpment marked the start of the Macquarie Pass. The road twisted and turned as it climbed through the subtropical rainforest.

'It says the pass is notorious for accidents,' said Melanie, reading from the brochure.

I had read that but thought it best to keep it to myself.

'Really?'

The road was particularly narrow in some sections and some of the hairpin bends were very challenging. It reminded me a bit of Galicia except our hillsides are usually covered with vineyards. After eight kilometres of coercing the Kia through tight bends we reached the summit of Mount Murray.

En route to Corbett Gardens we passed through Robertson, a large village in the Southern Highlands.

'Guess what this place is called?' asked Melanie as we drove past a road sign.

'Robertson.'

'Not the village, the area.'

How was I supposed to know?

'I give in.'

'Wingecarribee Shire.'

Australian place names are brilliant.

Robertson's one claim to fame is that it was the location for the film *Babe*; even I had to look that one up. From there we drove on to Bowral, site of Corbett Gardens. The gardens are famous for their annual tulip festival. Unfortunately, the event is held in spring. To say we were underwhelmed is an understatement.

'That was rubbish,' said Melanie.

It seemed a little unfair to blame the oversight on her but I couldn't resist teasing.

'If it's tulips you're after, try Amsterdam.'

'Very funny.'

From Bowral we drove through Moss Vale and on to Fitzroy Falls. Entry to the falls was free whereas the carpark cost three dollars.

'Let's have lunch before we walk to the falls,' I suggested.

Melanie unpacked the picnic and we tucked in. The leafy carpark provided much-needed shade from the midday sun. Fed and watered, we set off through the Visitor Centre and along the West Rim walking track to the Twin Falls Lookout.

The track undulates through a fascinating forest of ancient trees interspersed with bright green bracken the size of which we'd never seen before. We paused at a termite mound, two metres in diameter and a metre and a half tall. The track allows fleeting glimpses of Fitzroy Falls which plunges eighty-one metres down a sandstone cliff into the Yarrunga Valley. The view from the lookout platform was jaw-dropping. Mile after mile of subtropical rainforest punctuated by Mount Scanzi, Mount Carrialoo, and in the distance the Ettrema Wilderness. This view alone was worth the drive.

'Where next?' asked Melanie, as we strolled back to the car.

'Kangaroo Valley.'

I was really looking forward to this part of the drive. Seeing kangaroos in captivity is one thing; I couldn't wait to see them in the wild. What better place to do that than Kangaroo Valley?

'Keep your eyes peeled,' I said, as we drove past a sign indicating the start of the valley.

The cabin fell silent as we waited in anticipation of seeing troops of kangaroos.

'Where are they?' asked Melanie, as time slipped by.

'Perhaps they sleep during the day,' I suggested.

'They're kangaroos, not owls.'

'Well I don't know. Perhaps the bloke who discovered the valley killed them all.'

'Aw, don't say that.'

Unfortunately, humans have a habit of destroying anything they don't want or understand.

'Look!' I called.

'Where?'

'There at the side of the road.'

'I can't see any kangaroos.'

'Not kangaroos, pies.'

'Pies?'

'There's another.'

I'd driven past a placard with the words "The World's Best Pies" emblazoned across it. If the claim was true, this was an opportunity not to be missed.

'Let's stop and take a look.'

Kangaroo spotting was placed on hold; there was far more important research to conduct.

Established in 1880, the Old Barrengarry Store is a heritage listed shop and lays claim to being home to the world's best pies. Walking into the shop is like stepping back in time. Old wooden display shelving showcased interesting and unusual products but their speciality is an extensive range of homemade pies: beef and red wine, steak and mushroom, country lamb and veg, and creamy chicken, to name but a few. I was drawn to the Traditional Aussie, packed with savoury minced beef, enhanced with a touch of onions and flavoured with a secret blend of herbs and spices.

'What can I get you today?' asked a cheery sales assistant.

'I'll have a Traditional Aussie, please.'

'Make that two,' said Melanie.

We ordered two chocolate milkshake floats and made our way outside to a quiet garden at the rear of the shop. The pies lived up to their billing; they were delicious. Before leaving we bought a bottle of traditional cream soda to take home.

Our self-drive tour had been a great success. We'd been on the road for almost six hours and covered over 200 kilometres. We'd successfully navigated one of the most dangerous roads in Australia, seen the magnificent Fitzroy Falls, wandered through a magical subtropical rainforest and eaten one of the world's best pies. What more could we ask for?

'It's a pity we didn't see any kangaroos,' said Melanie.

Oh yes, kangaroos.

That evening we called a taxi to take us into town. Tonight's gastronomic delight was Chinese. Under normal circumstances the starters would have been disappointing; given our recent experience we put on a brave face. The main courses, however, were delicious.

'Would you like to go for a drink before we head back?' I asked as we stepped onto the high street.

'That's a good idea.'

Opposite the restaurant was a lively bar with groups of young men and women enjoying their Saturday night.

'Somewhere a bit quieter?' I asked, tipping my head toward the bar.

'I think so.'

We set off walking along the main street in the direction of home. The night air was pleasantly warm and it felt good to stretch our legs after such a filling meal. In the space of a few hundred metres, the environment changed from a lively centre into a ghost town and it wasn't yet 10:00 pm.

'Where is everyone?' asked Melanie.

I'd no idea.

We'd been walking for a good fifteen minutes and hadn't seen another pub. All the shops were closed, all the restaurants were closed and there wasn't a soul in sight.

'What do Australians do at the weekend?'

'I've no idea,' replied Melanie.

'What's that?' I said, pointing at a blue neon sign ahead.

We picked up the pace. As we neared, the faint thump of music floated on the warm air.

'I think it's a pub,' said Melanie.

She was right. The heavy bass beat was accompanied by the wailing strings of a rock guitar and a vocalist belted out an unfamiliar tune. Standing around the entrance was a group of ageing, leather-clad rockers and parked outside were a few unloved muscle cars and half a dozen motorbikes. Had we not been gasping for a drink, we would probably have walked past. As it was, we couldn't wait to get inside.

The volume increased as we pushed open the door. The four-piece band were squeezed onto a small stage to our right. The lead guitarist wrestled with his instrument as the singer screamed into the mic. A few enthusiastic members of the audience tossed their heads back and forth while others looked on emotionless. In our present attire, Melanie and I stood out like vicars in a strip club. Avoiding direct eye contact, we made our way to the bar. A denim clad barman tipped his head as if to say, what do you want?

'Two minis (half pints of beer),' I shouted at the top of my voice.

My knowledge of the local lingo failed to impress but garnered the right result. I paid for the beers and we moved to a less conspicuous place nearer the exit. Better safe than sorry.

The cold beer hardly touched the sides. It felt like we'd been walking for hours, but the noise was continuous and deafening.

'Let's move on,' I suggested.

'What?' screamed Melanie.

'Let's go!'

Melanie agreed. Away in the distance, a halo of light emanated from a large modern building.

'Is that the hospital?' I asked.

Arnold's home was a five-minute walk from the hospital and by the look of things, we were close.

'Look,' said Melanie, pointing at a street sign, 'Wollongong Hospital.'

Ten minutes later we were back at Arnold's.

It was too early to turn in so we sat outside on the decking with a glass of wine, pondering the merits of a society whose city centres are deserted by 10:00 pm on a Saturday night.

23

Ships in the Night

Australia was full of surprises. Discovering the world's best pie shop in Kangaroo Valley was one example. Time was passing at an alarming rate. Four weeks and four days sounds like a long holiday but tomorrow marked the end of our first week and the start of our four-day trip to the Blue Mountains. Between now and then we had to make plans to visit the remaining two destinations on our wish list, Phillip Island and the Great Ocean Road.

By lunchtime, we'd made the arrangements and reserved the accommodation. A 3,000-kilometre road trip over nine days, staying at seven locations, in three different states. I for one couldn't wait to get started.

That afternoon we drove to the seafront in Wollongong to find a suitable venue for our Teatime Taster. White horses skipped across a turquoise blue ocean and the afternoon sun felt warm and comforting. We made our way to Beach Cove, a picturesque harbour protected from the ocean by manmade jetties. Colourful boats bobbed gently on the calm water. The Harbourfront Restaurant looked like the perfect place to watch the setting sun. We took a seat and waited to be served.

'Sorry mate, I can't serve alcohol unless you order a meal,' explained the waiter.

I looked around. There wasn't another bar or restaurant in sight. I wouldn't have minded but the place was almost empty. I doubt I'll ever understand the mindset of a nation that fails to appreciate the spiritual merits of a Teatime Taster.

In the end we ordered an ice cream from a street vendor and sat on a park bench overlooking the sea. Very pleasant but not quite the same.

The following day we decided to take the scenic route to the Blue Mountains. From Wollongong we drove through Appin, Campbelltown, Harrington Park, and Penrith before reaching the Rest Easy Motel in Wentworth Falls.

'Would you like to book a table for dinner?' asked the receptionist after we'd checked in.

'What time does service begin?'

'A quarter past six,' she replied.

We'd had a late lunch so declined.

The room was a good size, light and airy with a king-size bed, sitting area, and a small balcony with distant views across the Blue Mountains.

We dropped our bags and headed out to Katoomba, self-styled capital of the Blue Mountains tourist industry.

'Look,' said Melanie, as we wandered down the main street, 'it's the booking office for the Explorer Bus.'

We popped inside and picked up a leaflet. Having got our bearings, we drove on to the neighbouring suburb of Leura before driving back to the village of Wentworth Falls to find somewhere to eat.

'This looks good.'

Melanie was standing outside the Canton Palace restaurant, looking at a menu in the window. We decided to give it a go. The food was OK but nothing to write home about. Before turning in we sat outside on the balcony, sipping wine and listening to the hypnotic sounds of night-time insects.

'Where's that Explorer Bus leaflet?' I asked.

Melanie pulled it from her handbag.

'Here you go.'

I took a sip of wine and flicked through the information.

'What do you think?' she asked.

'It looks interesting. Perhaps we ought to give it a whirl.'

To make sure we didn't miss breakfast, Melanie set the alarm clock. At 7:30 am it jolted us into a new day.

'What time is breakfast?' I asked.

'Between eight and nine.'

'And what time does the Explorer Bus arrive?'

'Nine thirty.'

The dining room was quite busy when we arrived. A couple of waiters were racing around clearing tables.

'Over there,' said Melanie.

The buffet-style breakfast ran the full length of one wall. For an all-inclusive package, the selection was fantastic.

'Are you sure you've got enough?' remarked Melanie, when I returned carrying a plateful.

'For now.'

The selection on offer included a range of health foods but an army marches on its stomach and we had a busy day ahead. I opted for lean rashers of bacon, scrambled eggs, a couple of pork sausages, fried tomatoes and baked beans. Having downed that I couldn't resist two rounds of toast, strawberry jam and fruit juice. Ready for the day ahead, we marched off to catch the Explorer Bus.

A small crowd had gathered around the bus stop. The weather was warm and dry. By the look of things, it had rained earlier but the clouds were lifting. The wait gave

Melanie the opportunity to flick through the leaflet. The crowd's relaxed mood changed as soon as the bright red ex-London Transport double-decker came into view. Jostling for position seemed unwarranted; this was the first pickup of the day. Melanie and I waited for the mêlée to subside before presenting our voucher to the driver, along with the required fee. He handed us our bus passes and we climbed the stairs to the top deck.

The Explorer Bus follows a twenty-nine-stop route and takes an hour to complete. Two buses, half an hour apart, cover the route. Passengers can hop on and off as they choose knowing the next bus will be along shortly.

'What do you want to see?' asked Melanie.

The Scenic World attraction was a must, but other than that, I wasn't sure.

'Why don't we stay on the bus for the first circuit and get our bearings?' I suggested.

'OK.'

The driver's running commentary made it easy for passengers to know exactly where they were and what there was to see. The views from the upper deck were excellent and the scenery awe inspiring. Australia was like nowhere else we'd ever been. Even on a busy bus, the vastness of the wilderness gave me a feeling of isolation, almost as if I was the only person in the world to have seen this boundless panorama. The land is ancient, the forests prehistoric. At any minute I half-expected a herd of diplodocus to pop their heads above the treetops and sing out across the valley.

After completing a full circuit, we picked our first attraction.

'Let's stop at Scenic World. We can start with a ride on the Skyway,' I suggested.

Scenic World is the premier tourist attraction in the Blue Mountains. One of its activities is the Skyway, a glass-bottomed cable car suspended 270 metres above the rainforest. It travels 720 metres from a cliff top and finishes in the Visitors' Centre. En route it provides excellent views of the Three Sisters rock formation, Katoomba Falls and the Jamison Valley.

'I'm not sure I'll like it,' said Melanie.

'You'll be fine. Compared to the Oriental Pearl Tower, this will be a walk in the park.'

When the bus came to a stop we were in such a rush to get off we didn't notice the weather. Conditions had been improving throughout the morning but a stubborn layer of mist blanketed the valley floor.

'We can't go on it in this,' I said. 'We won't see a thing.'

Melanie was happy to postpone the trip. That left us betwixt and between.

As you might expect, the entrance to the Skyway is situated in quite an isolated location.

'Come on, let's walk to the next bus stop.'

A leisurely stroll helped pass the time.

The next bus to arrive was another ex-London Transport vehicle but unlike the first, this was a single-decker bendy bus.

'What would you like to do now?' asked Melanie, as we took our seat.

I glanced at my watch.

'What about a beer?'

'That's a good idea.'

Despite our lofty location, humidity remained high. The slightest effort gave rise to a dry throat and raging thirst. According to the map, we were five stops from Solitary, a converted cottage transformed into a restaurant and café.

'Solitary restaurant and café,' rattled over the PA as the bus came to a stop.

The views from the garden to Mount Solitary, Kings Tableland, the Jamison Valley and across to the Southern Highlands were breathtaking.

'Let's sit over there,' said Melanie, pointing at a table on the edge of the garden.

We took a seat and waited in silence, drinking in the jaw-dropping scenery.

'What can I get you?' asked a young waitress.

We were so intoxicated with the panorama, we hadn't seen her approach.

'Two beers please,' I replied.

'I'm sorry sir but we're not allowed to serve alcohol without a food order.'

I glanced at my watch, 11:40 am.

'Can we have a drink while we read the menu?' I asked.

'Certainly sir,' she replied, before heading back to the cottage.

'What happens if we drink the beer and decide not to order anything?' asked Melanie.

'I think they transport you to the colonies,' I whispered.

The gourmet menu was quite a surprise. Fingers crossed the chef could deliver on his promises.

By the time we'd placed our order the clock had ticked around to midday and we were ready for another beer. More diners arrived, staring enviously at our prime location. The food lived up to its billing. Complex dishes lovingly prepared and beautifully presented.

'This is delicious. How's yours?' asked Melanie.

'Really good.'

I knew what was coming next.

'Can I have a taste?'

'Certainly dear.'

Solitary is one of those special places that requires a real effort to leave. We'd been fed and watered in style, bathed in the afternoon sunshine and submerged in the stunning scenery but all good things must come to an end and we had a bus to catch.

'Where now?' asked Melanie.

As well as the Skyway, Scenic World has a number of other attractions. Time was moving on and the last bus back to the Rest Easy Motel left Katoomba Station at 4:45 pm. With this in mind, we decided to postpone our visit to

Scenic World until tomorrow in favour of the Three Sisters rock formation.

The sandstone cliffs in the Blue Mountains are over fifty million years old. The Three Sisters are three sandstone stacks sculptured by natural erosion and the passage of time. They're best viewed from Echo Point Lookout, so we hopped on a bus and enjoyed a leisurely ride to the viewing point.

Our first full day in the Blue Mountains reminded me of *The Wheel of Fortune*: round and round she goes; where she stops nobody knows. Riding on the bus reignited childhood memories. It had been great fun and we'd seen some unforgettable sights. Tomorrow we would venture out with a much clearer picture of where to go and what to see.

Bright sunshine coaxed us gently into a new day. A hearty breakfast prepared us for a day of exploration. First stop, The Edge cinema. Somewhat uncharacteristically, we'd taken advantage of the two for the price of one offer to watch the 1996 film, *Wild Australia – The Edge*. Filmed in the Blue Mountains, this forty-minute documentary explores the relationship between humans and their environment. The cinematography was outstanding and the IMAX production was almost as surreal as emerging from a cinema at ten-thirty in the morning.

We only had one venue in mind for lunch, the Solitary café. Imagine our disappointment finding someone else occupying our favourite table. This time we looked on enviously.

We'd reserved the entire afternoon for our visit to Scenic World. We began our adventure on the Skyway cable car. The views of the rainforest through the glass floor were spectacular. If only Melanie had found the courage to open her eyes. The Skyway floats effortlessly from a rocky outcrop into the Scenic World Visitors' Centre.

'What now?' asked Melanie.

Scenic World boast four attractions, the Skyway, the Walkway, the Cableway, and the Railway. The last two provide access to the Walkway.

'Let take the Railway down to the Walkway and the Cableway back,' I suggested.

The Railway claims to be the steepest passenger railway in the world. It falls 310 metres at an angle of fifty-two degrees, passing through a tunnel during its spectacular descent. Passengers disembark on the forest floor and join the Walkway, a 2.4-kilometre elevated pathway through a section of ancient Jurassic rainforest which ends at the Cableway.

'I'm not going anywhere near that railway,' insisted Melanie.

'You'll be fine. Everyone is strapped in.'

'You can if you want but I'll take the Cableway and meet you at the bottom.'

Melanie's suggestion seemed like a reasonable compromise. I waited in line to board the train and Melanie looked on, waving me goodbye as it began its slow descent. The train journey was over in the blink of an eye which was somewhat disappointing. The footpath through the rainforest to the Cableway was clearly signposted. The forest floor was fascinating; the plants looked like they'd been plucked from the set of *Jurassic Park*. I half-expected to see dinosaurs running around.

Before I realised, I'd strolled its length and hadn't seen sight nor sound of Melanie. I'd stopped a few times along the way to take photos but kept an eye out. The Cableway is capable of transporting eighty-four passengers from the top of the escarpment to the floor of the Jamison Valley, 510 metres below. It had just started its descent so I waited. Trust Melanie to be late.

The huge glass-panelled car was by no means full but I couldn't see Melanie. Perhaps she'd changed her mind.

As it slowed to a stop, I was caught in two minds. Should I go back to the Visitors' Centre and search for her or wait here to see if she turned up? Who knows; perhaps we'd passed on the Walkway like ships in the night. If only I'd made a note of her new phone number, I could have given her a ring.

Dilemma, dilemma.

My indecisiveness was quickly overshadowed by a pang of guilt. What if she'd been too scared to board the Cableway and I'd abandoned her in her time of need? Guilt succumbed to logic.

The entry fee to Scenic World included one pass to travel on each of the three modes of transport. If I used my Cableway pass to return to the Visitors' Centre and she wasn't there, I'd have to pay to get back to the valley floor and then pay a second time to get back up. Was she worth it? Of course she was.

After the briefest hesitation I boarded the Cableway and headed back to the Visitors' Centre. The view from the cable car was breathtaking as it climbed above the rainforest and up the escarpment.

As soon as I disembarked I looked across at the queue waiting to descend and watched as one by one they boarded. The last person stepped on and the door slid closed. I moved away and wandered around the busy Visitors' Centre searching for her. I checked the café but nothing and hung around outside the ladies' for five minutes, still nothing. My initial frustration melted into mild concern.

Where could she be?

The information desk seemed like my last hope but did I have the courage to admit to misplacing my wife?

What else could I do?

Before submitting myself to such an embarrassing claim I made one final sweep but nothing. Oh well, here goes.

Two young ladies were standing behind the desk directing a family to the Skyway.

'Hi sir, my name's Tracy, how can I help you today?'

A polite and well-rehearsed response.

'Erm... I seem to have lost my wife, and I wasn't even trying to.'

My attempt to make light of her disappearance failed to impress. My explanation of events proved far more useful.

'Don't worry sir, I'm sure we'll find her.'

A comedic response seemed inappropriate.

'Would Melanie Briggs please make her way to the information desk, Melanie Briggs,' blasted out over the tannoy.

My private embarrassment became a public broadcast. The harder I tried to blend into my surroundings the more conspicuous I felt.

Having made the announcement, Tracy returned to her normal duties. A few minutes passed before I summoned the courage to lift my head and take a look around.

'Mr Briggs,' called Tracy.

I turned to face her.

'We've found your wife. She's waiting for you in the rainforest at the end of the Railway. I've spoken with my colleagues and you're welcome to go and meet her.'

Her discovery was never in doubt but Tracy's timely message was gratefully received. By the time we were reunited, Melanie had worked herself into an emotional frenzy. Tears ran down her cheeks as she flung her arms around me and wept with relief. Once she'd calmed down we strolled back through the forest towards the Cableway.

'What happened?' I asked.

'It was awful, really awful. The path kept going down and down deeper into the forest. The foliage was so thick it was like night-time.'

'Where did you go?'

'When I got off the cable car I just followed everyone else.'

'Where to?'

'I don't know. I kept walking and walking. I was convinced we'd bump into each other. Before I knew it everyone else had gone and I was all on my own and scared.'

Tears welled in her eyes.

'Oh love, what did you do?'

'I sat down and started crying.'

'Oh Melanie, I'm sorry. What happened then?'

'A group of four people saw me and asked what was matter.'

'What did they say?'

'They said I'd walked the wrong way.'

Finally, we were getting to the crux of the matter. It turned out that after leaving the Cableway, the group she followed turned left into the rainforest instead of right toward the Railway. She could have walked forever and our paths would never have crossed.

By the time she'd retraced her steps and walked the 2.4 kilometres back to the Railway, I'd already reported her missing. When she asked staff if they'd seen me, they knew exactly who she was.

As luck would have it, we emerged from Scenic World just in time to catch the last bus back to the Rest Easy.

'I think we'll dine here tonight,' I said, as we strolled through the lobby.

'That's a good idea,' replied Melanie. 'I think we've had quite enough excitement for one day.'

The gentle pitter-patter of rain greeted our third and final full day in the Blue Mountains. We decided to give the bus a miss in favour of the car.

'Let's go a little further afield today,' I suggested.

The night before I'd been studying the map. The Blue Mountains National Park covers an area of over 2,500 square kilometres. We didn't have time to see it all but we could at least see a little more.

'OK but can we stop at Bygone Beautys on our way out?' asked Melanie.

Bygone Beautys is a privately-owned teapot museum and tearoom in the village of Leura. It lies on the Explorer Bus route but we hadn't found time to stop. We'd usually stay clear of such tacky sounding tourist attractions but an advert for Devonshire cream teas had piqued our interest. Both of us have fond childhood memories of indulging in this opulent treat. Such recollections are often better left in the past but the temptation was too strong.

'That's a great idea.'

'We can call there after we've been to Wentworth Falls.'

By the time we left the Rest Easy, the rain had stopped. The Falls are a short drive from the motel. We parked the car in a wooded area and walked along a forest path to a viewing point at the edge of an escarpment. The scenery was spectacular. Over millennia, the action of running water has created a dramatic series of waterfalls cascading down a horseshoe shaped rock formation, framed in an endless ocean of rainforests. I used to think the area around Huddersfield was hilly and wild until we moved to Galicia; Australia brings a whole new meaning to the word "wilderness".

'Ready for your elevenses?' I asked.

'Yes please.'

Five minutes after leaving Wentworth Falls we reached the village of Leura. We parked on the street and entered the Teapot Museum. Fascinating as it was, it's a once in a lifetime experience: once you've seen one teapot, you've seen them all. The Devonshire cream tea on the other hand was an absolute triumph. Two light, airy scones packed with plump sultanas, smothered with a generous blob of homemade strawberry jam and topped with a liberal dollop of clotted cream. All for just $5.50. Childhood reminiscences were free.

Our self-drive tour of the Blue Mountains took us to Lithgow and Richmond before returning to the Rest Easy. That evening we drove into Katoomba to eat at Anki's Indian Restaurant. Excellent food and BYO, a fitting end to a brilliant trip. Tomorrow we'd be heading back to Wollongong via the Hunter Valley wine growing region.

We decided to skip breakfast in favour of an en route stop. During yesterday's sightseeing tour of the National Park we'd driven past several cafés offering freshly made fruit pies close to the town of Bilpin. The area around the town is known locally as the "Land of the Mountain Apple".

The clock had ticked around to 9:00 am by the time we'd checked out. An hour and a half later, we pulled into the roadside carpark of the Tutti Fruitti café. I'm not one to break a confidence but its claim to be the best kept secret in the Blue Mountains might be in danger.

The café is housed in a beautifully appointed wooden hut with a traditional tin roof. Outside is a covered porch with tables and chairs on both sides of the entrance. The weather was perfect, warm and sunny, so we took a seat on the decking and waited to be served. The homemade apple pie was to die for: crisp shortcrust pastry, bursting with sweet apples.

Within two hours of leaving the Tutti Fruitti we reached the Hunter Valley wine growing region.

'Are we going to stop for a taster?' asked Melanie.

'Of course, we can't visit Hunter Valley and not try the wine,' I replied.

We'd entered the valley along Putty Road and then turned right down Milbrodale Road. The valley was much flatter and broader than I'd imagined with row upon row of grapevines, as far as the eye could see.

'What about there?' said Melanie, pointing at a sign.

The notice advertised wine tastings for six dollars per person at Nightingale Wines. How could we resist?

'Why not?'

We turned off the main road and drove through the vineyard to the winery. By the look of the foliage, the grapes had recently been harvested. As well as a visitors' reception, the winery offers a fine dining restaurant and rental units for visiting tourists.

'Let's stay for lunch,' I suggested.

'It looks a bit pricey,' remarked Melanie.

'We're on holiday and besides which diners get a free wine tasting tour.'

The menu looked amazing but one dish caught my eye: kangaroo fillet.

'I'm going to have the fillet,' I said.

'You're joking?'

She knew me better than that. We'd been in Australia for eleven days, covered over 1,000 kilometres and we still hadn't seen a kangaroo in the wild. I figured if I couldn't see one, I might as well eat one, and what better place to try such a delicacy than in a top restaurant.

The fillet was delicious and no, it doesn't taste like chicken.

Before leaving, the winery manager accompanied us on a wine tasting tour and gave us an insight into the facility's capabilities. Learning about the different harvesting techniques was fascinating. Unlike the Ribeira Sacra where all the grapes are handpicked, in these vast flat vineyards, mechanical pickers strip the vines. The wines they produce are very good with clean, predictable flavours but for me, there's more to winemaking than mechanised management and scientifically controlled fermentation.

By the time we arrived back in Wollongong we'd been on the road over seven hours and covered almost 550 kilometres. We'd had a fruity breakfast, a bouncing lunch, and were just about to order a Domino's pizza. Before then, there was the small matter of the week's washing to catch up with. The day after tomorrow we'd be heading off again.

24

A Period Feature

Since our arrival, Janet's father Arnold had been staying in Sydney with his son Ross. In a week's time the pair of them were heading off to explore Tasmania. Arnold asked if he could come home for a few days to prepare for the trip. We were happy to oblige.

Midway through Saturday morning, Ross dropped him off. Arnold was one of the nicest people you could wish to meet. We spent most of the afternoon sitting outside on the decking listening to his life story. Now aged ninety, he'd fought in the Second World War, helped establish the university in Wollongong, was a keen golfer and, up until his knees started playing up, had been a passionate surfer. His prowess with a golf club was evident in the two mounted golf balls proudly displayed on the sideboard, recognition of him twice holing out in one, a feat most golfers only dream of.

'Take a look at the photo hanging in the hallway,' he said.

Melanie and I wandered through into the hall.

'Recognise it?' he called.

The photo was of the Sydney Harbour Bridge with a group of school children walking across escorted by their teachers.

'It's Sydney Harbour Bridge,' I shouted back.

'Recognise anyone in it?' he asked.

The photo was an old black and white print; the edges had started to fade and the focal clarity reflected its age.

'He must be in it,' whispered Melanie.

'How are we supposed to recognise him amongst all those kids?'

'Are you in it?' called Melanie.

'I'm the lead teacher,' he replied.

Melanie and I bent closer, straining to see the facial features. To be honest, it could have been anyone but there was no doubting his veracity. We ambled back outside and Arnold recalled the day's events. On the day prior to the official opening, local school children had been given the opportunity to cross. It was amazing to think we were sitting in the company of one of the first members of the public to walk across Sydney Harbour Bridge. What to us is a period in history was an event in Arnold's life.

'They even had to move my sister's house to build it,' he added.

Arnold explained that when the government compulsorily purchased the land on the approaches to the proposed new bridge, residents were given two options: move into a brand-new house nearby or have their existing home moved to Richmond, on the outskirts of the city. His sister chose the latter.

'To this day you can see where they cut the house in two,' he said.

Being built of timber, the contractors sawed his sister's house in half, transported it to Richmond and joined it back together. Now that's what you call a period feature.

Arnold was one of the most interesting people I'd ever met. Not only had he lived through history but more importantly he'd participated in its making.

The following morning, Arnold had been up and about for quite some time before we showed our faces. While Melanie put the kettle on, I packed the car. Before saying goodbye, we enjoyed one last coffee together. By the time we returned, Arnold and Ross would be travelling the backroads of Tasmania in Ross's purpose-built off-road explorer. Living rough seemed to be part of the attraction.

The first stopover on our nine-day expedition was the seaside village of Marlo. We'd chosen it because it was halfway between Wollongong and Phillip Island. Australians use the term "unit" as a generic name for many types of residential properties, from studio apartments to detached family homes. The unit we'd booked was a two-bedroom bungalow on a contemporary residential complex.

Planning the route was straightforward: drive south along the Princes Highway for 610 kilometres and turn left until you reach the ocean. To date, the town of Berry was the limit of our southerly exploration, some sixty kilometres from Wollongong. We were about to discover that this section of the highway was one of the most interesting.

Mile after mile, hour after hour we tootled down the Princes Highway with nothing to see but trees. From Berry we passed through Nowra before reaching Mollymook where we enjoyed fleeting glimpses of the ocean. Next came Batemans Bay, Mogo, Moruya, Narooma, Bega, Merimbula, and Eden. Shortly after leaving Eden we crossed the border from the state of New South Wales into Victoria. On a map it's marked with a dashed line. In reality it's even less distinguishable. Next came Cann River and finally Orbost where we turned left, following the Snowy River into the coastal resort of Marlo. After such a long and uninteresting drive Marlo wasn't quite the picturesque coastal village we'd hoped for.

The property was described as being less than fifty metres from the sea which was true, if somewhat misleading. What they'd failed to mention was the natural flood barrier which obscured the ocean view. Inside the bungalow had a very bohemian feel. There were handcrafted mobiles hanging from the bedroom ceiling which featured a painted mural of the night sky. The second bedroom housed an early Ikea-style bunk bed and children's clothes were hanging in the wardrobe. Cleanliness is a relative term but this place needed a good scrub. Later that evening Melanie discovered that only one of the hob's three rings actually worked, but nevertheless she rustled up a very tasty chicken curry.

'Look on the bright side,' I said, as we readied for bed.

'What bright side?'

'From here on in, things can only get better.'

'Hmm,' she murmured, as I switched off the light.

After a good night's sleep, we were ready for off. One hundred kilometres south of Marlo we finally emerged from the never-ending forest into a landscape of open flatlands and arable fields. At the town of Sale we left the A1 highway and joined the A440. By lunchtime we'd reached the coastal town of Port Welshpool.

'Let's stop and get something to eat,' I suggested.

Melanie agreed.

I pulled off the main highway and followed the signs. The layout of the port and the style of the houses gave it the appearance of an out of season holiday park.

'There's a café,' said Melanie.

I pulled into a small carpark and we walked inside. The place was empty.

'What can I get you?' asked a bubbly assistant.

The menu consisted of an extensive range of pies and a variety of different burgers.

'I'll have The Lot Burger, please,' said Melanie.

This wasn't the first time we'd seen it on a menu but it was the first time we'd plucked up the courage to order one.

'Make that two,' I said, 'and chips.'

A strong sea breeze forced us to dine inside. When the waitress brought our burgers we were speechless.

'Enjoy,' she said, as she placed them on the table.

From bun to bun, the stacked burger stood fifteen centimetres tall. The thick, meaty burger was sitting on a bed of lettuce and sliced tomato and topped with cheese, pickled beetroot, two rashers of bacon, and fried onions. Its crowning glory was a fried egg, sunny side up with a scrumptious runny yolk. We could have done without the side order of thick-cut fries but we devoured the lot.

Having eaten our fill, we continued on our journey. Less than two hours later, we crossed the bridge from the town of San Remo on the mainland, to Phillip Island. We'd booked a two-night stay at the Cottages for Two resort in Cowes, the island's self-professed capital. With yesterday's hippy retreat fresh in our memory we approached the reception desk with a heightened sense of anxiety.

'Here it is,' said the shift manager who'd led us through mature gardens to our contemporary cottage.

A tall gate led onto a small private terrace with a gas barbecue tucked away in one corner.

'This looks more like it,' I commented, as I slipped the key into the front door.

Inside, the cottage looked like a modern apartment. It was bright and spotlessly clean with an open plan kitchen, dining room, and lounge. Three steps led to the bedroom which was large enough to dwarf a jumbo-sized bed. Carefully arranged pillows embroidered with the names Romeo and Juliet set the scene and the en suite bathroom featured a jacuzzi big enough to bathe the forward line of Australia's national rugby team. We couldn't have been happier.

After a good poke around we wandered back to reception.

'Can you tell us where we can buy tickets for the Penguin Parade?' I asked.

The receptionist directed us to the tourist information office in the centre of town.

'If you're quick you should catch them before they close,' he said.

At this time of day, people in Spain have only just returned to work after lunch. Here in Australia the working day was drawing to a close. Despite the lateness of our arrival, the tourist information centre assistant was very helpful and surprisingly enthusiastic. We purchased our tickets and she explained how to get there.

'How long are you staying on the island?' she asked.

'Two days.'

'You might wish to visit these attractions as well,' she replied, handing us some leaflets.

We thanked her for her time and left. Next stop the local supermarket for a few essential supplies.

'Let's have a barbecue tomorrow,' I suggested.

'OK. What shall we have?'

It seemed a shame to travel halfway around the world and not try some Australian lamb.

'What about lamb steaks?'

Melanie agreed.

'Look at these,' I said, pointing at a pack of sausages.

'What are they?'

'Kanga bangers.'

'You're joking.'

'No, look,' I replied, showing her the pack of six.

'What are they made of?'

'What do you think?'

'They're not.'

'They are, kangaroo.'

'I'm not eating them.'

'We've got to try them.'

'You can if you want but I'm not eating a kangaroo.'

If the fillet was anything to go by, these sausages would be delicious.

'Please yourself but I'm getting a pack.'

That evening we left the cottage at 7:30 pm. Entry to the Penguin Parade started at 8:00 pm and we didn't want to miss anything. We'd been looking forward to this since Melanie read about it in the guidebook Claire had bought us. Excitement flooded the car and all the chatter was of penguins.

Australia was surpassing all our expectations. We were convinced that tonight would be no different. The only disappointment so far was the lack of wild kangaroos. We'd passed a few lifeless specimens at the side of the road. Melanie preferred to think of them as sleeping as opposed to roadkill. As we sped towards the Penguin Parade, the headlights caught two staring eyes. I was so surprised to see a live kangaroo my brain collided with my speech.

'Penguin!' I blurted out.

'It's to be hoped not,' quipped Melanie.

'I mean kangaroo.'

The sighting passed in the blink of an eye and the animal disappeared into the twilight. Melanie burst out laughing.

'It's all this talk of penguins,' I explained.

'Are you sure you don't mean kangaroos?' She chuckled.

I'd never hear the last of this. I ignored her sarcastic remark and looked at the milometer.

Since landing in Sydney we'd covered over 3,000 kilometres and this was the first live kangaroo we'd seen in the wild.

Given the lateness of the hour, we were surprised by the number of cars in the carpark. Before being admitted to the beach area, a park warden instructed everyone in the etiquette of penguin watching. The thrust of his remarks involved the prohibition of cameras. Standing thirty centimetres tall (one foot), little penguins are the smallest species of penguin. By chance, our visit coincided with the breeding season. Young chicks were waiting in beachside nests for their parents to return with the day's catch. Flash photography could frighten these sensitive creatures into seeking new nesting grounds away from man's prying eyes. The warden's advice was duly noted.

A series of raised boardwalks stretched out across the beach from the reception centre. The expectant crowd fanned out, staring into the sea. At 8:30 pm the first sightings were made. Dark shapes silhouetted against the ocean dived under and over the waves as they made their way ashore. In the water, their grace and agility are matched only by their comical clumsiness out of it. One after another the little penguins waddled ashore. They reminded me of potbellied drunkards stumbling across the beach, occasionally falling over and rolling around on their tummies before staggering back to their feet.

In the space of half an hour their number grew from one to one hundred. A hundred little penguins wobbling their way home after an exhaustive day fishing. Under the light of a southern moon, Mother Nature created a production Walt Disney could only dream of.

The colony consisted of more than 1,100 penguins. As we strolled back to the reception centre we watched as families were reunited and dinner was served.

The clock had ticked around to 10:30 pm by the time we got back to the cottage. We sat outside on the terrace sipping wine and reminiscing about the evening's events. This was one experience we would never forget.

'What's that?' I asked.

Melanie had nipped inside and returned carrying some papers.

'They're the leaflets from the tourist information office.'

She handed me one.

'This looks interesting,' she said.

'What is it?'

'A koala conservation park. "Visit the koalas in their natural habitat",' she read.

'We could go there tomorrow morning and go here in the afternoon.'

'Where?'

'Churchill Island Homestead.'

'What's that?'

'Some kind of museum.'

Melanie's expression said it all.

'We can take a look for nothing,' I replied.

She smiled and nodded her agreement. We finished off the bottle of wine and turned in.

'Are you still there?' I whispered.

'Mmm.'

The bed was so big she could have done a runner and I wouldn't have known.

The following morning, we skipped breakfast in favour of a lie-in and a mug of coffee. By 10:00 am we were pulling into the carpark of the Koala Conservation Centre. The centre features a treetop boardwalk which weaves its way through a grove of eucalyptus trees, allowing visitors to get up close and personal with the resident koalas.

'Look,' said Melanie, pointing into the trees.

I stopped and stared into the foliage. Resting on a branch was an adult koala with a young joey clinging to it. There can't be many animals that look as cute at twelve weeks old as they do at twelve years. Puppies and kittens are gorgeous, their adult selves less so. Newborn lambs are adorable whereas adult sheep are ugly. As for humans, given their disproportionally large heads and tiny limbs, babies look more like visitors from another planet than a smaller version of their parents. Koalas, on the other hand, are cute when they're young, adorable as adults and possess a sympathetic vulnerability in old age.

'Look over there,' said an elderly man to a small party of pensioners.

His accent was unmistakable.

'Are you from Yorkshire?' asked Melanie.

'Aye lass, I am.'

Minutes later we knew his life story. An ex-Yorkshire miner forced to emigrate to Australia due to the destruction of his industry at the hands of Margaret Thatcher and an uncaring Tory government, he was one of the lucky ones. Now he was enjoying retirement in his adopted homeland.

The conservation park had been great fun and while koalas could never be described as lively creatures, getting up close and personal to their daily lives was a real privilege.

Back at the cottage, I fired up the barbecue and slapped on the lamb steaks.

'Here you go,' said Melanie, handing me the packet of kanga bangers.

The lamb was delicious. The less said about the bangers the better.

After a long lazy lunch, we drove to Churchill Island Heritage Farm. The farm gives visitors an insight into the daily lives of early settlers. The thing about Australian history is that from a European perspective it's not very historic. The church in our village was built 500 years before Captain Cook laid claim to the island and it wasn't until 1788 under the rule of King George III that England began to colonise its prize. Even today, this island fifteen times the size of Spain has less than half its population.

Our final sightseeing destination of the day was The Nobbies, an ecotourist centre located on the western tip of the island. It's said that from the lookout point, Australia's largest fur seal colony can be seen basking on the appropriately named Seal Rocks. I can only presume that when we visited it was either out of season or the whole colony had decided to take the day off. The views from the point, however, were stunning.

That evening we ate at the cottage before having an early night. Tomorrow we would swap our quiet island retreat for the urban energy of Australia's second city, Melbourne.

25

Signs of Age

We left Phillip Island with heavy hearts, delighted we'd visited but sad that we might never return. Back on the mainland we joined the M420, Bass Highway, heading towards Melbourne.

Motorists travelling through the city are required to use a series of toll roads managed by an automated system. Failure to register carries heavy penalties. Previous attempts to navigate their online prepayment system proved fruitless and we'd fared no better with the telephone helpline. The only remaining option was to purchase credit from a state post office.

'Keep your eye out for a post office,' I said.

Whether it's buses, pubs, taxis, public conveniences or in this case post offices, if you want one you can never find one; when you don't, there's one on every corner. We drove through town after town without seeing so much as a mailbox.

'Let's see if there's one in that shopping centre,' I said.

For the last few miles we'd driven past a series of placards advertising an out of town shopping centre. The last thing I wanted to do was make a detour but if we didn't find somewhere soon we ran the risk of picking up a fine, or worse still, Janet collecting one. The centre was vast. I parked the car and we wandered inside.

'Over there,' said Melanie, pointing at a floor plan.

The colour coded plan showed every outlet on all three floors.

'Post office, second floor, number twenty-eight,' said Melanie.

The application process couldn't have been simpler but by the time we got back on the highway we'd wasted the best part of an hour.

Tonight's accommodation was the Charsfield Hotel, a four-star establishment in the heart of the city. We were only staying one night so as soon as we arrived we dumped the luggage in the room and headed into the centre.

Our ride into the city came courtesy of a tram from a bygone era. It passed in front of the hotel and stopped directly opposite the city's iconic Flinders Street Railway Station. From its architecture to its populace, everything about Melbourne seemed familiar. A European-style city on the edge of the world.

As our time here was short, we decided to take a river cruise down the Yarra River to Williams Town, a peninsula on the Port Phillip Bay. A number of different operators run shuttle services to and from the island. We picked the next boat leaving, bought our tickets and boarded. The journey down the river runs through Melbourne's business district. Modern, high-rise office blocks line the banks of the river. Global brands such as Price Waterhouse Coopers and Ernst & Young claim title to these imperious glass towers.

Private motor launches drifted along the river and a women's coxed four sped past under the stewardship of an elderly gentleman wearing a white peaked cap, more evidence of the city's European heritage. Further downstream, upmarket apartment blocks lined the river and luxury motor yachts were moored in exclusive marinas. At the deep-water entrance to the river estuary, Chinese registered tankers were being loaded with tonnes of cement to feed the nation's building boom.

By the time we disembarked, we were ready for lunch.

'I'm starving,' said Melanie.

A statement rather than a prognosis.

'Me too. What about fish and chips?'

A noticeboard outside a takeaway in the harbour claimed "The Best Fish 'n' Chips" on the island.

'That sounds perfect,' she replied.

The shop's claim was justified: crispy batter, succulent fish and perfectly fried chips. The setting wasn't bad either. We'd wandered across to a public bench overlooking the quay. Small yachts and fishing boats bobbed up and down on their moorings. The afternoon sun skipped across a turquoise blue ocean and in the distance, Melbourne's city skyline formed a futuristic backdrop. An hour after arriving, the cruiser returned and we sailed back to the city.

'Let's take a city bus tour,' I suggested.

While researching what to do, I had come across the Melbourne City Tourist Shuttle, a free public bus service that circulates all the major tourist attractions and includes an en route commentary.

The nearest bus stop was a short walk away in Federation Square. The service departed at twenty-minute intervals. After a short wait we boarded the busy bus and took a seat. The complete tour takes about an hour and passengers can get on and off as they choose.

After taking in the sights we caught the tram back to the hotel and enjoyed an hour's rest before readying ourselves for dinner.

Earlier in the day, while we'd been waiting for the boat to depart to Williams Town, we'd spotted an Indian restaurant overlooking the river and decided to give it a go.

The food was excellent and the location stunning. In contrast to Shanghai's night-time skyline, Melbourne glowed with corporate neon signage. On our return to the hotel our hopes of a nightcap were dashed by the bar's opening hours. Perhaps an early night wasn't such a bad idea; we had a busy day ahead.

The Charsfield's full English breakfast would have passed muster at any British hotel. By 9:30 am we were back on the road making our way through busy city traffic. It's said that the journey is more important than the destination; that was certainly true today. Our destination was Eastern Reef Cottage in Port Campbell, and the journey was a drive along the Great Ocean Road.

'I'm going to fill up before we go any further,' I said, as we left Melbourne.

Janet had told us that petrol prices fluctuate wildly depending on the day of the week. From Thursday onwards, pump prices start rising as the weekend approaches. On Monday they begin to fall, bottoming out on Wednesday. My initial scepticism was quickly dispelled as we watched with interest her predictions coming true. Today was Thursday; with a bit of luck we might find a station that had yet to raise their prices from Wednesday's low.

'There,' said Melanie, pointing at a petrol station. 'It's only $1.32.'

The tank wasn't empty but we had a long way to go and every cent counted. While I pumped the petrol, the service station attendant walked across the forecourt carrying an aluminium ladder, leant it against the fuel price board, and climbed. As if to emphasise Janet's warning, before I'd replaced the nozzle the attendant had changed the price from $1.32 per litre to $1.47. As he walked past me, my expression prompted a response.

'Don't worry mate,' he said, 'yours is at the lower price.'

Before driving away, we double checked the receipt.

A stiff breeze transformed a damp and grey start into a bright, sunny morning. With a full tank of fuel, we were ready to navigate the Great Ocean Road, a 243 kilometre stretch of coastal road running from Torquay to Allansford. Its construction was begun in 1919 by servicemen returning from the Western Front. On its completion in 1932 the road was dedicated to those who died during the Great War and is recognised today as the world's largest war memorial.

The road is starting to show its age and is more suited to the handling of a Porsche 911 than a lumbering Kia Carnival. The surface was pretty good but tight bends and adverse cambers kept me alert.

The seaside resort of Apollo Bay marks the halfway point. It had taken over two hours to travel 100 kilometres and I was ready for a break. I made the mistake of ordering fish and chips for lunch. After yesterday's pick, they were destined to be second best.

West of Apollo Bay the road became even more challenging. It's far easier to carve up a nation with straight lines than it is to build a road with them. An hour and a half after leaving Apollo Bay we crossed into the Port Campbell National Park, an area best known for the Twelve Apostles rock formation.

The cliffs along this stretch of the southern coast are limestone, a relatively soft rock prone to shearing. This type of erosion produces dramatic rock formations or sea stacks: tall columns of rock stranded offshore. Today only eight Apostles remain although there were only ever nine. Even so, they formed an impressive sight from where we stood on the clifftop looking down the coast.

Given how far we were from civilisation and the fact it was Thursday afternoon, we were surprised how popular they were. Of all the tourist sites we'd visited, this was by far the busiest.

'Let's come back at sunset and watch the sun going down,' I suggested.

Eastern Reef Cottage is located on the outskirts of Port Campbell, less than a fifteen-minute drive from the Apostles. When we arrived, there wasn't a soul in sight.

'Look,' said Melanie, pointing at an envelope pinned to the door of a timber framed cottage.

It was addressed to us. The owners would return later, and in the meantime the door was open, the keys were on the table and we were to make ourselves at home.

The cottage had been built using reclaimed timbers and poured earth. It was well appointed and very comfortable.

We returned to the Apostles at sunset and watched in silence as their lengthening shadows danced on the breaking waves.

We'd enjoyed our stay at Eastern Reef Cottage but it was time to move on. Allansford marked the end of the Great Ocean Road and completed our list of must-see tourist destinations. From now on, we'd do what we do best: wing it.

'Let's nip across the border,' I suggested, as we left the cottage.

'What border?'

'Into South Australia.'

'How far away is it?'

'About 250 kilometres.'

'OK, why not?'

From Allansford we rejoined the A1 Princes Highway and headed for the state of South Australia.

'Is there anything to see near the border?' I asked.

Melanie flicked through Claire's tourist guidebook.

'There's a Blue Lake in a place called Mount Gambier,' she said.

'What's that then?'

'It's a lake, and it's blue.'

'Aren't they all?' I replied.

'No, I mean it's really blue, look.'

I glanced across at the guidebook.

'No way. That has to have been photoshopped.'

The photo in the guidebook pictured a lake occupying a volcanic crater. Its colour was the most vivid shade of cobalt blue I had ever seen.

'Well it states it's a natural phenomenon from December through to March and reverts to grey for the rest of the year.'

'Knowing our luck, it will already have changed colour,' I said.

'Why, what date is it?'

'The 29th of February, a leap year.'

'We could always visit the Umpherston Sinkhole instead.'

'The what?'

'Umpherston Sinkhole is an ornamental garden created in a natural sinkhole,' she read.

'Let's visit them both.'

If there was the remotest possibility that this lake was that blue, I wanted to see it.

Both the lake and the sinkhole were situated on the outskirts of the city of Mount Gambier. I'd expected to drive up the side of a volcano to view the lake but centuries of erosion had left it indistinguishable from the surrounding countryside. A shallow banking prevented us from seeing the water from the car so I parked and we climbed a small flight of steps to the top of the bank.

For a moment I thought I was imagining things. The photo in the guidebook failed to relay the vibrancy of the colour. It looked as if someone had filled the lake with gallons of cobalt blue dye. Melanie and I were speechless. This was a photo opportunity not to be missed.

From there we drove the short distance to the Umpherston Sinkhole. The geology of the ancient sinkhole provided the perfect environment in which to build a magnificent sunken garden. Once again, an unplanned detour had unearthed unexpected treasures.

An hour after leaving Mount Gambier we were back in Victoria in the sleepy town of Casterton looking for somewhere to have lunch. The menu at the Southridge Café took us by surprise.

'This looks good,' said Melanie, reading from a menu in the window.

Our lunchtime diet had so far consisted of bulging burgers, or fish and chips. The international dishes on offer here sounded delicious. Melanie chose a chicken and mushroom pasta dish with a cream sauce; I picked deep fried chicken with salad. The portions were enormous and the food was cooked to perfection. It seemed a shame that this small-town eatery had such a limited catchment area.

Tonight's accommodation was the Hamilton Town House Motel in Hamilton, comfortable and functional. The facilities included a small jacuzzi and a complimentary bottle of bubbly, both of which we took full advantage of.

Day seven began with a hearty breakfast. Since leaving the coast, the weather had been excellent, warm, sunny, and in the main very still, and that morning was no different. The route I'd chosen for our return trip to Wollongong was primarily based around today's destination and for no other reason than I loved the name: Kangaroo Flat. Where else would you find a town called that?

En route we took in the sights, which for the most part consisted of mile after mile of flat dusty arable land linked by small rural settlements. The Grampian mountains formed a picturesque backdrop. The route we'd chosen took us through Maldon, one of many towns established during the Victoria goldrush of 1851. The boom lasted until the late 1860s and attracted prospectors from all over the world. It marked a period of rapid population growth and great prosperity. At its peak, Melbourne Treasury received over two tonnes of gold every week.

One of the town's attractions is the railway station where an authentic steam heritage train transports passengers along the Victorian Goldfields Railway to the historic goldmining town of Castlemaine.

On the approach to Maldon a sign for the Mount Tarrengower Lookout caught our attention. We'd made good progress that morning so I suggested taking a look.

In an effort to attract tourists to the area the town council bought the lookout tower from a mining company in 1923. It was originally a poppet-head or steel frame constructed over a mine shaft and was used to hoist men and materials to and from the surface. On a warm summer's day, it took quite some effort to climb the stairs to the viewing platform but the views over the surrounding countryside made the effort worthwhile.

'Let see if we can find the railway station,' I said, as we strolled back to the car.

I'd been in two minds whether to include Maldon in our tour but Melanie seemed very positive. My reservations stemmed from Melanie's childhood experiences. Her dad, Geoff, had been an avid train spotter and liked nothing more than foisting his obsession onto Melanie and her brother Charles. An interest neither of them shared.

In more recent times we had happy memories of travelling on the North York Moors Steam Railway from Pickering to Whitby. In the end, I needn't have worried; services had been suspended due to maintenance and didn't start until tomorrow.

'Can we come back in the morning?' asked Melanie.

'If you like. We've got plenty of time.'

Maldon was only half an hour from Kangaroo Flat. We checked the timetable for the first train – 10:30 am – and continued on.

'Look,' said Melanie.

A road sign read Lockwood.

'We'll have to stop and take a photo,' she added.

This was an opportunity not to be missed. I'd spent the whole of my childhood growing up in Lockwood. We'd travelled halfway around the world and found another: coincidence or fate?

Tonight's accommodation couldn't have been more different from yesterday's salesman's stopover. The Whistle Inn is a privately-run bed and breakfast owned and operated by railway enthusiast Ken and his long-suffering wife Marion. The annexed guest accommodation is built in the style of a railway station. The theme continued inside with railway memorabilia at every turn.

'Will you fill these in when you get a minute?' asked Ken, handing us a breakfast checklist.

The options available were mind-blowing. Ken and Marion's idea of a cooked English breakfast wasn't just full, it was positively overflowing, limited only by our piggish embarrassment.

We spent the rest of the day relaxing in the sunshine on the private terrace. The perfect place to enjoy a night-time barbecue before hitting the sack.

At 9:00 am Ken tapped on the door and delivered our pre-ordered breakfast feast. Ken's cooking skills deserved congratulation and before we knew it we were running late. We threw the case into the back of the car, said goodbye and sped off toward Maldon.

'You've got to be kidding,' I said.

'What?'

'Roadworks.'

The diversion was well signposted but seemed to go on forever.

'What time is it now?' I asked, as we rejoined the deserted C277.

'Eight minutes past ten.'

Since Janet had handed me the keys to her beloved Kia Carnival I'd driven it with care and consideration. The time had come to find out what she could do.

Within sight of the station, a stack of steam erupted into the air as the engine pulled away from the station. We had been thwarted in our attempt to travel back in time on the goldrush express.

'Bugger!'

'Oh no. What are we going to do now?' asked Melanie.

'I'm sure we'll find something of interest along the way.'

Today's destination was the town of Lockhart. The drive took us through the heart of goldrush country to the city of Bendigo and the town of Echuca before we crossed the border into New South Wales.

Bendigo's status as a goldrush boomtown is reflected in the city's architecture.

'Let's stop and have a coffee,' I suggested. Bendigo was a photo opportunity not to be missed.

'OK.'

The city centre is littered with magnificent Victorian architecture, watched over by a marble statue of Her Majesty in the nearby Rosalind Park. It's hard to imagine a more British city outside of the United Kingdom.

An hour after leaving Bendigo we reached the border town of Echuca on the banks of the Murray River.

'What's Echuca got to offer?' I asked.

Melanie flicked through the guidebook.

'The National Holden Motor Museum.'

'That sounds interesting, what do you think?'

'A car museum, do we have to?'

'Well what else is there?'
'There's something called The Great Aussie Beer Shed.'
'What's that?'
'It's a museum.'
'Do you get to taste the beer?'
'It doesn't say so.'
'That's no good. What else is there?'
'This sounds interesting.'
'What?'
'The Port of Echuca Discovery Centre. It sounds a bit like the Australian equivalent of Beamish, an open-air museum reflecting life as it was in the late 1800s.'
'Let's go there then.'

We couldn't have made a better choice. It felt like we'd stepped back in time as we wandered through the streets of the re-created port.

'Look,' said Melanie, pointing at a placard advertising paddle steamer cruises up the Murray River.

'Let's get some tickets.'

The Murray wasn't the most picturesque river we'd ever travelled along but the old steamer more than compensated for the muddy brown water. On our return to the quay, we found a quaint eatery on the main street and watched horse-drawn carriages transport visitors around the port.

Echuca to Lockhart was a three-hour drive through a flat landscape of dusty, dry arable land. In all that time we hardly passed another vehicle. Lockhart itself is reminiscent of a scene from a fifties Hollywood road movie. Tonight's bed and breakfast stopover was the Bank and Stable, a historic heritage building filled with antiques and collectables. The building used to house the town's bank and the new owners traded antiques out of the stables at the rear.

After checking in we stretched our legs by walking down the main street.

'Would you like a beer?' I asked.

'Yes please.'

We'd reached the Commercial Hotel, a typically Australian pub less than fifty metres from the Bank and Stable. The owner had placed a few tables and chairs outside on the pavement. Melanie took a seat and I went inside. Save for the barman and two elderly gentlemen watching cricket on TV, the place was deserted. Carlton draught seemed to be the beer of choice.

'Two halves of Carlton please.'

'You're not from round here are you, mate?' asked the barman.

While he pulled the beers, I answered his question.

The first drink hardly touched the sides.

'Another?'

'I wouldn't say no. What are we going to do for dinner?' asked Melanie.

'I'll ask the barman.'

The cricket was progressing as cricket does, slowly, but the locals didn't seem to mind.

'Two more please,' I said, placing the empties on the bar. 'You wouldn't by chance know anywhere we can get something to eat?'

'What are you after?'

His question caught me by surprise.

'Do you serve meals here?' I asked.

'I can rustle you up steak and chips, if you like.'

'I'll just ask the wife.'

I took the beers and stepped outside.

'Do they do anything else?' she asked.

'He didn't say so. I think he's doing us a favour.'

'In that case, steak and chips sound delicious.'

When the steak arrived, it filled the plate and was cooked to perfection. By the time we headed back to the B&B we'd been sitting outside on the pavement for more than two hours. In all that time we hadn't seen another soul. Lockhart was our kind of town.

We spent the final evening of our road trip sitting outside on the covered balcony of the Bank and Stable, enjoying a bottle of Cabernet Sauvignon and reminiscing about our favourite bits of the tour.

26

Close Call

Once again, the alarm clock ensured we reached the dining room in time for breakfast. If nothing else, this road trip proved that Australians make great breakfasts and the Bank and Stable was up there with the best of them. We started with a fresh fruit platter followed by a perfectly prepared full English and ended with Vegemite on toast.

Today's drive lacked purpose. From Lockhart we drove through the marvellously named town of Wagga Wagga. From there we travelled 340 kilometres in three and a half hours without seeing another soul. Only when we reached Moss Vale did a signpost pique my interest.

'Would you like a pie for lunch?' I asked.
'A pie?'
'Not just any old pie, but the world's best pie,' I replied.
'Are we near Kangaroo Valley?'
'Next turning on the left.'
'That's a great idea.'

Half an hour later we were ordering two Traditional Aussies and two chocolate floats. A terrific end to a fabulous tour. We'd driven over 3,100 kilometres in nine days, spent more than forty hours behind the wheel, and I'd loved every minute of it. Australia's roads weren't up to much and driving hour after hour through eucalyptus forests wasn't exactly thrilling but the places we'd visited and the things we'd seen were unsurpassable. We'd met great people, enjoyed fabulous food and created memories that would last a lifetime.

That evening we relaxed outside on the decking listening to the intoxicating sound of chirping crickets.

'I thought we might go to Sydney tomorrow,' I said.

'That's a good idea. How will we get there?'

Everyone we'd spoken to advised against driving into the city.

'I thought we might catch the train.'

'Let the train take the strain.'

'Exactly.'

That night we set the alarm clock for 7:30 am and turned in early.

Da, d, da, d, da, da, da!

That sounded exactly like Melanie's phone.

Da, d, da, d, da, da, da!

'Hello.'

That was Melanie's phone.

'*Si... si... si... adios.*'

I rolled over and looked at the clock.

'Who was that?'

'BricoKing.'

For a moment I thought she'd said BricoKing.

'Who?'

'BricoKing.'

'It's 3:30 in the morning. What did they want?'

'The shower screens are ready to collect.'

'That's good,' I replied.

Beep, beep, beep, beep!

When I eventually gathered my thoughts, Melanie was nudging open the bedroom door carrying two mugs of coffee.

'Morning,' I said, 'I had the weirdest dream last night.'

'Don't tell me, it involved BricoKing and shower screens?'

'How did… it wasn't a dream, was it?'

'No, I forgot to switch off the phone before we came to bed,' she admitted.

Given the eight-hour time difference, staff in Monforte would have been halfway through their afternoon shift.

The train to Sydney Central left Wollongong at 9:15 am. Plenty of time to enjoy breakfast before hailing a taxi. To date, Australia's transport network hadn't exactly bowled us over. Imagine our surprise when an ultramodern train pulled into the station. Unfortunately, that's where the praise ends.

On a scale of one to ten with ten representing a ride on the Shanghai Maglev, Australia's South Coast Line was an emphatic zero. It takes a staggering two hours to travel fifty-six miles. It would have been quicker to cycle. The journey wasn't without its moments. Fleeting glimpses of the ocean helped calm our frustration and crowds of school children kept our interest. As for the girl's uniform, the jury is still out. The cute little pinafore dresses look adorable on girls ten years old but on a young woman of sixteen it seems inappropriately risqué.

Eventually, the train pulled into Central Station.

According to the locals, the best way to see Sydney is aboard a public ferry and Circular Quay is the city's hub. I looked around the station.

'Over there,' I said, pointing at a sign for the tube, known locally as the City Circle.

Three stops and eleven minutes later the tube arrived at Circular Quay. As the doors slid open, the unmistakable sight of Sydney Harbour Bridge greeted us. It felt surreal to be standing in front of such an iconic landmark. I was speechless.

'Look,' said Melanie excitedly.

I couldn't quite believe it. Across from the bridge is one of the most recognisable buildings on the planet, the Sydney Opera House. Architects seem obsessed with reaching for the stars, constructing ever taller edifices, but none can hold a candle to this unique and memorable structure. After regaining our composure and taking more snaps than you can poke a stick at, we went to take a closer look.

The quay was a hive of activity. With their dark green hulls and cream decks, the publicly operated ferry boats look like waterbound buses. The skill of the crews made docking and departing look like the boats were on rails. We bought two unlimited travel day rover tickets for sixteen dollars each and hopped aboard the next boat to Darling Harbour.

Darling Harbour is a tourist magnet, a lively place with an international feel. The clock had ticked around to lunchtime so we ordered a salad from one of the many harbourside cafés. After lunch we caught a ferry to Manly, had a few beers then returned to Circular Quay. Positioned along the quay were a number of vendors offering evening paddle boat cruises around the harbour including dinner and cabaret. They weren't cheap but it sounded like fun.

'That sounds interesting,' I said, pointing at an advertising board.

We'd seen a number of the replica paddle steamers moored at Darling Harbour and wondered what they were used for.

'We're not exactly dressed for a dinner party,' replied Melanie.

'We could come back tomorrow evening.'

Melanie gave me one of those "are you being serious" looks.

'We could,' she replied.

'Would you like to?'
'It's quite expensive.'
'I know but we are on holiday.'
'OK, let's do it.'

A return trip to Sydney meant enduring another two-hour train journey but we felt it would be worth it.

'What now?' asked Melanie.

'Let's catch the Woolwich ferry.'

The F8 Woolwich ferry starts and finishes at Circular Quay and takes an hour to complete. By the time we'd boarded, the clock had ticked around to rush hour and the ferry was busier than it had been all day. So too was the harbour with lots of smaller vessels enjoying a warm still evening.

We followed a restaurant recommendation that Bob and Janet had given us and ate dinner at the Zaaffran Indian restaurant in Darling Harbour. The food lived up to expectations and the setting was hard to beat. After dinner we caught the last ferry back to Circular Quay, the tube to Central Station and the very slow train to Wollongong. By the time I turned off the bedside lamp, the clock had ticked around to 2:00 am.

A lazy morning followed our late-night exploits, but by 3.00 pm we were back at Wollongong Station waiting for the 3:01 pm to Sydney. It eventually arrived twenty minutes late. By the time we reached Sydney, had taken the tube to Circular Quay and the ferry from there to Darling Harbour, passengers were boarding the paddle boat for a 7:00 pm sailing.

The evening was a great success. The food was delicious, the entertainment excellent, and Sydney Harbour at night is a sight not to be missed.

For the second day running we collapsed into bed at two in the morning.

There was a certain inevitability to our late start but a day of rest wouldn't do us any harm. Janet had invited us to spend the coming weekend with her and the family in Canberra. On the way back from there, I thought we might head inland in search of Australia's famous red centre. With this in mind I spent the rest of the morning planning a route.

'What do you think to this?' I said, leaning back from the computer screen.

'It looks alright,' replied Melanie.

Her lack of enthusiasm was understandable. The Lachlan Way Motel at Lake Cargelligo hardly sets the pulse racing but it was cheap and took us as far inland as we could reasonably expect to drive in a day.

'I thought we could stay there on our way back from Canberra.'

'Where is it?'

I showed her on the map.

'It's in the middle of nowhere.'

'That's the point,' I replied.

'OK. By the way, what would you like for lunch?'

'What have we got?'

'Not a lot.'

'In that case, let go for a pie in Kangaroo Valley.'

'Why not?'

The drive to the pie shop took just over an hour but was worth it.

The following morning marked the start of our final week. When we arrived in Australia, it felt like we had all the time in the world. From now on, we had to make every minute count. Unfortunately, no one explained that to the weather gods.

'It's not a very nice day,' said Melanie, as she bumped open the bedroom door.

'It might brighten up later.'

'So, what are we going to do today?'

'I'd like to drive over the Sydney Harbour Bridge,' I said.

'Are you sure?'

From what I'd seen of the city traffic, those advising against driving in Sydney had never fought their way through London's city streets or raced around the North Circular at rush hour. To say nothing of negotiating the Paris Périphérique or fighting a way through the middle of Madrid when the national football team is playing at the Estadio Santiago Bernabéu. To be honest, I'd seen more traffic on the Huddersfield Ring Road than I'd seen in Sydney.

'Piece of cake,' I replied.

My confidence was well founded and the roads running through the city were some of the best we'd travelled on. What I hadn't counted on was the tunnel. Everyone knows about the bridge but who knew that Sydney Harbour has a tunnel? Whether through an error of judgement or lapse in concentration, before I knew it we'd missed the road across the bridge and were driving under the harbour.

'We'll get it on the way back,' I assured Melanie.

North of Sydney we followed the coast road to an exclusive residential area overlooking Palm Beach. Its exclusivity extended to the six bucks public parking fee so we doubled back to Whale Beach and paid three.

The cloudy morning had developed into a beautiful sunny day. The beach occupied a classic c-shaped bay. The headlands either side were dotted with whitewashed houses with idyllic views of white crested breakers rolling onto a beach of fine golden sand.

'I'm going for a paddle,' said Melanie, as I drew to a halt.

I couldn't blame her. The turquoise blue ocean looked irresistible.

'It's freezing,' she said, as she walked back up the beach.

'Lunch?' I asked.

While Melanie had been splashing about in the surf, I'd checked out a beachside bar.

'I could murder a burger and chips,' she replied.

On the drive home, I kept my wits about me and fulfilled my earlier ambition to drive across Sydney Harbour Bridge. The views weren't as good as we'd hoped but the thrill of crossing this iconic structure more than compensated.

Our next trip to Sydney would be our last. Janet had kindly picked us up from the airport when we arrived but we had to make our own way back. We had two options, public transport or taxi. Our preferred choice was the latter but it would depend on the cost. The time had come to start making plans.

An internet search highlighted how complicated and time-consuming travelling by public transport would be. A phone call to our favourite Wollongong taxi company revealed the prohibitive cost of private hire.

'What are we going to do?' asked Melanie.

'I don't know but 150 bucks for a taxi is outrageous.'

'I know but the flight is long enough without spending three hours on public transport getting to the airport.'

She was right; an eleven-hour flight was bad enough.

'I've got an idea.'

'What?'

'Let's find out how much it will cost to hire a car here and drop it off at the airport.'

'Don't you have to pay extra to drop off at a different location?'

'We can find out for nothing.'

Melanie drifted off into the kitchen while I began my search. Half an hour later I'd unearthed a cost-effective alternative.

'Got it,' I announced, as I walked into the lounge.

Melanie was ironing some essentials for our weekend in Canberra.

'I hope it's not catching.'

'Ha ha, very funny.'

'What have you got?'

'We can hire a car on Thursday in Wollongong and leave it at the airport Friday morning.'

'How much?'

'That's the best part, it's only fifty-seven bucks.'

'Are you sure?'

'Certain.'

'You'd better book it then.'

Five minutes later, our transport to the airport was sorted.

'What time are we setting off?' asked Melanie, as I powered down the computer.

I looked at my watch. The time had ticked around to 11:30 am.

'Another hour?'

'What about lunch?'

'We'll get something on the way.'

An hour later we loaded a case of newly ironed clothes into the back of the Kia and headed off to the nation's capital, Canberra.

The M31, Hume Highway, was one of the better roads we'd travelled along. An hour into the drive I spotted the world-famous golden arches towering above the surrounding countryside.

'Let's stop for a McDonald's.'

Melanie looked surprised at my suggestion.

'Are you sure?'

'I can't remember the last time we had one.'

McDonald's burgers are one of those convenience foods we love to hate. We convince ourselves they're no good for us but every now and then we can't resist ordering one.

'OK, why not?'

I pulled into the service area and parked. We'd had some fabulous burgers during our stay and this didn't hold a candle to any of them. Despite that, there's something unique about a McDonald's and we enjoyed every morsel. Two hours later, we pulled up outside Janet's home and in true Australian fashion, Janet had a barbecue planned for dinner. What surprised us was the location.

'We're going to drive to a picnic area in the bush,' she said.

In a flurry of organised chaos, Janet, her eldest daughter Melissa and son Andrew loaded cool boxes and cartons into the back of Janet's car and off we went. Within half an hour we were unloading everything and carrying it to a public picnic area in the middle of nowhere. In fading light, we ventured into the bush in search of kindling. The whole experience was great fun, if somewhat bizarre.

By the time we headed home, twilight had given way to dusk. Janet was focusing on the road ahead. Out of the corner of my eye, I caught sight of something moving. In the darkness I made out the unmistakable silhouette of a group of kangaroos. As my eyes focused, one of them began to move towards the road, slowly at first but then it gathered momentum. Surely Janet had seen it but her speed remained constant. By the time I realised a 200lb (90kg) adult kangaroo was on a collision course with our family saloon, it was too late to say a word.

'Shit!' said Melanie, as the beast jumped the width of the road in one leap, missing the car by a matter of inches.

A sudden intake of breath was followed by a ripple of nervous laughter as the possible consequences sank in. Hitting a beast that size would have had disastrous consequences. On this occasion it only served to sharpen everyone's concentration.

Janet's middle child, Rachel, had missed the evening adventure due to a friend's birthday party. The following morning, Janet pressganged her into leading us on a kangaroo safari into the nature reserve that backed onto their house.

For Australians, tracking kangaroos in their natural habitat is as exciting as trainspotting. Somewhat reticently, she led the way. Within minutes she'd spotted our quarry.

'There,' she said, pointing at a patch of open grassland.

Melanie and I were gobsmacked. We'd travel thousands of miles through four states and seen more roadkill than we had live kangaroos. Standing less than a hundred metres away was a group of half a dozen. Bubbling with excitement I flipped the lens cover off my camera and started shooting.

'Let's get closer,' I said, walking slowly towards them.

Melanie followed and Rachel brought up the rear.

The leading male had caught sight of us long before Rachel spotted him and hadn't taken his eyes off us. Suddenly, he turned on his heels and leapt away, followed swiftly by the others.

'Come on,' I said, picking up the pace and hotfooting it after them.

Melanie raced after me, but Rachel was having none of it. It was far too warm to be running around in the undergrowth chasing a mob of kangaroos. If I didn't know better I'd say kangaroos are equipped with proximity sensors. Every time we got within fifty feet, the whole group stopped feeding and hopped away. After running around in the bush for half an hour I realised Rachel had a point. When we walked back to the house Melanie and I were still buzzing with excitement.

'Did you see any?' asked Janet.

'We chased a small group through the bush,' I replied.

'It was amazing,' added Melanie.

While we'd been chasing the local wildlife, Janet had prepared a picnic.

'I thought we'd take a ride out to Lanyon Homestead. It's a historic house museum managed by the National Trust.'

The homestead dates back to the first half of the 19th century which for Australia is ancient history. The museum was stacked with everyday items our grandparents had used. From there we drove into Canberra for a picnic lunch in Commonwealth Park on the banks of Lake Burley Griffin. A short walk from the picnic area was the Canberra and Region Visitors' Centre, an exhibition centre dedicated to the history of the country's capital.

A long running dispute between Sydney and Melbourne over which city should be the nation's capital was resolved in a rather unusual way. Both cities agreed the best solution was to build a new capital city. As if that wasn't strange enough, in 1912, the Department of Home Affairs organised an international competition to design it. One hundred and thirty-seven designs were received and a winner chosen. At this point, someone had second thoughts and a new plan was put before parliament incorporating elements from the winner, the two runners-up and a fourth design by architects based in Sydney. Looking at the final plan, it's difficult to imagine the freemasons didn't have a hand in the decision. It's certainly been planned upon the square. This bizarre episode ended with a second competition to come up with a suitable name. Needless to say, Canberra was the winner.

Our day ended with a boat trip around Lake Burley Griffin and a visit to Parliament House, which was closed. That evening we showed our appreciation by taking the family out for dinner. My abiding memory of Canberra will unfairly centre around that evening. After three failed attempts to find an Indian restaurant that was open, we settled on Chinese. The food was great, so too the company, but I couldn't help thinking that Canberra must be the only capital city in the world where three out of four restaurants are closed on a Sunday evening.

A nation's capital is more than pencil lines on a plan, it's the heartbeat of a country, a place that evolves and develops, that grows and changes through the passage of time. Perhaps in centuries to come Canberra will become that beating heart.

Melanie and I thought it best to keep out of the way on Monday morning. Melissa left early to visit the gym before going to work but Rachel and Andrew needed parental persuasion to get ready for school. By the time we'd eaten breakfast, packed the car, and said our goodbyes, the clock had ticked around to 11:00 am.

An eight-hour drive to Lake Cargelligo was punctuated with a lunch break in the town of Temora. The journey was one of my favourites of the entire holiday. Amy Winehouse kept us company as she had done throughout our trip. So impressed were we with her first album, *Frank*, we bought the second, *Back to Black*, during one of our many fuel stops.

Lunch at the pavement café in Temora provided a glimpse of rural Australian life. Later in the day we spotted two kangaroos sitting in the middle of a field in the shade of a leafy tree. They seemed as interested in us as we were in them. The further inland we drove the dustier the fields became. The earth changed colour from clay brown to a rusty red and a number of mini dust tornados twisted their way across the landscape. One even veered across the road, causing the car to rock. Throughout the drive the temperature had risen steadily. By the time we reached Lake Cargelligo it had topped 40°C.

The town of Lake Cargelligo sprang up around a natural lake of the same name. Our accommodation for the night was the Lachlan Way Motel, unremarkable in every way save the outstanding lake view.

'Let's take a closer look,' I suggested. We both needed to stretch our legs.

The area around the lake was beautifully landscaped with manicured lawns and tropical plants. Stepping out of our air-conditioned room felt like walking into an oven. The heat was so intense the road surface had started to melt.

'I can feel the heat through my shoes,' remarked Melanie, as we walked across the road.

'I wonder what people do for a living around here?' I asked.

This was the most isolated community we'd visited.

'What people?' quipped Melanie.

She was right. There wasn't a soul in sight.

That evening, as the temperature waned, we drove into the outback to watch the sun set over the red earth. Distant mountains formed a dark silhouette against a flaming sky. In the foreground, wiry bushes created a natural focal point. A stunning sunset made the long drive inland all worthwhile.

Dinner consisted of half a bag of crisps, left over from earlier in the day, and a small packet of complimentary biscuits left by the hotel. Once again, we'd fallen foul of Australia's early dining habits. We should have known the phrase "Open until late" was a relative term. The pizza takeaway had locked its doors two hours before we turned up at 9:00 pm.

Despite an early night, the sun was high in the sky by the time we checked out. The route back to Wollongong took us through Caragabal, Cowra and Boorowa where we stopped for lunch: cheeseburger and chips at a picnic area on the banks of the Boorowa River.

That evening we sat outside on the decking reminiscing about our adventures in Australia, a country that surprises visitors at every turn.

'What are we going to do tomorrow?' I asked.

'We'll have to start packing at some point.'

'We can do that on Thursday.'

Delaying the task helped postponed the inevitable.

'What time is the flight on Friday?' asked Melanie.

I hadn't got a clue.

'Hang on a minute, I'll take a look.'

I went inside to check.

'The flight leaves Sydney at 11:50 am and arrives in Shanghai at 19:10 pm.'

'It can't do.'

'Why?'

'That would make the flight less than eight hours.'

She was right.

It had taken the best part of eleven hours to get here.

'Don't tell me they've made a mistake.'

My heart rate quickened. Shortly after reserving our flights the booking agent notified us of a change. I was sure I'd checked the new tickets. All of a sudden, the answer struck me.

'It's the time difference,' I blurted out, 'between here and China.'

Melanie looked as relieved as I felt.

'So what time do we need to be at the airport for?' she asked.

'Nine o'clock will give us plenty of time.'

I took a sip of wine before remembering my original question.

'So, what are we going to do tomorrow?'

'I don't know but perhaps we should stay close to home.'

'What about taking a picnic to Mount Keira lookout?'

'That's a great idea.'

The following morning we enjoyed a leisurely start to the day, coffee in bed followed by breakfast on the decking. Melanie prepared a picnic and by midday we were heading out of town.

Mount Keira is part of the Illawarra escarpment and four kilometres from Wollongong. At 464 metres above sea level it's the highest peak in the area. From the summit, visitors can see for over fifty kilometres in all directions. On a good day, even the Blue Mountains come into view, some seventy-seven kilometres away.

The short drive made a pleasant change and the views from the lookout were every bit as good as advertised.

We spent our final day preparing for the journey home. Melanie finished the ironing while I gave the Kia Carnival a wash and brush-up. The old girl had done us proud. We'd travelled over 8,500 kilometres and she hadn't missed a beat. We decided to push the boat out for our last supper and booked a table at the Harbourfront Seafood Restaurant. My choice of fish and chips seemed a fitting finale to a fabulous holiday.

27

Manolo the Magnificent

An early night failed to provide the sleep we'd hoped for. By the time the alarm clock went off, I felt as if I'd been awake for hours and Melanie fared no better.

'Did you sleep?' I asked.

'Not really.'

By 9:00 am we were sitting in the departure hall of Sydney Kingsford Smith Airport waiting for the check-in desk to open. Two hours and twenty minutes later we were airborne. Eleven hours after taking off the undercarriage bounced down on the runway of Pudong International Airport in Shanghai. The passage of time had taken its toll on mind and body. The last thing we needed was an hour-long coach ride to our suburban overnight stopover.

By the time we arrived, dinner was being served. The hotel food was hideous. We ordered crispy duck. What we didn't expect was a whole bird, beak and all, charred to a carbon crisp and served with boiled rice, one lump or two. Thanks to the granite-like support of the mattress, we endured a restless night's sleep. Breakfast proved to be as inedible as dinner. Had this been our only experience of the Orient, our memories of China would have been very different. Fortunately, we'd had the foresight to make our outbound stopover a visit to remember.

When we landed in London Heathrow, my body felt like parts of it were still in transit. Local time was 8:00 pm, in Shanghai it was about 2:00 am and heaven knows what time it was in Wollongong.

After a day and a half realigning ourselves with the rest of the world, we drove to Huddersfield for an emotional reunion with Jazz. She was delighted to see us and we her. A day and a half later we left Huddersfield and drove back to London to stay overnight before catching the 6:35 am ferry from Dover to Calais.

Our drive through France was shorter than expected. Instead of turning right after disembarking the ferry, I mistakenly turned left. Forty minutes and sixty kilometres later, we crossed the border into Belgium. Realising my mistake, I turned around and headed back. Eight hours and 884 kilometres later, we reached Saintes for our overnight stop.

We left Saintes at 8:00 am. Three hours later we crossed the Pyrenees and entered Spain. Seven hours after that we drove through the village of Canabal and pulled into our driveway. In total, we'd been away from home for forty-nine days, driven over 13,000 kilometres and flown over 27,000 miles. We'd visited six countries on three continents and apart from the unruly garden, *El Sueño* looked the same now as the day we had left.

For the first few days, we felt like strangers in our own home. Nothing had changed but it would take time to settle back into our rural lifestyle. One of our first tasks was to check the progress at Vilatán. That too looked pretty much the same as when we'd left. A little disappointing but hardly surprising. While we were jetting around the world, Manolo underwent long-awaited surgery on his troublesome leg. Now we were back, it was up to us to re-energise our flagging restoration project.

On our way to the house we called at BricoKing to collect the shower screens they'd been so keen to tell us about. We tried to make light of the fact that they'd woken us in the middle of the night. The concept of time difference got lost in translation.

Manolo said very little when we arrived but seemed pleased to see us.

'I'll get off then,' said Melanie, after a quick look around.

Melanie was doing her best to catch up with the holiday laundry. Between loads, I'd asked her to phone the subcontractors to let them know we were back and find out when they'd be starting work. I continued varnishing the wooden ceilings, a rather solitary job. Melanie returned later in the day to pick me up.

'Elite-European rang this morning,' she said, as we drove home.

'Oh yes, what did they want?'

'The woman asked if we could pick the stuff up in Madrid.'

'Madrid! I hope you said no.'

I suspected something like this might happen when I'd made the booking. I'd told her Galicia was off the beaten track but she didn't seem interested.

'I did,' she replied.

'What did she say to that?'

'She didn't seem bothered.'

'I guess it's not her that has to drive the 1,000-kilometre detour.'

By the end of our first week back, it felt like we'd never been away. Memories of Australia took a back seat to managing subcontractors and working on the house. Days were filled with work. Visiting friends occupied our evenings. Carol and Gerry were here on holiday as were

Mitty and Rajan. Bob and Janet were due to arrive the coming weekend.

Since returning the weather had been bright and sunny but we knew from experience it was unlikely to last. At this time of year, Mother Nature lulls us into a false sense of summer only to dampen our spirits with April showers.

Melanie had managed to get hold of most of the subcontractors with one notable exception, Alfonso the stonemason. Ramon the plumber promised to be there on Friday to start installing the bathroom furniture. Manolo had already tiled the en suite bathroom and the shower room. José Metal had agreed to start fitting the new windows on Tuesday the 1st of April and José Kitchen would make a start that Friday.

When I arrived at the house on Monday morning Manolo was busy tiling the floor in the lounge. I continued varnishing the ceilings.

José Metal turned up on Tuesday as agreed and set about fitting the new windows. The transformation was quite remarkable. By the time he'd finished, the appearance of the house had changed from an empty stone shell into a warm and inviting home. I couldn't quite believe it; we finally seemed to be making real progress.

Toot! Toot!

Jazz ran to the French doors barking with excitement. I looked out of the window.

'Who is it?' called Melanie.

'It looks like our stuff has arrived,' I replied.

Sure enough, six years after moving to Spain, the last of our belongings had finally caught up with us.

The following day Bob and Janet called to see us.

'Can we take a look at the house?' asked Janet.

'We can go now if you like,' I replied.

When we arrived at Vilatán, Manolo's van was parked in the driveway. No sooner had Janet stepped from the car than she burst into tears.

'What's matter?' I asked. 'Don't you like it?'

Janet gathered her composure.

'It looks lovely,' she replied.

'What then?'

'I'm just thinking about your dad. He couldn't believe you'd bought such a dilapidated ruin. If only he could see it now.'

Janet's sentiment struck a chord. Dad thought we were mad to buy it and it didn't matter how many times I explained our plans, all he could see was the ruin in front of him. She was right: if only he could see it now. Some things are not meant to be.

The alarm clock had become an unwelcome companion following our return but without it, progress would have been unacceptably slow.

Beep, beep, beep, beep!

Melanie rolled over and hit the snooze button. Five minutes later it went off again. This time she switched it off, crawled out of bed and pulled on her dressing gown before wandering through into the kitchen. I dragged my aching frame to the bottom of the bed and flung open the window shutters. The day mirrored my mood: damp and overcast.

As soon as Jazz returned from her morning constitutional she ran into the bedroom and leapt onto the bed, tail wagging with excitement. A few minutes later Melanie returned with two mugs of coffee.

Ring, ring … Ring, ring.

'Who's that at this time in the morning?' said Melanie.

How would I know?

'*Hola*… OK… *Si*, OK… *Adios*.'

'Who was that?' I asked.

'José Kitchen.'

'What did he want?'

'He's not coming this morning because of the rain.'

José had promised to start fitting the kitchen today; what difference the inclement weather made was anyone's guess.

'Did he say when he would be starting?' I asked.

'Monday, probably.'

When it comes to subcontractors, probably is as good as definitely but neither reflect their true definition. Wait and see would be more accurate.

One person who did turn up as promised was the carpenter, José Manuel. He'd come to double check the measurements for the new *bodega* doors. We'd chosen *castaña* (chestnut) which in joinery terms is the Spanish equivalent of English oak. A hardwood with an enviable reputation for strength, durability, and quality.

'The other doors are finished if you'd like to come to the workshop and take a look,' he said.

That lunchtime we called in. The unvarnished doors looked stunning. When fitted, we were confident their beauty would more than justify the additional expense.

As if to contradict his earlier excuse José Kitchen turned up on Monday the 8th during a particularly heavy shower and immediately set to work fitting the kitchen. Nevertheless, I was pleased to see him. While he made a start on the kitchen, I began painting the shower room and Manolo created a chimney breast around the brick-built chimney. It was nothing like I'd expected but fitted perfectly with the character of the house.

'Have you heard from Marmoles Grande?' asked Manolo before he left for lunch.

'What about?'

'The granite for the staircase.'

Marmoles Grande were supplying the granite steps for the internal staircase. Until Manolo had fitted them, he wouldn't be able to pour the concrete floor in the entrance lobby or the utility room.

'Not yet. I'll give them a call this afternoon,' I assured him.

Manolo's question came as a timely reminder to get back in touch with Felix. Before Manolo poured the concrete floors, we needed him to install the switches, sockets and lighting on the ground floor.

Progress continued apace. Within a week of contacting Felix all the ground floor electrics had been installed. I'd given each ceiling two coats of varnish and made a start on the exterior woodwork. José Kitchen had all but finished fitting the kitchen and Ramon the plumber had completed all the internal pipework and fitted the bathroom furniture. All he had to do now was connect the pipe from the borehole into the house and the waste pipes from the house into the new septic tank.

'*Hay una problema* (There's a problem),' said Ramon.

I scampered down the ladder and followed him to the front of the house.

'What's matter?' I asked.

Ramon opened the valve at the wellhead but nothing came out, not a single drop. My heart sank. Had we run out of water?

We'd known from the start that without water, all we owned was a pile of stones in the middle of the Galician countryside. As things stood, we now owned a very expensive pile of stones. If the borehole had run dry, all this work would have been for nothing.

'Have we run out of water?' I asked.

I crossed my fingers and waited for his reply.

'Come here,' he said.

I moved closer to the wellhead.

'Listen.'

I crouched down. A faint drone echoed through the housing at the top of the borehole.

'What is it?' I asked.

'I'm not sure but we're going to have to pull the pump out and take a look.'

This was all we needed.

'I'll ring Chanquero,' I replied.

Chanquero had drilled the borehole and fitted the pump. Perhaps he could shed some light on the problem.

Ramon and his partner Luis made a start while I spoke to Chanquero.

'I'll come and take a look,' he said.

'Now?'

'I'll be there in ten minutes.'

Fortunately, he and his crew were working nearby.

Hauling a twenty kilogram (44lb) submersible pump 200 metres up a borehole is no mean feat. Anxious to find out what the problem was, I lent a hand. Anyone watching would have thought we were a three-man tug of war team grappling with a thirty millimetre diameter tube that was attached to the pump. We soon reached the limits of our land. Ramon hopped over the wall into the field next door. The black polypropylene pipe snaked back and forth across the field.

'*Para* (Stop)!' shouted Luis who was standing at the wellhead.

At a depth of about 125 metres, he'd found something.

Luis took the strain while Ramon and I rushed to take a look.

'*Madre dios* (Chuff me)!' said Ramon.

The wall of the pipe had burst like an overinflated inner tube, preventing water from rising above that point. Neither Ramon nor Luis had ever seen anything like it.

'Does this mean we have enough water?' I asked.

'Yes,' replied Ramon.

What a relief.

No sooner had we discovered the fault than Chanquero and his two sidekicks turned up. To be doubly sure this was the only problem they pulled the pump to the surface and checked it out. The damaged section of pipe was replaced and the pump gently lowered back down the borehole.

By the time Melanie arrived at lunchtime, the drama had passed and Ramon and Luis were heading home.

'So, there's definitely enough water?' asked Melanie, after I'd explained what had happened.

'Definitely.'

'Do we have running water in the house?'

'We do indeed.'

That in itself was a milestone.

'I'm going to try it,' she said excitedly.

'You can't.'

'Why not?'

'We might have running water but the waste pipes aren't yet connected.'

Melanie looked disappointed but this wasn't the first time she'd had to wait one more day.

When Alfonso the stonemason had originally agreed to rebuild the boundary walls, he'd made it clear that working for us would have to fit in around his commitments to bigger contractors. Considering the standard of his work and his prices, we were happy to wait but there are limits to even our patience.

'I'll be there on Monday,' he'd said when I rang him.

When I rang back on Tuesday to find out why he hadn't showed up, he blamed the excavator driver for being unavailable.

'I'll definitely be there on Friday,' he'd said.

The following Monday I rang him again.

'I thought you were starting work on Friday.'

'I'll definitely be there this week,' he'd replied.

This went on for the best part of a fortnight before he finally showed his face on Monday the 14th of April.

'*Hola*,' he said, in a chirpy tone.

Alfonso's arrival coincided with a change in the weather; April showers had returned. Despite the occasional heavy downpour, it's amazing how much progress a professional stonemason and his colleague can make in a day, which was just as well. Two days after arriving they disappeared.

'The excavator is needed on another job,' he said. 'As soon as it's available we'll be back.'

'How long might that be?' I asked.

'I'm not sure but I'll call you as soon as it's free.'

If that was a polite way of saying "Don't call me I'll call you", he had another think coming.

An unavoidable consequence of Alfonso's two-day stint was the quagmire created by manoeuvring an eight tonne excavator back and forth across the rain sodden meadow. Manolo was not a happy man; deliveries were difficult enough to unload at the best of times.

Through trial and error, the drivers from Ramon Ortero's builder's merchant had worked out the only way to access the narrow driveway was to drive past the entrance, turn around, drive back up the lane and reverse into the driveway. When it comes to judging distances, lorry drivers seem to possess a sixth sense.

On the morning of the 17th one such driver followed his usual routine and despite the appallingly muddy conditions managed to reverse into the driveway without so much as a wheel spin. What he hadn't counted on was the lightness of his vehicle once he'd unloaded.

'Craig!' shouted Manolo.

Until this point, I'd been blissfully unaware we'd even had a delivery, never mind it getting into trouble.

'Yes,' I called.

'There's a problem.'

'What's going on?' asked Melanie.

'I've no idea.'

We left what we were doing and went to take a look. The delivery lorry was exactly where I would have expected it to be given it had just unloaded its cargo. What we didn't expect to see were the rear wheels spinning like Catherine wheels and torrents of mud shooting into the air.

'Can you help me push him?' asked Manolo.

My first thought was you've got to be joking, but Melanie beat me to it.

'You've got to be joking,' she said.

Manolo was having none of it and I felt obliged to give him a hand. Melanie looked on from a distance. She knew as well as I did our feeble frames wouldn't make the slightest difference. After a three-minute mud shower even the driver realised the futility of our efforts. Discussions followed. Raised voices and exaggerated arm movements heralded a new plan of action. A half-hearted attempt to place a few rocks under the rear wheels was followed by a more sustained effort. This time our endeavours bore fruit and the lorry gradually moved forward, slipping and sliding on its way towards the narrow entrance. As it did the lorry skidded dangerously close to Alfonso's newly built drystone wall.

'Stop,' hollered Manolo.

'Stop,' repeated Melanie, who'd been watching events unfold.

The driver was revving the engine so loud he couldn't hear a thing. Manolo ran to the cab and banged on the door.

'Stop, stop.'

He caught his attention just in time. The driver jumped down from the cab and surveyed the impending catastrophe. The rear of the lorry had slipped to within ten centimetres of the wall; any movement forward or backwards would undoubtedly end in disaster.

Galician folk are rarely stuck for words of advice, be it sound or otherwise. On this occasion the four of us stood in silence, staring at this unfathomable problem.

Minutes passed before Melanie came up with a suggestion.

'What about Ramon?' she said.

Manolo and the lorry driver turned to face her, desperate to hear a translation.

'What about Ramon?' I asked.

'Perhaps he could tow it out with his tractor.'

The word tractor caught their attention. While Melanie went in search of Pablo's father-in-law Ramon, I explained her fiendish plan. The pair gave it a cautious thumbs-up. Had the idea been theirs, I suspect they would have been more enthusiastic. A few minutes later she returned. Following lengthy and animated discussions, Ramon fetched his tractor and the extraction began.

Avoiding a collision with the wall proved impossible but the damage was minor and the granite gatepost remained intact and upright. By the time the lorry left, the morning had gone. Manolo packed up and headed home for lunch and Melanie and I weren't far behind.

In common with many countries, the 1st of May is a public holiday in Spain. We used our day off to drive to Portugal in search of furniture.

First thing on Monday morning I was back on the job. Melanie stayed at home to chase Marmoles Grande and find out when Alfonso was planning to return.

Within an hour of my arrival, José Manuel appeared with the new doors. My joy soon turned to despair when they started installing them. To fit the new doors into the old stone doorways, a certain amount of coaxing was required. This took the form of an angle grinder. It's said that a thimbleful of liquid looks more like a gallon when it's spilt, but compared to the dust created from grinding granite, it's more like a drop in the ocean. The floor was blanketed with a thin layer of grey grit, the newly painted walls were covered and it clung to the varnished ceilings like iron filings to a magnet. All our hard work would require hours of cleaning to restore its beauty. As for the newly fitted kitchen, I could hardly bring myself to look at it.

'José Manuel has started fitting the doors,' I announced on my return.

'How do they look?'

'They look fantastic. I'm so glad we chose hardwood.'

'But?'

Melanie could sense I had my reservations.

'I wasn't expecting so much mess.'

'We'll soon have a few wood shavings swept up,' she replied.

'That's not the problem.'

'What then?'

'Dust.'

'Dust?'

'Dust… It's everywhere.'

'Dust?'

'Yes. They used an angle grinder to straighten the doorways.'

'An angle grinder?'

'An angle grinder.'

'I'm sure it's not as bad as you think,' she replied.

I hadn't the heart to contradict her.

'Anyway, how did you get on?'

'Marmoles Grande are useless. We're going to have to go down and speak to them.'

'And Alfonso?'

'He said Tuesday.'

'Do you mean tomorrow?'

'No, next Tuesday.'

'*A ver* (We'll see).'

By Wednesday, José Manuel had fitted all the doors and they look stunning. Melanie and I could now begin the clean-up. Three days later the house looked as good as new. We were still waiting for Marmoles Grande to deliver the steps but Manolo kept himself busy by building the internal walls for the entrance lobby and utility room.

On Monday afternoon we had the clearest indication yet that Alfonso was about to start work. Out of the blue he turned up and dropped off his cement mixer.

'*Hasta mañana* (See you tomorrow),' he said, before leaving.

I couldn't quite believe it when he showed up the following morning. Having him back on site was an opportunity not to be missed. Melanie and I had a clear idea of how we wanted to landscape the meadow: a top lawn supported by a low retaining wall and a lower bottom lawn. Running between the two a long driveway with a turning area close to the house. We discussed our plans with Alfonso.

'I should have enough time to build the retaining wall after I've finished the boundary,' he replied.

That was great news.

The following morning, I booted up the computer and almost fell off my chair. The date read May the 14th. I'd been so busy over the last few weeks, Melanie's birthday had completely slipped my mind. Shock turned to panic. I had two days to rectify my oversight. How I'd missed the pile of unopened greetings cards on the sideboard was anyone's guess.

'I'll see you at lunchtime,' I said, as I left.

Work would have to wait; Melanie was far more important. Before returning home for lunch I'd bought a gift and a card and arranged for a group of us to meet at our favourite restaurant on the evening of the 17th. Best of all, Melanie was none the wiser.

On the Monday after Melanie's birthday the granite steps finally arrived. Our elation was short-lived.

'They're too wide,' said Manolo.
'What are?'
'The steps.'

We'd waited the best part of two months only to find out they'd cut them to the wrong size.

'What can we do?'
'I'll have to cut them.'

Throughout the morning the scream of an angle grinder echoed through the house. As if that wasn't bad enough, plumes of grey dust settled on every surface.

'Look at the mess,' said Melanie, in between cuts.

I felt her pain. Once again, we had to clear up someone else's mess.

By the end of the month, Manolo had finished the staircase and it looked superb. Alfonso had completed the garden walls and I'd made a start on preparing the ground for seeding. Both bathrooms were finished and functioning and the new fitted kitchen looked amazing.

Our attention turned to the driveway, something we hadn't given much thought to until recently. If we weren't careful, choosing the wrong material would spoil the entire look of the property. After weeks of deliberation and numerous quotes, we decided to go with Alfonso's suggestion of reinforced concrete paved with irregular granite slabs.

On the 10th of June, Manolo left the job having completed all the work we'd contracted him to do. He'd done a fantastic job, making the vision of our mind's eye a reality. He'd surpassed our expectations at every turn. Melanie and I could work our magic on painting the interior and dressing the house. Over the last two years we'd collected all manner of household goods. Each passing day brought us one step closer to completing our dream of providing luxury accommodation for the discerning traveller.

We had some way to go before we could accept bookings and as expected, we would miss this year's rental season but we could start preparing for next year. In order to do that, we needed to name our creation.

'What about *Casa Tranquilo*?' said Melanie.

Her suggestion had a familiar ring to it.

'I don't think so.'

We smiled.

'We need a name that English-speaking tourists can pronounce,' I said. 'What about *Campo Verde*?'

'*Campo Verde*,' repeated Melanie. 'Yes, I like it.'

And *Campo Verde* was born.

HASTA PRONTO

Continue the Journey

The following is an excerpt from book six in The Journey series

The Discerning Traveller

Let every new day broaden your horizons

1

Indemnity Assured

Travel broadens the mind. Unfortunately, it has the same effect on my waistline. Gingerly I stepped onto the bathroom scales, exhaled, and peered down at the digital display. The chant "Who ate all the pies?" sprang to mind. I blamed the pie shop in Kangaroo Valley and their self-proclaimed World's Best Pies, but I needn't have worried. Within a month of returning from Australia, Melanie and I were back to our fighting weights. Renovating a Spanish farmhouse tends to have that effect.

'What's for dinner?' I asked, as we watched the setting sun dip behind the woody knoll.

'I thought we'd have a barbecue,' replied Melanie.

That's exactly what Spanish summers are designed for and a rumbling stomach demands.

'I've been thinking.'

'Really.'

Melanie rolled her eyes. What harebrained scheme had I come up with now?

'Yes.'

'And what exactly have you been thinking about?' she asked.

'Christmas.'

'Christmas!'

Her response was understandable.

'I know it's only June but if we're going to go away, we need to start making plans. What do you think?'

'What do I think to what?'

'Going away for Christmas.'

'Sounds like a great idea.'

'How does a month sound?'

'A month!'

'Why not?'

On our recent trip to Australia we'd been away from home for seven weeks. In all that time nothing untoward had happened to the house. I figured we could easily go off for a month without any problems. Besides which, I liked the idea of a longer holiday.

'Can we afford to go away for a month?'

'That depends on what sort of deal I can negotiate.'

'And where were you thinking of going?'

Winters in Galicia can be harsh and my joints aren't getting any younger. Four weeks in the sun would do both of us the world of good. We'd spent the last two Christmases on the Mediterranean coast. The weather had been warm and sunny and it's a destination we can drive to which is a major consideration when travelling with a dog.

'I thought we might go to Mijas again.'

The municipality of Mijas, on the Costa del Sol, sits between Fuengirola to the east and Marbella to the west.

'I like the sound of that,' replied Melanie.

'OK, I'll email Maria tomorrow morning and see what she has to offer.'

Maria is the owner-operator of Just Mijas, a boutique property rental company based in the village of Pueblo Aida. This modern holiday resort is situated in the hills overlooking the coastal town of Fuengirola and has been built in the style of a traditional Andalucian village.

The setting sun had painted the evening sky subtle shades of pastel pink. Time for dinner. While Melanie prepared a seasonal salad, I grilled some sausages on the barbie.

'What have you got planned for tomorrow?' asked Melanie as we tucked in to our alfresco feast.

'I thought we could get the entrance lobby and the staircase ready for painting.'

'Will you need me?'

'Yes please, unless you have something better to do.'

Since returning from Australia all our energy had been focused on finishing our property project. We'd christened the house *Campo Verde*. It suited its rural location and rolls off the tongue regardless of nationality. Manolo, the main contractor, had finished his work at the end of May and we were delighted with the results. Our task was to convert this brand-new restoration into a warm and inviting home. We were too late to take advantage of this year's letting season but were determined to start marketing the house as soon as possible.

'What is there to do?' asked Melanie.

'We need to mask off everything that doesn't need painting.'

Using a roller gives a professional finish to new plaster but makes a hell of a mess.

'I want to get the lobby painted before José Manuel starts fitting the false ceiling,' I added.

We'd decided to have a false wooden ceiling in the downstairs entrance lobby to match the look of the upstairs living accommodation. José Manuel is a skilled carpenter. He'd done a great job crafting the external doors so we'd asked him to do the work.

The sound of magpies tap dancing on the roof tiles eased us gently into a new day. I flung open the window shutters to reveal a bright summer's morning. Before setting off to work I emailed Maria with our Christmas holiday dates.

'Are you ready?' I asked, as I stepped into the kitchen.

'Ready when you are.'

The summer sunshine made the twenty-minute drive to the village of Vilatán a joy. The route took us through the low lying plain of the Val de Lemos and up into the surrounding hills. A landscape of pine forests, grassy meadows, and natural woodlands are stitched together with drystone walls and sprinkled with tiny hamlets and isolated farmhouses. Before long we were trundling through the narrow lanes of the village and into the driveway.

Masking off the entrance lobby was quite straightforward; the staircase proved far more challenging. At its highest point it measures six metres from floor to ceiling. To reach the top of the stairwell I cobbled together a working platform using two ladders. The first I leant against the wall at the foot of the stairs. The second bridged the gap from the first-floor landing across to the other ladder.

'Do be careful,' said Melanie, as I made my way cautiously along the makeshift platform.

In situations like this I convince myself there are no other options.

As I edged towards the centre of the ladder my trembling knees caused it to shake. One false move and I'd end up in intensive care. I inched forward, determined to overcome my fear. Melanie looked as terrified as I felt.

Eventually I made it to the far end and paused for breath. After regaining my composure, I began. First one side and then the other. Within the hour I'd masked off the ceiling and successfully made my way back to the safety of the landing. By the end of the day the lobby and staircase were ready for painting. First thing tomorrow I would make a start.

Lengthening summer days gave us plenty of time to relax after a hard day's work. Before smothering myself in suntan lotion I checked to see if Maria had replied to my email. She had but the news was mixed.

'There's a problem,' I announced, as I stepped outside.

Melanie was lying on a sunlounger reading Jodi Picoult's latest novel.

'What problem?'

'We've had an email from Maria.'

'What did she say?'

'The apartment we stayed in last year is already booked over Christmas.'

Melanie looked disappointed.

'She's given us a couple of options,' I added.

The first was a ground floor apartment that was available for the whole month. Alternatively, we could spend the first ten days in a one-bedroom penthouse and the remainder of the holiday in the two-bedroom apartment we'd had last year. I explained the options to Melanie.

'Penthouse, is that the same as a top floor flat?' she asked.

We both smiled. Pretentiousness is not a Yorkshire trait.

'That's right,' I replied.

On closer scrutiny the ground floor apartment had an east facing aspect which is ideal during the hot summer months but less appealing in winter. The penthouse was directly above the two-bedroom apartment, both of which were south facing. To offset the inconvenience of moving from one apartment to the other, Maria had offered us a generous discount. For a couple of thrifty Yorkshire folk, that proved the clincher.

The very next morning I confirmed the booking. Christmas was sorted.

AVAILABLE NOW FROM AMAZON

About the Author

Craig began writing a weekly column for an online magazine in 2004. He has written a number of articles for the Trinity Mirror Group and online publications such as CNN, My Destination, and Insiders Abroad.

In 2013 he published his bestselling travel memoir, *Journey To A Dream*. It told the story of a turbulent first twelve months in Galicia. Since then he has added *Beyond Imagination*, *Endless Possibilities*, *Opportunities Ahead*, *Driving Ambition*, *The Discerning Traveller*, *A Season To Remember*, *An Excellent Vintage*, *Life In A Foreign Land*, *The Accidental Explorer*, *Seasons To Be Cheerful*, and *Here To There And Back Again* to The Journey series.

As well as writing, Craig is an enthusiastic winemaker and owns a small vineyard.

Printed in Great Britain
by Amazon